HOW TO REDUCE THE TAX YOU PAY

Planning
HOW TO
through 2004,
REDUCE
plus tips
THE TAX
for 2003 returns
YOU PAY

KEY PORTER BOOKS

Copyright © 1988–2003 Deloitte & Touche and Samson Bélair/Deloitte & Touche.

Deloitte & Touche refers to Deloitte & Touche LLP and related entities.

All rights reserved. No part of this work covered by the copyrights hereon may be reproduced or used in any form or by any means— graphic, electronic or mechanical, including photocopying, recording, taping or information storage and retrieval systems—without the prior written permission of the publisher, or, in the case of photocopying or other reprographic copying, a licence from the Canadian Copyright Licensing Agency.

National Library of Canada Cataloguing in Publication Data

The National Library of Canada has catalogued this publication as follows:

How to reduce the tax you pay

Annual.
[1988]–
ISSN 1187-0028
ISBN 1-55263-258-X (16th ed.)

I. Deloitte & Touche.

HJ4661.H68 1988–   343.7105'2'05   C91–090997-0

Key Porter Books Limited
70 The Esplanade
Toronto, Ontario
Canada M5E 1R2

www.keyporter.com

Electronic formatting: Heidi Palfrey

Printed and bound in Canada

03 04 05 06 07 08 6 5 4 3 2 1

Acknowledgements

How to Reduce the Tax You Pay was compiled by a team of writers from Deloitte, one of Canada's leading professional services firms, providing a full range of audit, tax, consulting, and financial services through more than 6,600 people in more than 46 locations across the country. Our firm's professionals have been developing effective business solutions for Canadian and international companies for more than 150 years. We are dedicated to helping our clients and our people excel. Internationally, Deloitte is a global leader in professional services with more than 119,000 people in over 140 countries.

NUMBER ONE FOR TAX ADVICE IN CANADA

In the *International Tax Review*'s annual survey for 2003, our Canadian tax practice is ranked Number One by tax executives. We received top honours in the survey's two overall categories of **Tax Planning** and **Tax Transactions**, as well as first place in all six of the specialty service categories: **Mergers and Acquisitions**; **Transfer Pricing**; **Capital Markets**; **Cross-Border Structuring**; **Indirect Taxes**; and **State and Local Taxes**. In addition, five of our partners were included on a list of the most highly recommended Canadian practitioners: **Albert Baker** and **Alain Orvoine** of our Montreal office; and **Leon Bleiwas**, **Andrew Dunn**, and **Charles Taylor** of our Toronto office.

EXECUTIVE EDITORS

Mark Robinson, Toronto
Danielle Lacasse, Montreal

PRODUCTION EDITORS

Gisèle Archambault, Montreal
Bill Sherman, Toronto

CONTRIBUTORS

Brian Anderson, Winnipeg
Jean-Luc Beauregard, Montreal
Susan Beuerman, Kitchener
John Bowey, Kitchener
Brian Cardinal,
   Hamilton-Halton
Cara Celotti, Toronto
Charles Evans, Kitchener
Heather Evans, Toronto
Karen Gangnier,
   Hamilton-Halton
Marc Gravel, Montreal
René Huot, Montreal
John Hutson, Kitchener

Brian Janzen, Winnipeg
Anne Jewett, Toronto
Tracy MacKinnon, Vancouver
Anne Montgomery, Toronto
Keith Pitzel, Winnipeg
Len Sakamoto, Toronto
Brian Taylor, Saskatoon
Doris Trevisani,
   Hamilton-Halton

PRODUCTION SUPPORT

Junia Fulgence, Toronto

DISCLAIMER

The information and analysis contained in this book are not intended to substitute for competent professional advice. Planning your tax and financial affairs to reduce the tax you pay is a complex process—one that is unique to you or your business. The material that follows is provided solely as a general guide to assist you in understanding the main income tax provisions you can use to minimize your tax burden. No action should be initiated without consulting your professional advisors. This book reflects the law and legislative proposals to November 1, 2003.

Contents

How to Use This Book	12
Tax Calendar	13

1. TAX PLANNING—GETTING STARTED — 15
What is Tax Planning?	15
Where to Begin	16
Get Started	17

2. TAX PLANNING FOR TODAY— THE BASIC CONCEPTS — 18
The Concept of Income	19
The Three Basic Types of Income	19
Other Income	20
Non-Taxable Income	21
Canada's Graduated Tax System	23

3. THE SIX FACES OF TAX PLANNING — 24
The Key Planning Concepts	24

4. LONG-TERM TAX PLANNING—ESTATE PLANNING   29

Objectives	32
Your Changing Estate Plan	35
Your Will	37
Taxation on Death	40
Planning Techniques	44
Taking Advantage of Tax Provisions	50
Succession and Estate Planning for Business Assets	54
Beginning the Process	65

5. FILING TIME   66

Tax Credits versus Deductions	66
Personal Tax Credits for Canadians	67
Tax Filing Time	72

6. IF YOU ARE AN EMPLOYEE   75

Employment Income—What Is Included?	76
Credits and Deductions	80
Planning Opportunities	86
Do You Qualify for a GST Rebate?	95

7. IF YOU ARE A BUSINESS OWNER   98

If You Are a Sole Proprietor or in a Partnership	99
Deductions	102
Planning Opportunity	105
If You Have an Incorporated Business	105
Planning Opportunities	117

8. IF YOU OWN INVESTMENTS   123

Income from Capital Property	124
Income in the Form of Interest	136
Income from Dividends	138
Credits and Deductions Related to Investments	139

9. IF YOU INVEST IN TAX SHELTERS OR OFFSHORE — 142

How Can You Protect Yourself?	143
Limited Partnerships	143
Mineral Exploration and Oil and Gas Shelters	144
Multiple-Unit Residential Buildings (MURBs)	144
Canadian Films	145
Farming as a Tax Shelter	145
Provincial Tax Shelters	146
General Rules for Offshore Investment Reporting	146

10. IF YOU OWN YOUR OWN HOME — 150

Principal Residence Exemption	150
Planning Opportunities	153

11. IF YOU HAVE A SPOUSE — 156

Definition of Spouse	157
Credits and Deductions	157
Planning Opportunities	158
Consequences of Marriage or Common-Law Relationship Breakdown	170

12. IF YOU HAVE CHILDREN — 174

Common-Law and Same-Sex Couples	175
If You Have Children or Grandchildren Under 18: Credits and Deductions	175
Planning Opportunities	177
If Your Children Attend Post-Secondary School and/or Are Over 18: Credits and Deductions	179
Planning Opportunities	182
If Your Child Has Special Needs: Credits and Deductions	183

13. IF YOU HAVE AN RRSP — 185
- Making an RRSP Work for You — 187
- Contribution Rules and RRSP Mechanics — 188
- RRSP Investments — 203
- Special Situations — 206
- Maturing Your RRSP — 209

14. IF YOU DRIVE A CAR FOR BUSINESS — 217
- Tax Aspects for Employees: Employee-Provided Vehicles — 218
- Tax Aspects for Employees: Company-Provided Vehicles — 225
- Tax Aspects for Employers and Self-Employed Individuals — 228
- Planning for Business Use of Automobiles — 231

15. IF YOU ARE A SENIOR — 232
- The Taxation of Seniors — 232
- Credits and Deductions — 234

16. IF YOU PROVIDE CARE FOR YOUR PARENTS — 237
- Credits and Deductions — 237
- Accessing Personal Tax Information — 240

17. IF YOU MAKE POLITICAL OR CHARITABLE CONTRIBUTIONS — 241
- Credits and Deductions — 241

18. IF YOU LIVE IN QUEBEC — 246
- Credits and Deductions — 247
- Tax Incentives — 249
- Consequences of Marriage Breakdown — 256
- Corporate Tax Issues — 256

19. FACTS AND FIGURES FOR CALCULATING 2003 TAXES — 260

- Maximum Combined Rates for 2003 — 260
- Federal Rates of Tax for 2003 — 261
- Quebec Personal Income Tax Measures — 261
- Combined Federal and Provincial Personal Income Tax Rates for 2003 — 265

Index — 273

Deloitte Offices — 279

How to Use This Book

Do you want to pay more income tax than the law requires?

Of course you don't—but that is exactly what many Canadians do. Some may fail to understand the tax rules and amendments, or how they are applied. Others miss out on tax planning opportunities that the law provides, or fail to take advantage of specific tax incentives that are readily available. Far too many taxpayers make errors in completing their tax returns, errors that the tax department may not be able to identify or correct. And finally, some people just can't seem to meet the deadlines imposed under the law, and therefore end up paying interest and penalties on top of what they owe.

> We think this book can help you to avoid costly mistakes, and to reduce or defer your tax burden through intelligent planning—both for your 2003 return and throughout 2004.

THIS EDITION

This is the 16th edition of this book. If you are looking for a "big picture" view of the taxation of income in Canada, we invite you to read this guide from cover to cover. If, on the other hand, you are looking for information specific to your situation, you can quickly access the most up-to-date data in the chapter or section relating to your situation.

Tax Calendar[1]

December 31, 2003	Due date for single instalment of 2003 taxes for farmers and fishermen.
January 30, 2004	Last day to make interest payments to meet income splitting loans exceptions.
February 29, 2004	Last day for filing 2003 T4 and T5 summaries and sending slips to payees.
March 1, 2004	Last day for RRSP contributions eligible for deduction from 2003 personal income tax.
March 15, 2004	Due date for 1st quarterly instalment of 2004 personal income taxes.
April 15, 2004	Due date for 2003 U.S. personal income tax returns and last day for filing for extension.
April 30, 2004	Due date for filing 2003 personal income tax returns and for payment of balance of 2003 income taxes. Self-employed individuals and their spouses must pay their taxes, even if they have until June 15 to file their tax returns. Where a taxpayer died in 2003, the terminal return is due on the later of April 30, 2004, or six months following the date of death.
June 15, 2004	Due date for 2nd quarterly instalment of 2004 personal income taxes. Filing due date for self-employed individuals and their spouses for 2003. Note that tax for 2003 was due April 30, 2004.

September 15, 2004	Due date for 3rd quarterly instalment of 2004 personal income taxes.
November 2004	Good month for taking a final look at your tax planning for 2004.
December 15, 2004	Due date for 4th quarterly instalment of 2004 personal income taxes.
December 31, 2004	Due date for single instalment of 2004 taxes for farmers and fishermen.

---

[1] Remittances of amounts deducted or withheld are considered to be received on the date they are actually received and not the date they were mailed. Note that if the payments are made at a chartered bank, they are considered to have been received by the Canada Customs and Revenue Agency (CCRA) at that time.

CHAPTER ONE

Tax Planning—Getting Started

WHAT IS TAX PLANNING? / 15
Tax "Loopholes" / 16
Time Value of Money / 16

WHERE TO BEGIN / 16
Setting Your Goals / 16
Getting Personal / 17

GET STARTED / 17

WHAT IS TAX PLANNING?

Effective tax planning is the core principle behind this book. Throughout this guide, we will show you the essential steps that all taxpayers should know in planning to reduce their taxes. No one, including you, should pay more tax than the law requires. The best way of ensuring that you pay only your fair share of taxes is through tax planning.

Don't mistake effective tax planning with tax evasion. Tax evasion is any manoeuvre undertaken to hide income otherwise subject to tax; for example, failing to declare all your interest income on your tax return. Tax planning, on the other hand, involves reviewing your financial goals, and arranging your activities to achieve those goals in the most tax-effective manner. By "tax-effective," we mean that you take advantage of the existing tax rules that permit you to reduce or defer taxation, increase deductions, or avoid tax traps.

Tax "Loopholes"

Most people assume that you can save your tax dollars only through loopholes—those inadvertent errors in the design and structure of the *Income Tax Act*. In fact, our *Income Tax Act* contains tax incentives that encourage certain tax-planned activities. If you take advantage of these incentives, you are doing precisely what the government encourages you and other taxpayers to do. These provisions, most of which we cover in this book, are therefore the exact opposite of loopholes.

Time Value of Money

Tax planning, and the resulting tax savings, enables you to optimize the time value of your money. The essence of this concept is that one dollar received today is worth more to you than the same dollar received in the future. For example, if you receive one dollar today, you can invest it to earn interest. After one year, you will have one dollar plus the interest income. If you do not receive that dollar until the end of the year, you have lost the opportunity to earn the interest. Similarly, paying one dollar in taxes today is more expensive than doing so in the future because you lose the interest that dollar could have earned.

WHERE TO BEGIN

Usually, the first step in effective tax planning is to find out where you stand today. Chapter 19 contains statistical tables to help you to determine your tax position for 2003. Use these tables to calculate your approximate tax liability for this year. Later, refer back to these tables after reading the various strategies explained in this book to determine your potential tax savings.

Setting Your Goals

Your primary tax objective should be to ensure that the taxable income you earn is recognized at a time, and in a form, in which it will be most favourably taxed. There are limits to the benefits of tax planning, however.

Caution: A particular tax incentive or tax plan cannot convert a bad investment into a good one.

Suppose an investment generates tax deductions of $100, resulting in a real tax saving of about $48 for taxpayers in the top bracket. If you anticipate losing the full amount you invested, your real economic cost, after the tax saving, is 52 per cent of the cost. This is not smart tax planning, nor is it a "tax shelter." This is a foolish investment!

Getting Personal

The process of setting tax-saving goals requires that you understand the basic concepts of how income is taxed in Canada. We'll discuss these concepts in the next chapter. Other factors to consider in your planning include current interest rates, projected inflation rates, current income tax rules, and the possibility of future legislative changes. After referring to this guide, put your tax plans on paper and then sit down with your spouse and/or children. Discuss your family finances and tax plans together in such a way that everybody can understand your objectives. Open discussions will both encourage and educate your family about financial and tax planning, both of which are important lifetime lessons. Once you have considered all the factors relevant to your situation, you and your family can implement your tax plan.

GET STARTED

Despite all the hoopla, tax planning is essentially a simple process with a few basic elements. It is a year-round activity. Make it an integral part of your regular financial planning and personal budgeting process. Unless you have planned carefully throughout the year, opportunities for reducing your tax bill become more and more restricted as the end of the year approaches. Tax planning is most effective if begun immediately.

Get started!

CHAPTER TWO

Tax Planning for Today— The Basic Concepts

THE CONCEPT OF INCOME / 19

THE THREE BASIC TYPES OF INCOME / 19
Employment Income / 19
Business Income / 20
Property Income and Capital Gains / 20

OTHER INCOME / 20
Alimony and Maintenance Payments / 21
Child Support Payments / 21
Annuities / 21

NON-TAXABLE INCOME / 21
Gifts and Inheritances / 22
Lotteries, Gambling, and Other Prize Winnings / 22
Specifically Exempt Income / 22
Exempt Persons / 22

CANADA'S GRADUATED TAX SYSTEM / 23
Marginal Tax Brackets / 23

Understanding the underlying principles of how we are taxed in Canada, how government-legislated tax incentives work, and, finally, how to choose the tax strategy best suited to you will enable you to plan effectively. In this chapter, we look at how income is taxed in Canada.

THE CONCEPT OF INCOME

All taxpayers resident in Canada must declare their income from all sources, including those outside Canada, and must pay tax on their taxable income. The general category of taxpayer includes individuals, corporations, and trusts. In each case, the responsibility to report all income, earned both in and outside Canada, rests with the taxpayer. Even non-residents are responsible for reporting and paying tax on income earned in Canada.

"Income" is not specifically defined in the *Income Tax Act*. You determine your taxable income after you calculate your income from all sources and make the appropriate deductions. Different types of income are calculated differently, however. For this reason, the first step in tax planning is to identify your sources of income. There are three main categories of taxable income: employment income, business income, and property income and capital gains. With few exceptions, if you have received a benefit of any kind from any activity, it is likely to be taxable as income.

THE THREE BASIC TYPES OF INCOME

Employment Income

Most Canadians earn the bulk of their income through employment. Independent contractors, professionals (including lawyers and accountants), and other freelance workers are not considered employees because there is no employer-employee relationship. They earn business income, which is discussed below.

Employment income includes all benefits you receive in connection with the services you provide to your employer. Benefits, in this sense, include any bonuses, gratuities, or honorariums, as well as any retiring allowance you receive when you leave a job. Your employer will withhold and remit to the Canada Customs and Revenue Agency (CCRA) on your behalf your income tax and other required payments. At tax filing time, you include the T4s issued by your employer with your annual tax return.

Business Income

If you earn income from a business activity, your taxable income is the "profit" of the business. You calculate your profits by subtracting your expenses incurred in generating earned revenue from your earned revenue. In certain situations, if you realize a business loss, this loss may offset income from other sources, including employment and investment income. Farming income receives different treatment than regular business income and the deductibility of farming losses from other sources of income is restricted.

If a revenue-generating activity creates income through the disposition of property, for example, the sale of real estate, the income will be considered either business income or a capital gain and eligible for a partial exclusion. The determination of this issue depends on the nature of your business. For example, if your business regularly buys and sells real estate, income earned from any disposition of property will likely be business income.

Property Income and Capital Gains

The third major income category is income from property, including interest, dividends, and rent. Capital gains are connected with property income, but are subject to special rules for the taxable amounts. We'll talk further about these in Chapter 8.

Gains from transfers of property (through sale, gift, etc.), including gains from sales of property used solely for personal purposes, are generally taxable. The primary exceptions to this rule are certain tax-deferred transfers between spouses, certain transfers of farm property to children, and gains from the sale of a personal residence if you designate it as your principal residence.

OTHER INCOME

Most income from sources other than employment, business, or property is probably taxable. While we cannot cover all of the possibilities in this book, here are some of the more common alternative sources of income for Canadians. If you are in doubt, we recommend that you seek professional advice.

Alimony and Maintenance Payments
Discussed further in Chapter 11.

Child Support Payments
Discussed further in Chapter 11.

Annuities
An annuity is an agreement under which one party purchases the right to receive periodic payments over a specified period from another party. Whether you purchase the annuity with after-tax or before-tax dollars determines if income earned from the annuity is taxable. If an annuity payment is received from a contract purchased through a tax-exempt fund or plan, the full amount of the payment is taxable as income in the year you receive it. Most common examples of such annuity payments include amounts from pension plans and registered retirement savings plans (RRSPs). On the other hand, if you use your savings to buy an annuity contract, you use after-tax dollars. As a result, a portion of each payment under the contract is excluded from your taxable income. The portion of each payment that corresponds to your original investment in the contract is excluded because you already paid tax on those funds. See Chapter 13 for further discussion of RRSP annuities.

NON-TAXABLE INCOME
You might be surprised to learn that it is possible to receive income that is not taxable at all. The general rule is that the *Income Tax Act* must specify a source of income for it to be taxable. Here are some examples of tax-exempt income.

Gifts and Inheritances

A gift or inheritance is not taxed as income to the person receiving the property. The CCRA considers that the individual making the gift, with certain exceptions such as spousal transfers, sold the property at its fair market value on the date of transfer. As a result, if the property has increased in value, the individual making the gift may realize a capital gain, while the recipient will be treated as having acquired the property at the fair market value on the date of transfer. If the recipient sells or transfers the property at a future date, a further capital gain may accrue to the recipient if the property increases in value from the date of the gift.

Lotteries, Gambling, and Other Prize Winnings

Gains resulting from games of chance (such as lotteries and gambling) are not included in income. If you receive prizes related to your employment, however, the value of the prize will likely be added to your employment income.

Specifically Exempt Income

Several categories of income are specifically exempt from taxable income. These include certain military and RCMP pensions, income from personal injury awards, and expense allowances received by elected members of the federal and provincial governments, by elected officers of municipal governments, and by certain officers of municipal government bodies.

Exempt Persons

Finally, certain categories of persons, including individuals, corporations, and trusts, are specifically exempt from paying tax in Canada, regardless of what kind of income they earn. They include:

- diplomatic staff from other countries;
- municipally or provincially owned corporations;
- boards of trade and chambers of commerce;
- charitable organizations and foundations;

- non-profit organizations;
- labour organizations and benevolent or fraternal benefit societies; and
- trusts under various deferred income plans.

Naturally, the rules for qualifying as an exempt person are very strict and are strictly enforced by the CCRA.

CANADA'S GRADUATED TAX SYSTEM

Marginal Tax Brackets

Canada's personal income tax system features a built-in fairness system in the form of graduated rates of tax. As your taxable income increases, the percentage of tax you pay also increases. In other words, income that falls into a higher tax bracket is more heavily taxed than income that falls into a lower tax bracket. Different tax rates at different income levels result in marginal tax brackets. Knowing your marginal tax bracket means that you will be able to calculate how much will be paid to the federal government in taxes from each additional dollar of taxable income you earn.

Understanding the concept of marginal tax brackets is essential for successful family income planning, in particular income splitting. For example, if the primary earner in the family is in a 45 per cent tax bracket and can transfer income to a family member who is in a 25 per cent bracket, the family will save 20 cents for every dollar of taxable income transferred, provided that the lower-income earner does not move up into the next tax bracket.

Marginal tax brackets also tell us how much we will save if we incur costs that are tax-deductible. If your marginal tax bracket is 45 per cent and you can deduct one dollar from that taxable income, you will save 45 cents in taxes; this 45-cent saving means that the actual after-tax cost of spending that tax-deductible dollar is 55 cents. Because of marginal tax brackets, tax-deductible expenditures are more valuable to high-income taxpayers than to low-income taxpayers.

CHAPTER THREE

The Six Faces of Tax Planning

THE KEY PLANNING CONCEPTS / 24
Income Splitting / 25
    The Attribution Rules Defined / 25
    Getting Around the Attribution Rules / 25
Income Shifting / 26
Investment Selection / 26
Tax Deferral / 27
Income Deferral / 27
Tax Shelters / 28

THE KEY PLANNING CONCEPTS

Tax planning can be broken down into six main strategies:

- *income splitting*—transferring income from a taxpayer in a high tax bracket to one in a lower tax bracket;
- *income shifting*—transferring income from a high-tax-rate year to a lower-rate year; or shifting deductions from a low-rate year to a high-rate year;
- *investment selection*—transforming income from a fully taxed source to one that is eligible for full or partial exemption;
- *tax deferral*—delaying taxation of income;
- *income deferral*—deferring the recognition of income for tax purposes to future years; and
- *tax shelters*—using tax law incentives to maximize deductions and minimize taxable income.

Income Splitting

Income splitting is achieved when income that normally would be taxed entirely in your hands is instead successfully transferred in whole or in part by you to another person with a lower marginal tax rate. Most often, the other person is either your spouse (including a common-law spouse) or your children. If the difference in marginal tax rates is 20 per cent, the family's tax saving is $200 for every $1,000 of income transferred to the lower-rate individual. Successful income splitting also requires that the income transferred does not bump the lower-rate individual to a higher tax rate and that the attribution rules are observed.

The Attribution Rules Defined. The government is aware of the benefits of income splitting and the *Income Tax Act* contains provisions, called attribution rules, that are designed to discourage income splitting. If a provision of the *Income Tax Act* is contravened because of a transfer of taxable income and the attribution rules are applied, the transferred income will be attributed back to the taxpayer who made the transfer. The transferring taxpayer will then be taxed on the income, despite the fact that the transferring taxpayer did not personally receive it.

Getting Around the Attribution Rules. Generally, because of the scope of the attribution rules, it has become difficult, if not impossible, to have large amounts of income taxed in your spouse's or children's hands rather than in your hands over a short period. For this reason, it is important to begin your income splitting program as early as possible and continually update it to take advantage of the remaining opportunities. Refer to the various planning options discussed in Chapters 11 and 12, but remember that these strategies operate under the assumption that you have and will continue to have a higher tax rate than your spouse and children.

> **Caution:** The income-splitting tax, or "kiddie tax," has been in effect since 2000. The targeted group consists of individuals who are under age 18 and are Canadian residents throughout the year, with a parent resident in Canada during the year.

Specifically, the tax focuses on certain income earned by minor children:

- taxable dividends and other shareholder benefits derived from owning (directly or indirectly) unlisted shares of Canadian and foreign companies, and
- partnership or trust income derived from providing goods or services to a business owned directly or indirectly by a relative of the individual.

If the tax applies, income earned by the minor child is taxed at the top marginal rate, and only the dividend and foreign tax credits are available. The tax will apply to existing arrangements, unless the child holds shares of a private corporation that were inherited from a parent. Alternatively, if the child sells the shares and purchases investments in a public corporation, the rule will cease to apply. Finally, capital gains income will not be subject to the tax.

Income Shifting

To gain a tax advantage through income shifting, you must be able to forecast your current year's and future income, as well as opportunities for controlling the timing of your income flow. Business owners and professionals have more opportunities to shift income than do most employees.

Investment Selection

This strategy requires knowledge of how the different types of income are taxed in Canada. For example, dividends received from Canadian corporations and capital gains are treated more favourably from a tax perspective than interest income. Consequently, if returns on investment are otherwise equal, investing in Canadian dividend-earning equities is more tax-efficient than investing in an interest-earning investment, such as a bond. While this strategy is relatively easy to implement for future investments, before you divest yourself of your interest-earning investments, account for any costs you will incur in shifting your investments. For example, you may have to pay a penalty to transfer an investment from an interest-bearing account to one that will provide income in the form of capital gains. If the penalty outweighs the tax benefit, seek other options.

Tax Deferral

Postponing the payment of taxes is tax deferral. The longer we are able to do so, the longer our money remains available for investment and other activities. The concept of the time value of money plays a significant role. By postponing the payment of taxes, you can take greater advantage of current investment opportunities.

Income Deferral

Income deferral simply means deferring the recognition of income for tax purposes to future years. Your benefit is that you postpone paying tax, again taking advantage of the time value of money. It is sometimes said that tax deferred is tax saved. If, for example, you can defer $1,000 of tax payable for one year, and earn 5 per cent during that time, you have "saved" $50 (less, of course, any tax payable on that $50 of income).

Over the past few years, there has been a significant reduction in the number of opportunities available to defer income, especially with respect to interest income, which must be reported annually even if it has not yet been received. These rules affect all taxpayers, including individuals and trusts with individuals as beneficiaries. Income earned in deferred income plans, including registered retirement savings plans, deferred profit sharing plans and registered pension plans, is not affected by these rules, however.

Tax Shelters

Many upper-income Canadians have discovered the hard way that the "quality of the investment" in a tax shelter is by far the most important element, overshadowing all other considerations, including immediate tax savings. Receiving a deduction for the money you put into a tax shelter is no consolation if you end up losing your money because the investment is of poor quality. If you are considering investing in a tax shelter, obtain professional advice before committing your funds and future state of mind to these high-risk investments.

CHAPTER FOUR

Long-Term Tax Planning— Estate Planning

OBJECTIVES / 32
Financial Considerations / 32
Preparing to Meet Your Estate Planning Advisor / 33
Components of an Estate Plan / 34
Planning Objectives / 34

YOUR CHANGING ESTATE PLAN / 35
Estate Planning Early in Life / 35
Planning in Middle Age / 36
Pre-Retirement Planning / 36

YOUR WILL / 37
Choosing the Executor / 38
Dying Intestate / 39
Reviewing Your Will / 39

TAXATION ON DEATH / 40
Deemed Disposition Rules / 41
Optional Tax Returns / 43
Taxation of the Estate / 43
Foreign Death Taxes / 44

PLANNING TECHNIQUES / 44
Gifting / 44
Income Splitting / 46
The Use of Trusts / 46

Preferred Beneficiary Election / 47
Deemed Disposition Rule for Trusts / 49
Estate Freezing / 49
   Direct Sale / 49
   Corporate Freeze / 50

TAKING ADVANTAGE OF TAX PROVISIONS / 50
Principal Residence Exemption / 50
Registered Retirement Savings Plans / 51
Spouse and Spousal Trust Rollovers / 52
Life Insurance / 53

SUCCESSION AND ESTATE PLANNING FOR BUSINESS ASSETS / 54
Exemption of Tax on Capital Gains on Shares
  of Small Business Corporations / 55
    The Alternative Minimum Tax / 56
Rollover of Farming Property / 57
Estate Freezing Techniques for Corporate Assets / 57
   Direct Sale / 58
   Sale to a Holding Company / 59
   Asset Freeze / 61
   Internal Freeze / 61
   Choosing the Best Freeze Vehicle / 62
   Sales to Third Parties / 62
Insurance / 62
   Buy-Sell Agreements / 63

BEGINNING THE PROCESS / 65

Much of this book focuses on how you can plan today to save you and your family tax dollars this year. Planning today can also save tax dollars far in the future, but it requires formulating a plan right now. In this chapter, we look at what you and your family need to know to create a workable and effective retirement and estate strategy.

Long-Term Tax Planning—Estate Planning ▶ 31

Retirement and estate planning is a matter of money management, both current and future. When you retire, the amount of income you will earn at that time will depend in large part on what you do today, as well as how you manage your tax position in the future. Similar issues affect your estate.

Although you might be inclined to skip this chapter, you are mistaken if you believe that you are neither old enough nor rich enough to have an "estate" that is worth planning. Virtually everyone over the age of majority should think about what will happen to his or her assets in the event of death, and should make arrangements to ensure that financially dependent family members are as adequately provided for as possible.

> **Caution:** Each year, thousands of Canadians die in accidents or through sudden illness, and many of them die without a will. Although the odds are that you will live to a ripe old age, you owe it to yourself, and to your family, to "put your house in order."

Estate planning is the ongoing process of creating and maintaining a program designed to preserve your accumulated wealth and ensure that it is distributed to succeeding generations efficiently and in accordance with your wishes.

Several developments over the last decade have affected virtually all existing estate plans and those who are contemplating an estate planning program:

- The abolition of the $100,000 lifetime capital gains exemption in 1994 altered the taxation of assets passed on to succeeding generations.
- The constant tightening of the rules limiting income splitting among family members can necessitate the restructuring of many estate planning approaches.
- The Alternative Minimum Tax affects a number of upper-income Canadians, particularly those with "tax shelter"-type investments.

- New or revised family law or similar legislation in several provinces affects the transfer of assets from one generation to the next. In particular, the province of Quebec legislated specific changes to successions when the Civil Code was amended in 1994.

OBJECTIVES

In general, the objectives of effective estate planning are to:

- ensure that you and your family are adequately provided for now and in the future, and that your heirs are adequately provided for after your death;
- distribute assets according to your wishes, both during your lifetime and on your death, with a view to ensuring that the maximum benefits available accrue to your beneficiaries; and
- minimize various forms of wealth erosion, such as taxes, both now and in the future.

Your estate planning objectives should be realistic. More importantly, you should review your estate plan regularly to ensure that it remains flexible enough to accommodate unexpected changes in your financial or personal situation, as well as changes beyond your control, such as new legislative developments.

Financial Considerations

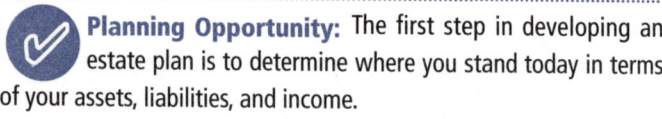

Planning Opportunity: The first step in developing an estate plan is to determine where you stand today in terms of your assets, liabilities, and income.

You should try to create projections for the future direction of your affairs, including possible inheritances, asset liquidations such as the sale of a business or property, the paying off of mortgages, education costs for children, and the acquisition of a recreation or retirement property. At the same time, educate yourself on how the economy's performance might affect your assets and income in the future. One useful prediction tool is the "rule of 72." For example, if inflation averages 4 per cent a year, one dollar today will be worth 50 cents in today's dollars in approximately 18 years (i.e., 72 divided by 4) and be worth 25 cents in 36 years.

Preparing to Meet Your Estate Planning Advisor
A professional estate planner needs accurate and up-to-date information concerning your financial affairs, as well as a clear understanding of your financial and personal objectives. He or she must be as well informed about your financial affairs as you are. Once you have selected the estate professional(s) who will manage your estate plan, most often an accountant and/or lawyer (notary in Quebec), ensure that you provide comprehensive information about your finances and future plans. This includes providing:

- lists of your assets and heirs;
- mortgage documents and deeds;
- shareholder and partnership agreements;
- RRSP and life insurance forms;
- prenuptial and domestic contracts; and
- candidates to be your executor(s).

An effective estate plan requires the cooperation and input of a number of individuals, including your accountant, lawyer, insurance agent, financial advisor, and to some extent your business associates. As with your overall tax plan, you should involve your spouse in setting your estate planning objectives. If your affairs are complicated and your spouse is expected to manage them upon your death as an executor, involving him or her now makes good sense.

Components of an Estate Plan

To be effective, your estate plan must be tailored to suit your individual needs. The tailoring aspect requires careful consideration, planning, and preparation of a combination of the following documents:

- a will, which is the core document to any estate plan;
- trust(s), both *inter vivos* (created during your lifetime) and testamentary (created through your will);
- life insurance, which will ensure that your dependants are not faced with a heavy financial burden caused by your tax liability or funeral expenses;
- power of attorney for finances, or mandate in Quebec, which allows an individual of your choice to take over your financial affairs should you become unable to manage them;
- power of attorney for health care, or mandate in Quebec, which allows an individual of your choice to make medical decisions for you on your behalf;
- a living will, which enables you to predetermine your medical care, in particular the application of continuing life support;
- organ donor cards, which enable you to choose whether your organs will be salvaged for transplant or medical research;
- funeral arrangement instructions and pre-paid plan, which will relieve your family members of the burden of deciding how you would like to be remembered; and
- a business succession plan—a key estate planning document for any small business owner.

Wills and trusts are discussed below. Business succession plans are covered in Chapter 7. It is most crucial that you and your estate plan advisor determine which of these documents will best suit your long-term plans.

Planning Objectives

From a tax perspective, your estate planning objectives should be to:

- minimize and defer taxes now and in the future in order to preserve your accumulated wealth;
- shift any potential tax burden associated with a particular asset to your heirs so that taxes become payable only when your heirs eventually dispose of the asset; and
- minimize taxes at death so that as much as possible of your accumulated wealth passes to your heirs.

YOUR CHANGING ESTATE PLAN

Your approach to planning for your estate will change through the various stages of your life. Because your own estate plan will depend on your particular circumstances and those of your family, we can only outline general considerations. The following are intended as descriptions of typical family situations.

Estate Planning Early in Life

During the period from your mid-20s to age 40, you will likely settle down and start a family, will have little in the way of substantial assets, and will be establishing yourself in your career or business. In this case, your goal is to protect your dependants in the event that you or your spouse should die or otherwise become unable to provide for them.

> **Planning Opportunity:** Your estate plan may extend no further than paying down the mortgage on the family home and ensuring that you have sufficient life insurance (likely term insurance) and long-term disability insurance in place.

At this stage, it is likely that, in your will, you would leave all your assets outright to your spouse.

Once you have more income, you will want to start saving for future acquisitions, for your children's education, and for your retirement. These added expenses also affect your estate plan.

✓ **Planning Opportunity:** The higher-income-earning spouse should contribute to registered retirement savings plans (RRSPs) for both spouses.

At some point, you may be able to budget to pay the higher premiums to obtain the added security and investment benefits available with permanent life insurance.

Planning in Middle Age

From your 40s to your mid-50s, you may well have more substantial assets as a result of a larger family income. However, you may also be facing increased expenditures, such as post-secondary education for your children.

✓ **Planning Opportunity:** During this period, continue contributing to a retirement plan, whether it be an RRSP or a registered pension plan. You may choose to discontinue your term life insurance policy, while continuing with coverage under a permanent policy.

This is a good time to restructure your business affairs and investments to reduce current taxes and facilitate the accumulation of savings and other assets for your retirement.

Pre-Retirement Planning

Once you have reached your mid-50s, it is time to give serious consideration to planning for your retirement, if you have not already done so.

⚠ **Caution:** You must ensure that you secure sufficient retirement income to cover your needs, as well as sufficient savings to cover unforeseen events in the near future.

You should continue with contributions to your pension fund through an RRSP or pension plan, and you will probably continue to make additional investments. You might want to determine what type of retirement income best suits your needs once your RRSPs and pension plans have matured. If you have a business, you may wish to sell it to further supplement your retirement income, or create a succession plan to pass the management of it to others.

> **Caution:** It is important to keep your will up to date with your family's situation as well as the legislation. Ensure that you have a succession plan if you are a business owner.

The deemed disposition rules in the *Income Tax Act*, which impose a tax on unrealized capital gains at the time of your death, could seriously erode the value of your assets. However, you may be able to minimize the tax consequences of the deemed disposition rules through the careful disposition of your assets during your lifetime and with a carefully drafted will. You may want to consider gifting some of your assets to your heirs during your lifetime, or establishing trusts for their benefit to take effect either during your lifetime or after your death.

YOUR WILL

A will is the primary estate planning tool. In fact, without it, you and your family will be completely unprepared to deal with the financial, in addition to the emotional, consequences of your death.

When you create your will, you are the testator if you are a man, or the testatrix if you are a woman. In your will, you appoint the executor(s) of your estate, name your beneficiaries, and create a distribution plan for your assets. It is important that you consult your spouse in the preparation of your will so that he or she understands the reasons for the provisions that are included. If your spouse does not agree with the terms of the will, many provincial family law statutes allow a spouse to claim to have the same division-of-asset rules apply that are provided upon marriage breakdown. This procedure can be expensive and protracted, and you should try to avoid this outcome wherever possible. Communicating your wishes to your spouse beforehand, and possibly drafting a domestic contract to deal with the division of assets, can prevent such a challenge.

Choosing the Executor

The role of the executor under a will involves onerous responsibilities. You should consider not only the willingness of the person to serve, but also his or her appropriateness for the position. Two of the major criteria are the familiarity of the person with your affairs and his or her technical and financial competence to manage your estate.

> **Caution:** The executor is charged with interpreting your wishes as expressed in your will and in other documents, and carrying them out to the best of his or her ability. Ensure that your will provides clear instructions.

The executor is often empowered by the provisions of your will to make virtually all decisions that you have not anticipated concerning your estate. These discretionary powers are especially important because your executor is charged with maintaining the value of your estate until assets are distributed to the beneficiaries. For example, if the executor believes your business would benefit from outside management help before your beneficiaries take it over, your will must empower him or her before the executor can undertake this arrangement. If these powers are not conferred, and your spouse or your children are incapable of managing the business once they gain control, there is little the executor can do but advise them to bring in outside expertise, or perhaps to sell the business before its value seriously declines.

Much of what happens to your assets after your death depends on the arrangements you have made before you die. If your instructions are not specific enough, your executor, although acting in good faith, may misinterpret your wishes or have his or her powers contested in court.

Dying Intestate

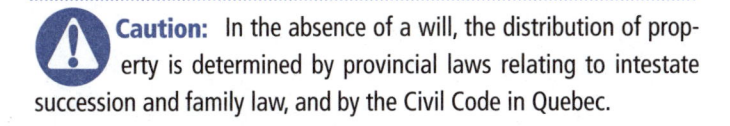

> **Caution:** In the absence of a will, the distribution of property is determined by provincial laws relating to intestate succession and family law, and by the Civil Code in Quebec.

Such laws vary from province to province. For example, the law in several provinces provides that if a person dies without a will, a reserve must be set aside for the surviving spouse after the individual's debts and liabilities are paid off. The spouse receives an amount equal to the reserve and shares the balance with the children, if any. Since this type of distribution is arbitrary, in most circumstances it will not satisfy the wishes of the deceased or the needs of individual family members. Creating a will gives you the opportunity to make your own choices for the division of your assets.

Reviewing Your Will

A good rule of thumb is that your will should be reviewed, and revised if necessary, at least every five years. Your will should be revised immediately in the event of the death of an intended beneficiary or the executor, or because of changes in your family situation or financial circumstances. Quebec's Civil Code provides additional reasons why Quebec residents should have a professional review and, if necessary, modify their will.

Changes in the law may also affect the validity of your will. For instance, in some provinces, such as Quebec, legislation regarding division of matrimonial property will override the provisions of your will. Furthermore, legislation in most provinces (not including Quebec) provides that you may not totally disinherit your spouse or a dependant. Remember to review all the other parts of your estate plan, such as insurance policies and retirement savings and pension plans. When circumstances demand, remember to change beneficiary designations, or a substantial part of your estate may go to someone you may no longer wish to benefit.

To avoid pitfalls and difficulties with your will in the future, professional legal advice should be sought in all cases from lawyers (notaries in Quebec) experienced in wills and family law. Your tax advisor should also review the will before you sign it.

TAXATION ON DEATH

If you understand how taxation applies on death, you will be better equipped to decide how to provide effectively for the distribution of your assets in your will and how to distribute assets during your lifetime, if that is your choice.

Technically speaking, there are no Canadian death taxes (estate or inheritance taxes), federal or provincial, levied on the value of the assets that pass to beneficiaries. Only income amounts received (or deemed to be received) by the deceased and capital gains realized (or deemed to be realized) are subject to income tax.

Apart from income tax, however, each province levies fees called probate fees. These are charged to the estate of an individual as part of the process of receiving court approval for a will and appointment of an executor, or court approval for the appointment of an administrator, where there is no will. These fees are calculated on the value of the estate. While they vary between provinces, they can range as high as 1.5 per cent. Probate fees are a debt that the estate must pay before the executor can take over and distribute the estate assets to the beneficiaries. Planning for these fees now will ensure that your estate and your beneficiaries do not face undue financial hardship upon your death.

Once the executor takes over administration of the estate, four distinct taxpaying entities may result: the deceased, the estate (during the estate settlement stage), any ongoing trusts created under the deceased's will, and, finally, the beneficiaries.

Deemed Disposition Rules

In the year of death, an individual's taxation year runs from January 1 to the date of death. Your executor must file a final return of income, known as the "terminal return." The terminal return must report all income earned from January 1 of the year of death to the date of death. Income includes interest, rents, royalties, annuities, remuneration from employment, and other amounts payable on a periodic basis that were accrued but not due at the time of death, as well as amounts due but not paid. Also included are net taxable capital gains or losses realized prior to death and not included in income in a previous year. A significant difference between the terminal return and a normal tax return is that the Alternative Minimum Tax, discussed below, is not payable in the year of death, although carryforwards from prior years may be applied in calculating the terminal tax liability.

In addition to actual earned or realized income, the *Income Tax Act* contains provisions that create deemed income, which must be reported as income in the terminal return. Specifically, the deceased is deemed to have disposed of all capital property immediately before death for consideration equal to its fair market value immediately before death. These deemed dispositions can result in capital gains and losses, as well as a terminal loss or recapture of depreciation already claimed, which must be included in the terminal tax return.

"Recapture of depreciation" is a term that relates specifically to capital property used to earn income. Taxpayers are entitled to claim a capital cost allowance (CCA) to offset the purchase cost of capital property. CCA acts like depreciation in that it is claimed over time against the income earned through the use of the property. The *Income Tax Regulations* determine the CCA rates. If you sell or transfer capital property for a price greater than its depreciated value, you must account for that gain by including the excess amount as income. That income is considered a recapture of depreciation.

A large tax assessment on the "profit" from these deemed dispositions may result. Because we are dealing with a deemed as opposed to an actual sale, no money has changed hands and the estate may have difficulty paying any taxes that are levied.

> **Planning Opportunity:** An individual may avoid some of the adverse tax consequences of the deemed disposition rules by transferring property to a spouse or spousal trust and by transferring any farm property or an interest in a farm property to children through a will.

If property of any kind is transferred by will to a spouse or spousal trust, no capital gains, recapture of depreciation, etc., arise on death, unless the estate elects to claim a gain on the transfer. Effectively, the spouse or spousal trust inherits the deceased's tax cost (i.e., the cost at which the deceased acquired or was deemed to have acquired the property). Before choosing this method of relieving taxes, ensure that your executor claims any of your remaining exemption room in the $500,000 lifetime capital gains exemption. When a principal residence is transferred to a spouse or spousal trust, the spouse or spousal trust retains the deceased's principal residence exemption.

If you bequeath farm property, an interest in a family farm partnership, or shares in a family farm corporation to your child, grandchild, or great-grandchild in your will, there is a complete tax deferral on the transfer and the child assumes your tax cost. Your estate can elect to preclude full or partial deferral of tax, which increases the tax cost of the farm property for the child. Ensure that, during your lifetime or upon your death, you or your executor fully claims the $500,000 lifetime capital gains exemption.

The transfer of property to a spouse and the transfer of farm property to a child through a will are commonly known as "rollovers." Your heirs assume any potential tax liability for the property, which will be payable only when they dispose of or are deemed to dispose of the property.

Optional Tax Returns

Depending on the source of income, your executor has the option of filing three additional, separate returns. Specifically, if, prior to death, you were the proprietor of or a partner in a business, a beneficiary of a testamentary trust, or you earned "rights or things" (which are generally unrealized income amounts at the date of death), these returns may be filed.

> **Planning Opportunity:** The advantage in filing these separate returns is that each return treats the deceased as a separate person, allowing additional use of tax credits and access to graduated rates of taxation.

Full personal tax credits can be claimed on each return, allowing for potential tax savings. The splitting of income among the different returns then produces a further saving because of the graduated tax rate system.

Taxation of the Estate

Once the will comes into effect, the estate will hold income-producing assets in trust before they are passed to specific beneficiaries. Generally, all income earned and received by the estate from the date of death is taxed in the estate. The beneficiaries pay tax on the income of the estate only when income is payable or distributed to beneficiaries or the estate makes an election to attribute income to a preferred beneficiary.

Your will should be drafted to empower the executor of your estate to undertake some testamentary tax planning where possible. For example, controlling the timing of gifts or deciding which assets will pass through the rollover provisions (see page 52, "Spouse and Spousal Trust Rollovers") may reduce taxes in your terminal return and reduce the impact of taxes on your beneficiaries.

Foreign Death Taxes

If you have any assets located in the United States, or if you or any of your beneficiaries is a citizen or resident of the United States, U.S. federal and state estate taxes may apply.

Provisions of the Canada-U.S. Income Tax Treaty contain the rules on death taxes with respect to U.S. property held by Canadian residents who are not U.S. citizens. If you own U.S. assets, consult with your tax advisor to determine what steps, if any, might be taken to reduce or eliminate the U.S. estate tax exposure.

PLANNING TECHNIQUES

As you consider some of the estate planning strategies outlined below, understand that there are costs involved that go beyond financial. A tax saving could be accompanied by loss of control over the related asset, or perhaps the overall flexibility of your estate plan will be impaired to some extent. The tools and techniques that you use depend on your personal and financial situation and your estate planning objectives.

Gifting

The most direct method of accomplishing the more common estate planning goals is to gift assets to your potential heirs during your lifetime. Since ownership is transferred, the future capital appreciation of the assets and the related future tax liability are also transferred. There are three drawbacks to gifting, however.

First, if the asset is transferred to your spouse or a related child under the age of 18, you will be subject to the "attribution rules." In other words, any investment income (i.e., interest, dividend, and rental income) earned on the property is taxed in your hands until the marriage breaks down (by death, divorce, or separation) or until the year the child turns 18. Also, when an asset is transferred to your spouse, the capital gain on the subsequent sale of the transferred property is attributed to you.

Second, since ownership of the asset is transferred, you lose control over the asset and you no longer have access to its future income-earning capability.

Third, when you gift an asset to any person, except your spouse, during your lifetime, you generally are deemed to have received proceeds of disposition equal to the fair market value of the asset at the time of the gift. Consequently, you will be immediately liable for any tax resulting from a capital gain.

As in the case of deemed dispositions that occur on death, there are certain exceptions to this deemed disposition *inter vivos* (i.e., during your lifetime) rule. You may be able to defer the tax via a rollover when:

- property is transferred to a spouse or a spousal trust (although future capital gains and losses will be attributed back to you); or
- farm property is transferred to a child, grandchild, or great-grandchild.

If you are a shareholder of a Canadian private corporation that uses all or substantially all of the fair market value of its assets in an active business primarily in Canada, or you own qualified farm property, you may qualify to claim the $500,000 lifetime capital gains exemption on the disposition of shares of the company or farm (refer to Chapter 8). This exemption may be limited to $400,000 if you have already taken full advantage of the $100,000 cumulative capital gains exemption.

> **Planning Opportunity:** If you have not already used up your $500,000 capital gains exemption, you may want to gift enough of your shares in the private company to your children to trigger a $500,000 capital gain and thereby use the exemption.

This strategy may not make sense if you are planning to sell the company to outsiders, however. It might be better to save the exemption for the arm's-length sale, rather than use it for a "paper transaction" between family members. Keep in mind that this exemption may suffer the same fate as the $100,000 personal capital gains exemption. Plan now.

Income Splitting

The primary objective of income splitting is to have income that normally would be taxed in your hands, at a high tax rate, taxed instead in the hands of a relative, usually your spouse or child, at a lower tax rate. See Chapter 3 for a definition of income splitting and a discussion of the attribution rules. See also Chapters 11 and 12 for income splitting strategies.

The Use of Trusts

In its simplest form, a trust results when one person holds property that has been transferred by another person to be held on certain conditions for the benefit of a third person. In more technical terms, a trust is created when a settlor transfers property to a trustee, who holds the property for the benefit of a beneficiary. A trust may be either testamentary (i.e., arising upon your death) or *inter vivos* (i.e., arising during your lifetime).

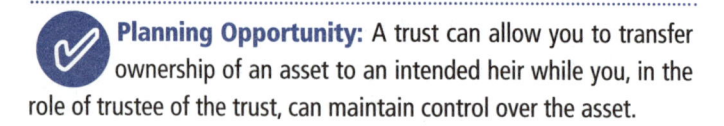

> **Planning Opportunity:** A trust can allow you to transfer ownership of an asset to an intended heir while you, in the role of trustee of the trust, can maintain control over the asset.

Trusts enable you to accomplish many of your estate planning goals. They may be used for such varied purposes as funding a child's education, providing for mentally or physically disabled children, or obtaining professional property management services.

Two conditions must be satisfied to achieve a tax saving. First, you must create a valid trust and relinquish ownership of the assets held by the trust. Remember that, as trustee, you may still control the management and operation of the trust itself. Second, you must avoid the attribution rules.

> **Planning Opportunity:** An *inter vivos* trust is generally taxed at the top personal rate. Testamentary trusts are taxed more favourably at the progressive tax rates applied to individuals.

Because of the difference in the tax treatment of trusts, you must be very selective about the purpose behind creating your trust and the kinds of assets that you place in your trust. For example, if you intend to create a source of future income for your spouse and are considering transferring investment assets to a trust, you might also consider creating a self-directed spousal RRSP. A professional tax advisor can assist you in this choice.

If trust income is distributed to a beneficiary either directly through an actual distribution, or indirectly, as with the preferred beneficiary election (see below), such amounts are deducted from trust income and taxed in the hands of the beneficiary, assuming the attribution rules do not apply. This can result in some overall tax savings if the beneficiary is taxed at a lower marginal rate.

The *Income Tax Act* provides that certain forms of income earned in a trust retain their character when distributed to beneficiaries and taxed in their hands. For example, eligible Canadian taxable dividends received by a trust and distributed to a beneficiary are eligible for a dividend tax credit claim by the beneficiary.

Preferred Beneficiary Election. When this election is made, income earned by the trust is taxed in the hands of the beneficiary, even though the income remains in the trust. Since 1997, this election has been restricted to beneficiaries who are eligible for the disability tax credit or adult beneficiaries who can be claimed as dependants because of a mental or physical impairment. In addition, a preferred beneficiary must be a Canadian resident and one of the following:

- the settlor of the trust, or his or her spouse or former spouse;
- a child, grandchild, or great-grandchild of the settlor; or
- the spouse (but not former spouse) of a child, grandchild, or great-grandchild of the settlor.

The settlor must also contribute more to the trust than any other taxpayer.

The restriction of the preferred beneficiary election has curbed the use of trusts for minor children. The Canada Customs and Revenue Agency (CCRA) has granted some leeway, however. Many trusts empower their trustees to make payments to third parties for the benefit of the beneficiaries. Historically, the concern was that these payments would not qualify as payments to the beneficiaries and the trust would still be responsible for the tax. The CCRA will allow third-party payments to qualify as payments to the beneficiaries if the payments are made at the request of the parent/guardian of the child. As a result, a family trust can be structured to pay the discretionary expenses of the beneficiaries while the parent(s) cover the basic necessities of life. Discretionary expenses include tuition for private school, the cost of lessons, memberships, travel, etc.

The CCRA will also consider third-party payments paid to cover the necessities of life as payments to the child in very limited cases. A trust may pay for the basic necessities of life, either directly to a third party or through reimbursement to the parent/guardian. When calculating its taxable income, the trust may claim a deduction for the payments, and the minor beneficiary would include the amount of the payments as income. The parents would not attract any added tax liability, provided that the attribution rules do not apply. Because of the precise nature of these arrangements, seek professional advice on this issue.

Deemed Disposition Rule for Trusts. Special rules prevent trusts from holding property for an indefinite period. This restriction prevents the long-term deferral of capital gains from income. The general rule provides that every 21 years, there will be a deemed disposition by the trust of all of its capital property for proceeds of sale equal to the fair market value of the property. Because the rule is a deeming provision, the proceeds, which might only be on paper, will still affect the trust's tax position.

Estate Freezing

An estate freeze is generally undertaken when an individual seeks to reduce the tax consequences of owning assets that are likely to increase substantially in value over the long term. An effective freeze can eliminate or defer immediate tax in your hands, ensure that future growth of the asset will benefit your children, and allow you to maintain control of the asset.

An estate freeze is not a gift. If assets are gifted to a child, no value is received in return and control is lost. Under an estate freeze, you retain, or at least have access to, the current value of the frozen assets. Only the future increases in value are transferred to the child. It is also possible for you to retain control over those assets. Unlike estate freezing, gifting assets to your child eliminates tax on your death, but it also may result in an immediate tax liability, possibly outweighing the long-term benefits.

Direct Sale. Selling an asset to your child, the simplest of estate freezes, may achieve some or perhaps all of your estate planning goals. Tax is eliminated on death, but you must include any capital gain in income for tax purposes in the year of the sale. Normally, you would take back a note payable from the child as payment of the sale price. You need not charge interest on the note; however, if your child is a minor, the attribution rules will apply to any income earned on the transferred asset. By selling, you can dispose of a growth asset and obtain a fixed-value asset in its place.

> ⚠ **Caution:** Legal issues are associated with the sale of an asset to a minor.

With a direct sale, you can claim a reserve (i.e., not recognize the full capital gain) if you have not received all proceeds from the sale and the unpaid proceeds are not yet due. The taxable capital gain must be brought into your income over a specified period, depending on the type of asset sold. Further, depending on the asset sold, when the reserve amount is included in income, it may be eligible for the $500,000 lifetime capital gains exemption.

The fact that you can demand partial or full payment on the note at any time may represent some form of control over the asset. Further, transferring the asset to a trust of which the child is a beneficiary may permit you to exercise more control over the asset if you are the trustee.

Corporate Freeze. For an asset freeze to be truly successful, the assets used must increase in value in the future, and the bigger the increase, the better. As a result, the most common "frozen" assets are business assets. In particular, business assets in the form of shares of a private corporation controlled by the individual are often ideal for a freeze. Using a corporation in an estate freeze provides the individual with considerable flexibility and, if properly structured, enables him or her to achieve each of the estate freezing goals mentioned above.

TAKING ADVANTAGE OF TAX PROVISIONS

Principal Residence Exemption

Detailed rules on the principal residence exemption are contained in Chapter 10. A number of estate planning options involve changes to the ownership of a principal residence.

If two residences are currently owned by a married couple (e.g., a city home and a summer cottage), the couple should consider transferring ownership of one property to adult children or grandchildren who reside in the residence for at least part of the year. The more common example involves transferring the cottage. This may involve a slight cost currently, for example, tax on the capital gain from the property that has accrued since 1981. Any future gain realized on the disposition of the other property retained by the couple will generally be tax-free under the principal residence rules.

Of course, if you sell or gift the cottage directly to the children, you and your spouse no longer have any legal right to occupy it. Taking back a demand note as consideration on the sale may give you some control over the property, but perhaps not enough to suit your wishes. One solution might be to transfer the property to a discretionary trust for you and your children. The trust agreement could be structured to permit you to give the cottage to a particular child at some time in the future, while ensuring that the future increase in value accrues to the ultimate owner.

Registered Retirement Savings Plans

RRSPs are probably the most common tax deferral vehicles in use today (also refer to Chapter 13). The immediate tax benefit of an RRSP is that it reduces annual income for tax purposes (within specified limits) by the amount of the annual contribution. The longer-term benefit is that an RRSP shelters the income accumulating in the plan from taxation.

For estate planning purposes, if you name a beneficiary in your RRSP, the assets in your RRSP will pass to the named beneficiary outside of your estate and will not be subject to probate. Further, if you name your spouse as your beneficiary, your estate will not incur any tax liability on the transfer to your spouse. Further, your spouse will be able to defer tax on the transfer if he or she transfers the assets to his or her own RRSP.

> **Planning Opportunity:** Even if you have a surviving spouse, you can name a financially dependent child or grandchild as a beneficiary. If your child or grandchild is over age 18, he or she must also qualify for the impairment credit. On the transfer of assets to the dependent child or grandchild, there will be no tax to your estate. A qualifying child or grandchild over 18 can also transfer your RRSP assets to his or her own plan. A child or grandchild under 18 can transfer assets to an annuity with a term that ends when he or she turns 18.

Spouse and Spousal Trust Rollovers

If you bequeath capital property directly to your spouse or a qualifying spousal trust, the property can be rolled over (i.e., transferred) at your tax cost with no resulting taxation at the time of your death. For these spousal rollover rules to apply, certain criteria must be met:

- You must have been resident in Canada immediately before death.
- The ownership of the property must actually be transferred to your spouse or a qualifying spousal trust.
- If the transfer is to your spouse, he or she must have been resident in Canada immediately prior to your death.
- The spousal trust must be testamentary (i.e., created by your will) and must be resident in Canada when the property vests (i.e., property is fully transferred) in the trust.
- Vesting in the spouse or spousal trust generally must occur within 36 months of your death.
- If the property is transferred to a spousal trust, your spouse must be entitled to receive all the income during his or her lifetime and no other person may receive or have the use of any income or capital during that period.

Your executor can undertake a certain amount of tax planning after your death. For example, he or she may elect that the spousal rollover provisions not apply to selected assets. This election will enable your executor to use previous years' losses and, if the election is made with respect to qualified property, your $500,000 capital gains exemption. Because all or part of the capital gains that have accrued up the date of death are used through losses or the exemption, your spouse's future tax liability will only include any gains that accrue on the property after the transfer date.

Life Insurance

Life insurance plays an important role in estate planning. It can be used for a variety of purposes:

- to provide a base for generating investment income to replace earnings;
- to accumulate as a tax shelter and provide a tax-free payout on your death to your beneficiaries, provided that it is properly structured;
- to help the surviving shareholder of a closely held corporation finance the purchase of shares from the estate or heirs of a deceased shareholder;
- to provide liquidity on death to cover the payment of income taxes and other debts and expenses;
- to provide additional assets to bequeath to children who are not involved in a family business. In the absence of the insurance funds, those children might otherwise receive shares of the family business, creating a possible disruption in the operation of the business.

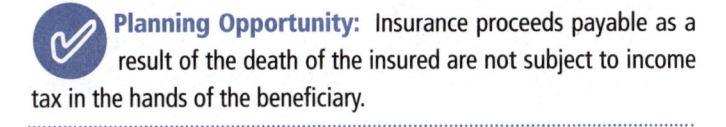

Planning Opportunity: Insurance proceeds payable as a result of the death of the insured are not subject to income tax in the hands of the beneficiary.

Your financial situation and the future needs of your family will dictate the type and quantity of life insurance you should have. While your insurance agent can provide you with details of the wide variety of individual policies available, bear in mind that there are two basic types of life insurance: term policies and permanent policies.

The premiums of a term policy are generally less expensive for a younger person, but there are a number of disadvantages. For example, you receive no benefits if either you or the insurer cancels the policy. There is usually no obligation for an insurer to continue coverage, and the policy likely will not be renewed beyond a certain age. Of course, insurance companies now offer many variations on the term policy that have additional features, such as options that guarantee your insurability to almost any age.

While a permanent policy (often referred to as a "whole-life" or "universal" policy) initially involves higher premiums, it has the advantage of also serving as an investment vehicle. For example, you can usually borrow against your insurance savings at a favourable rate, and you may receive a lump sum if you decide to cash in the policy at a future date. Most permanent policies are structured so that accruing income is not taxed annually; however, borrowing against the cash surrender value or "cashing in" the policy could result in tax.

Insurance arrangements involving the purchase of a deceased shareholder's shares by the surviving shareholders are more complex and require careful planning.

SUCCESSION AND ESTATE PLANNING FOR BUSINESS ASSETS

If you are a business owner or have an interest in a business, this asset could be your largest source of current as well as retirement income. Converting your business interest into retirement income requires the implementation of a succession plan. You may foresee eventually transferring control of the business to your children, or you may wish to sell the business to a partner or third party on your retirement, or arrange for professional management while ownership remains with your family. Whatever your goals, be aware of the planning techniques that can result in substantial tax savings for you and your family.

Most financial planning, including tax and succession planning, involves incorporated businesses. If your business is not incorporated, but can be, discuss the situation with your professional advisor to determine if you would benefit from such a change in business structure.

Before choosing the planning techniques best suited to you, consider a number of factors, such as the abilities of your spouse and/or children to manage the business, the level of their participation in control and ownership, the time frame for transfer of control, the role of key employees, and your own financial needs after retirement.

Planning Opportunity: The remainder of this chapter examines three major succession and estate planning techniques that focus on business assets:
- claiming an exemption of the tax on capital gains on the transfer of shares of an eligible small business corporation and deferring and/or claiming an exemption of tax on capital gains on the transfer of eligible farm property (and, in Quebec, eligible fishing property) to your children;
- applying one of the methods of corporate estate freezing so that the tax consequences of all or part of the future growth in the business are passed to your heirs; and
- using insurance to fund certain succession planning transactions.

Exemption of Tax on Capital Gains on Shares of Small Business Corporations

The deemed disposition rules consider capital property, including shares, to be disposed of for proceeds equal to fair market value immediately before death. As well, on the gifting of the shares to anyone other than your spouse, you are deemed to receive proceeds of disposition equal to the fair market value of the shares.

If the value of the business has increased significantly over the years, a large capital gain will generally result from the transfer of the corporation's shares. If the capital property qualifies, such a gain is eligible for the lifetime $500,000 capital gains exemption. If you owned capital property prior to 1994, you may already have claimed the $100,000 personal capital gains exemption. In this case, your lifetime exemption is restricted to $400,000. This exemption applies to gains realized on the disposition of "qualified farm property" or "qualified small business corporation shares," terms defined in the *Income Tax Act*. In Quebec, the exemption also applies to gains on the disposition of eligible fishing property. Generally speaking, if your business is an active business carried on primarily in Canada, and at least 90 per cent of the fair market value of assets of the corporation are used in the business, chances are that it would qualify for the $500,000 capital gains exemption. If your spouse owns part of the small business corporation, he or she also has access to the $500,000 exemption, which means that tax on up to $1 million of capital gains may be eliminated. If the gain is realized in one year, however, you may be subject to the Alternative Minimum Tax (AMT) on the "untaxed" part of the gain.

The Alternative Minimum Tax. The AMT is an alternative method for calculating income tax. It was created in 1986 to prevent high-income Canadians from sheltering taxable income with deductions, credits, and shelters. Although recent changes have mitigated its impact, the AMT should always be considered in tax planning. You must calculate your taxable income using both the regular and AMT methods for the current year and pay the greater tax amount. Under the AMT, 80 per cent of any capital gain is added back (70 per cent in Quebec). Some relief is available if you can claim that the income or deduction that gave rise to AMT was a result of timing. Any overpaid AMT can be carried forward for seven years against your future tax liability to the extent that regular income tax exceeds AMT. In addition, AMT is not payable in the year of death.

Rollover of Farming Property

To encourage the children of farmers to continue to operate the family farm after their parents' retirement or death, special rules permit the transfer of farming assets from one generation to the next without incurring a tax cost. Similar rollover rules also apply to the transfer of shares of a family farm corporation (or a holding corporation that owns such shares) and to the transfer of an interest in a family farm partnership. Also, the $500,000 capital gains exemption is available for gains realized on the disposition of qualified farm property (and, in Quebec, eligible fishing property), to the extent that it has not been used to shelter gains from the disposition of qualified small business corporation shares.

Rollover provisions do not eliminate taxation, but merely postpone the taxation of a gain. However, transferring the property under the lifetime exemption will increase the child's tax cost of the property, resulting in a smaller capital gain when the child does dispose of the property. The child may use the $500,000 lifetime exemption to shelter future gains when the property is sold, provided the exemption still exists at that time.

Estate Freezing Techniques for Corporate Assets

After deciding on the objectives that best suit your estate planning needs, particular techniques must be chosen that will achieve your intended objectives with the optimum tax advantage. The techniques briefly discussed below all involve "freezing" the present value of your business so that all or part of the future growth and the resulting tax consequences are deferred to your heirs. These techniques can also be used to freeze the value of almost any assets having inherent taxable capital gains.

Recall that an estate freeze is a method of organizing your affairs to permit any future appreciation in the value of selected assets to accrue to others, usually your children, and not to you. From your tax perspective, the value of the asset is frozen on the day of the transaction. Because these freezing techniques involve corporate assets, seek professional advice before undertaking any of these strategies.

The choice of technique used to freeze the assets will depend on a number of considerations, including:

- nature of the assets to be frozen;
- size of the estate;
- extent of control you wish to exercise over the frozen assets;
- number of parties to be involved in the freeze;
- immediate tax cost, if any, that might result from the freeze, taking into account the $500,000 lifetime capital gains exemption on qualified property;
- your tolerance for complexity in your financial arrangements;
- professional fees that will be incurred; and
- degree of flexibility and reversibility desired.

The following discussion assumes that your active business assets are owned by a corporation controlled by you. In general, the corporate structure facilitates effective succession and estate planning. If your business assets are not held by such a corporation, it is usually a relatively simple matter to arrange a transfer under professional guidance.

Direct Sale. Perhaps the simplest method of freezing your interest in shares of a privately held company is to sell the shares directly to your adult children. In the most common scenario, the sale would take place at fair market value, and you would take back a promissory note for the balance of the sale price not received in cash. There should be an agreement of purchase and sale that outlines the details of the sale, such as terms of payment, the due date of any unpaid amount, whether the unpaid balance is subject to interest, etc. Although it is not necessary to charge interest on the unpaid balance owed by your children, you should be aware that the attribution rules will apply if no interest is charged because the arrangement occurs between non-arm's-length parties.

There are some disadvantages to a direct sale. First, you will be taxed on any capital gain realized in excess of any gain eligible for your $500,000 lifetime capital gains exemption. You also may become subject to the Alternative Minimum Tax. However, you may claim a reserve (i.e., exclude from income) on a portion of the taxable gain if you do not immediately receive all proceeds of disposition. You may claim a capital gains reserve on the unpaid purchase price for up to five years, or 10 years if you sell to your child. When amounts claimed under the reserve provisions are eventually brought back into income for tax purposes, they will be eligible for your $500,000 lifetime capital gains exemption. Remember that even if you gift the shares to your children, you will be deemed to have received proceeds of disposition equal to the fair market value of those shares.

A second disadvantage of a direct sale is that you could lose control of the business if sufficient voting shares are sold to your children. This obstacle may be overcome if you subscribe for new voting preferred shares that carry more votes than the existing common shares. Alternatively, you may be able to exercise some control by placing the common shares in escrow (i.e., maintaining possession and control of them) until the demand note has been entirely paid off.

Another disadvantage of a direct sale accompanied by a promissory note is that, unless cash is paid for the shares, the amount owing to you remains in the corporation and may therefore continue to be at risk. To avoid this, have your children take out a loan to pay for the shares, rather than accepting a demand note from them. Accepting the full payment would necessitate recognizing the entire capital gain almost immediately for tax purposes, however, as well as risking the triggering of the Alternative Minimum Tax. As a compromise, the consideration could be part cash (from the outside loan) and part note (from the children).

Sale to a Holding Company. A common method of freezing the value of shares in an existing company involves the use of a new holding company specifically set up to acquire such shares. The children involved in the freeze would incorporate a company and acquire all its common shares for a nominal amount. You would transfer your shares in the operating company to the newly incorporated holding company, which generally can be done on a tax-deferred basis. You would take back voting preferred shares (with a value equal to the shares transferred into the holding company) in the new company as consideration for the transfer.

> **Caution:** Family law statutes in certain provinces require the equal division upon marital breakdown of assets acquired by a couple during their marriage. While gifts and inheritances are generally excluded, assets that are sold to a child could form part of the marital property and thus could be transferred to the former spouse of a child.

To avoid this possibility, the parent could acquire all the common shares of the holding company, as well as the preferred shares. The parent would then give the common shares to his or her children. Making a gift typically excludes the common shares from the matrimonial property of the married child in most cases, because assets inherited or received by way of gift are excluded from matrimonial property. In Quebec, shares of a private or public company are not included in matrimonial property. In certain provinces, an appropriately worded deed of gift can also exclude from matrimonial property any income derived from the gifted property (such as dividends on gifted shares).

Any future appreciation in the value of the business operations now accrues to your children. You could retain control of the operating company by holding voting preferred shares in the holding company. This permits you to set dividends and a reasonable salary according to your income requirements and allows you to run the business much as you did before.

One disadvantage of the use of a holding company in an estate freeze is that a capital gain or deemed dividend may arise on the redemption or disposition of the preferred shares (that you acquired as consideration for the transfer of your shares) during your lifetime. All or a portion of the capital gain could be exempt under your $500,000 lifetime capital gains exemption, however, if the shares were considered qualified property at the time of redemption or disposal. It might be necessary to obtain a professional valuation of your shares.

Asset Freeze. As an alternative to transferring the shares of an operating company to a holding company, consider freezing the value of these shares by selling the underlying operating assets to a new company incorporated by your children. This method of estate freezing may involve considerable work and expense, and sales or other transfer taxes could result. However, in some situations an asset freeze is the best approach. It works well if you own a multifaceted business and you want to break it up into separate corporations, each to be owned by one child.

Internal Freeze. It may be possible to reorganize the existing share capital structure of your company to accomplish an estate freeze. Where applicable provincial or federal company law permits, you may exchange all your existing common shares for voting preferred shares of a certain type. After the exchange, a new class of common shares would be created and purchased by the children at a nominal amount. The result of this type of reorganization is that you freeze the current value of your holdings in the operating company, and your children participate in the future growth in value of the company through their ownership of the common shares. This type of freeze is relatively simple, does not require a new corporate entity, and provides you with preferred shares that should give you a fixed income through dividends, if desired. Of course, as with other freezes where no cash is received, there is always the problem that the money owed to you is tied up in the corporation and therefore exposed to some risk.

Choosing the Best Freeze Structure. The freeze structure chosen should not be based solely on income tax considerations. For example, a partial estate freeze should provide better protection from future inflation than a complete freeze. In all cases, consult your professional advisors before making a final decision. An estate freeze requires careful planning, not only because of the tax consequences involved, but also because it may be difficult to thaw (i.e., unwind).

Sales to Third Parties. If you own a business, you may consider transferring it to unrelated parties, such as other shareholders, partners, or key employees, rather than to your children or spouse. Your spouse or children may be unable or unwilling to run the business, or the partners or other shareholders may not want the children involved. Alternatively, you may have little choice because such an arrangement may also be a binding condition in an existing shareholder's agreement governing your company's shares (see opposite, "Buy-Sell Agreements").

Selling your shares to your fellow shareholders will ensure that the company remains private and thus eligible for the small business tax benefits.

Arranging a sale to employees may bind your best employees to the business, relieve you of some management headaches as you get older, and assist in an orderly transfer of ownership. A sale could be coupled with a long-term employment contract should you wish to remain involved in the company.

Insurance

Insurance arrangements for business purposes are complex and require careful planning. The purpose of business insurance in the context of estate planning is to ensure that sufficient funds are on hand at your death for the business to be dealt with in accordance with your wishes.

Depending on your estate plan, a properly constructed insurance plan will ensure that your estate has sufficient liquid assets on hand to pay tax on any taxable capital gains realized on your death. Furthermore, such a plan will enable your partner or another shareholder in the corporation to purchase your share of the business upon your death, if that is your wish.

Buy-Sell Agreements. A buy-sell agreement is basically a contract between business partners or shareholders of a corporation. It is frequently used in estate planning to extend to surviving shareholders the right or obligation to purchase the shares of a deceased shareholder. It is advantageous both for the surviving shareholders, who may not want a stranger to buy into the corporation, and for the family of the deceased, who might otherwise have difficulty selling the shares.

The spousal rollover rules are not applicable to shares that are subject to a compulsory buy-sell agreement. Tax is paid in the terminal tax return by the deceased shareholder on any resulting capital gain if the $500,000 lifetime capital gains exemption cannot be fully used. If the buy-sell agreement is structured in such a way that the surviving shareholder has an option to buy, and the surviving spouse has an option to sell, the shares can first pass to the spouse on a rollover basis. Any capital gain arising on the subsequent sale of the shares by the spouse would be recognized in his or her hands. The gains would, however, be eligible for the spouse's own $500,000 lifetime capital gains exemption, if it is still available and provided that the shares are qualified shares at the time.

Whichever buy-sell method is employed, one thing remains certain—unless there is some method of funding the transaction, the agreement may not be consummated. It is common for life insurance to be used to provide the funds to finance the sale, and there are three common methods of employing life insurance as the funding mechanism for a buy-sell agreement.

- *Criss-Cross Insurance.* This is an insurance arrangement where each shareholder of a corporation acquires a life insurance policy on the life of every other shareholder. On the death of one shareholder, the survivors receive the tax-free proceeds of the policy and use the funds to purchase the deceased's shares from his or her estate or beneficiaries. One disadvantage of this method is that the cost of the insurance to each shareholder can vary widely, depending on the ages and health of the other shareholders.
- *Corporate-Owned Insurance.* With this type of policy, the corporation insures the lives of its shareholders and receives the proceeds on their deaths. The advantage of this method is that the corporation pays all insurance premiums and the cost to the shareholders is shared in proportion to their shareholdings. The proceeds are used by the corporation to purchase the deceased's shares, either from the deceased's estate or from the surviving spouse. Generally, neither the deceased nor the spouse will be subject to tax on the buy-back if the arrangement is properly structured. Specifically, the surviving shareholders will avoid an increase in the cost base of their shares upon redemption, which in effect means the deceased shareholder's gain has been transferred to them. This situation could be compensated for by reducing the redemption price so that more cash is retained in the corporation or by increasing the amount of the insurance coverage.

The legislation is complex, however, and, in spite of some protective measures, the deceased could be subject to tax. Existing succession plans should be reviewed to see if they qualify for the protection, while business reorganizations should be structured to alleviate the impact of the new rules.

Obtaining professional advice is strongly recommended.

- *Split-Dollar Insurance.* Split-dollar insurance is a combination of both criss-cross and corporate-owned insurance. Each shareholder purchases a whole-life type of policy on the other and assigns the cash value of the policy to the company. On the death of a shareholder, the company receives the cash value of the policy while the surviving shareholders receive the face value less the cash value, and use these proceeds to purchase the shares. The advantage of this method is that the company pays most of the premiums.

The use of buy-sell agreements, combined with life insurance funding, should be considered where shares of private companies are owned and two or more shareholders are dealing with each other at arm's length and also in some non-arm's-length situations. In all cases, the insuring method employed should not be chosen without the assistance of a professional advisor.

BEGINNING THE PROCESS

Estate planning is not a once-and-for-all exercise. It is an ongoing process, involving a variety of techniques over the years, to match your changing circumstances. This chapter has focused on the tax aspects of estate planning. There are other factors to consider that are of equal or greater importance. Above all, don't rush into a tax-motivated estate plan without giving full consideration to your personal and financial circumstances. Keep in mind that few things in life turn out exactly as we plan them. Your estate plan must have sufficient flexibility built into it so that you can adapt it to accommodate unforeseen future events.

CHAPTER FIVE

Filing Time

TAX CREDITS VERSUS DEDUCTIONS / 66

PERSONAL TAX CREDITS FOR CANADIANS / 67
For All Taxpayers / 67
    Single Status / 67
    Medical Expenses / 67
    Refundable Medical Tax Credit / 71
For Employees / 71
For Taxpayers with Spouses / 71
For Taxpayers with Children / 71
For Seniors / 72
For Canadians with Elderly Parents / 72
For Canadians Who Make Charitable or
   Political Contributions / 72
The GST Credit / 72

TAX FILING TIME / 72
Tax on Income / 72
Amending Your Previous Years' Returns / 73
A Word on Tax Audits / 73

TAX CREDITS VERSUS DEDUCTIONS

The difference between a tax credit and a tax deduction can be described simply.

A tax deduction is part of the calculation of taxable income. It decreases taxable income and saves tax based on the marginal tax bracket. For example, a $100 expenditure that qualifies for a deduction from income will save an individual in a 40 per cent bracket $40, but will save an individual in a 22 per cent bracket only $22.

A tax credit is part of the calculation of the tax levied on taxable income. The result is an amount subtracted from tax to arrive at the actual tax due. Tax credits provide the same dollar benefit to each taxpayer claiming a particular credit because the credit is subtracted directly from the individual's tax payable. If, however, the individual has no tax payable from which the credit can be deducted, and the credit is not refundable, the value of the credit is lost.

While many of us have some degree of familiarity with the personal credits listed in our tax returns, the rules for many of the credits are modified and updated regularly. In this chapter, we list the various personal tax credits available to all Canadians. With the exception of the single status and medical expenses tax credits, most of the credits and deductions are discussed in detail in other chapters that deal with specific tax topics.

PERSONAL TAX CREDITS FOR CANADIANS

The credits discussed below represent only the federal portion of the tax credits.

For All Taxpayers
Single Status. For the year 2003, the single status credit for all Canadians is $1,241 for the full year.

Medical Expenses. The federal medical expenses tax credit for 2003 is calculated by subtracting the lesser of $1,755 or 3 per cent of your net income for the year from your total qualifying medical expenses. You then multiply this amount by 16 per cent to arrive at the final credit value. You must include your receipts for your medical expenses when you claim the tax credit, and you cannot claim expenses already claimed in a previous return.

If a claimant dies within the year, the medical expenses must be paid within any 24-month period including the date of death. In any other case, they must be paid within any 12-month period ending in the taxation year.

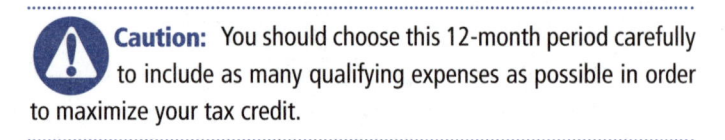

> **Caution:** You should choose this 12-month period carefully to include as many qualifying expenses as possible in order to maximize your tax credit.

The *Income Tax Act* contains extensive provisions detailing the nature of expenditures that qualify as medical expenses, which include but are not limited to the following services and products:

- medicine, including fees for doctors' visits, prescription drugs and lab tests;
- dentistry, including dentures;
- osteopathy;
- chiropody or podiatry;
- chiropractic;
- naturopathy, including acupuncturists;
- dietetics;
- therapeutic science (physiotherapy and occupational therapy);
- optometry;
- psychoanalysis;
- psychology;
- Christian Science;
- pathological or audiological speech therapy;
- sign language interpreter fees and sign language training fees;
- private health plan premiums;
- prescription eye glasses;
- devices for incontinence;
- ambulance fees;

- expenses related to bone marrow or organ transplant, including costs of searching for a suitable donor and including such costs incurred by a donor;
- expenses related to the acquisition, training and care of a guide dog or other companion animal, including travel and training of the disabled person;
- medical devices, equipment, or prostheses;
- equipment designed to improve the mobility or communication ability of persons with mobility or communication disabilities;
- certain non-medical equipment, such as a special furnace or water filter, modified to help lessen the effects of certain medical or physiological conditions, such as severe chronic asthma or immune system disorders;
- a maximum of $1,000 or 50 per cent of the value of an air conditioner, humidifier, or air cleaner necessary to help an individual cope with chronic ailments, disease, or disorders;
- 20 per cent (to a $5,000 maximum) of the costs of adapting a van to transport a wheelchair-bound individual;
- expenses incurred to alter the driveway of an individual's principal residence, where the individual has a severe and prolonged mobility impairment, to allow the individual access to a bus;
- expenses incurred for moving to accessible housing (to a $2,000 maximum);
- transportation expenses, provided that the patient must travel at least 40 kilometres (alone or with an attendant), and other related travelling expenses, provided that the individual must travel at least 80 kilometres (alone or with an attendant);
- incremental expenses related to the construction of a principal place of residence or reasonable expenses for renovations to a dwelling where special features are incorporated to enable the individual to gain access to, or be mobile or function within, the home.

- part-time attendant care up to $10,000 per year ($20,000 in the year of death);
- expenses related to full-time attendant care at home (but not paid to a spouse or to someone under 18 years of age), or for care in a nursing home;
- expenses for care, or care and training, at a school or institution equipped to provide such care or care and training;
- expenses related to the training of an individual in connection with providing care to an individual with a mental or physical infirmity. To be eligible for the credit, the taxpayer must be providing care to an individual who is related to the taxpayer, and that individual must have a mental or physical infirmity and be a member of the taxpayer's household or dependent on the taxpayer for support;
- expenses related to therapy for individuals with severe and prolonged disabilities;
- expenses related to the care and supervision of disabled persons living in a group home; and
- expenses related to the tutoring of persons with learning disabilities or other mental impairments, including the costs of spoken books prescribed by a doctor for people with disabilities.

Specifically excluded from this credit are the following products and services:

- toothpaste;
- non-prescription birth control devices;
- wigs, unless they have been made for an individual who has suffered extreme hair loss as a result of disease, treatment, or accident;
- maternity clothing;
- antiseptic diaper services;
- funeral expenses;
- illegal medical treatments or operations;

- food and beverages, unless they must be ingested as treatment for an illness;
- gym, spa, or hotel health programs;
- scales for weighing food; and
- payments to a municipality, in cases where the municipality has employed a doctor to administer to the community.

Refundable Medical Tax Credit. In addition to the normal non-refundable medical expense tax credit, you may be eligible to claim a refundable tax credit for the year equal to the lesser of $544 or 25 per cent of eligible medical expenses. The credit is reduced by 5 per cent of adjusted income exceeding $20,621. To qualify, you must be a Canadian resident, be age 18 or over, and have income of at least $2,719 for the year.

For Employees (See Chapter 6)
CPP/QPP and Employment Insurance contributions

For Taxpayers with Spouses (See Chapter 11)
Spouse credit
Mental or physical impairment
Tuition fees
Education
Student loan interest
Infirm dependant
Age 65 and over
Pension income

For Taxpayers with Children (See Chapter 12)
Infirm dependant
Mental or physical impairment
Tuition fees
Education
Student loan interest
Eligible dependant

For Seniors (See Chapter 15)
Age 65 and over
Pension income
Mental or physical impairment

For Canadians with Elderly Parents (See Chapter 16)
Eligible dependant
Infirm dependant
Mental or physical impairment
Caregiver

For Canadians Who Make Charitable or Political Contributions (See Chapter 17)
Charitable donations
Political contributions

The GST Credit

All Canadians must pay a 7 per cent Goods and Services Tax (GST) (or a 15 per cent Harmonized Sales Tax (HST) in Nova Scotia, New Brunswick, and Newfoundland and Labrador) on most goods and services. In Quebec there is also a 7.5 per cent Quebec Sales Tax (QST). Since the QST is applicable on the price plus GST, its effective rate is 8.025 per cent.

To offset GST paid by lower-income taxpayers, a GST credit is available. To receive the GST credit, an individual, or the lower-income spouse of a family, must file a tax return and fill out the appropriate information (number of dependants and spouse's net income) box on the return. The credit is paid out in four instalments over the following year.

TAX FILING TIME

Tax on Income
All provinces and territories now use a tax on income system for calculating personal income taxes. Taxpayers continue to

file a single income tax return, with federal and provincial income tax calculated separately. Note, however, that Quebec requires a separate provincial income tax return to be filed.

Amending Your Previous Years' Returns

You are required by law to keep your tax records and documentation for the six previous years. In addition, clients who file by computer or use computer-assisted accounting programs (namely corporations) are required to keep an electronically readable computer version even if a paper version is also kept. At first glance, this might seem like a needless hassle, but there is also an opportunity here. If you find, as a result of implementing a tax plan, that you did not take advantage of certain deductions or credits, or you made a mistake in a previous year's return, you can resubmit your revised return. There is a time limit, however. In most instances, the Canada Customs and Revenue Agency (CCRA) will reassess for errors or omissions within three years of the original filing date, even if the reassessment would be in the taxpayer's favour. Beyond this limit, the CCRA has discretion under the Fairness Package to reassess a taxation year at the request of a taxpayer.

A Word on Tax Audits

Similarly, the tax authorities have three years from the time your tax return is initially assessed to review the information and make any reassessment of your taxes. Although there is an excellent chance that you never will be audited, it is important to be able to explain the information on your return if you are asked. For this reason, good record-keeping is an essential element of your tax planning. Document the intent and the details of your various transactions and all aspects of your business and financial activities. This documentation will assist you in remembering in several years' time exactly what occurred. Should you be audited, this detailed documentation will provide evidence of careful and businesslike planning, an important protective stance in an audit.

There is no need to fear a tax audit if your tax plans are well designed and well documented in accordance with tax law. If you have made misrepresentations through neglect, carelessness, or wilful default, or if you have committed fraud, however, you do have something to worry about. There is no time limit for assessment on such activities.

CHAPTER SIX

If You Are an Employee

EMPLOYMENT INCOME—WHAT IS INCLUDED? / 76
Fringe Benefits / 76
Employee Loans / 77
    Commercial Rate Rule Exception / 78
    Home Purchase Loans / 78
    Home Relocation Loans / 79

CREDITS AND DEDUCTIONS / 80
CPP/QPP and Employment Insurance Credit / 80
Expenses Connected with Employment—The General Rules / 81
Deductible Expenses / 81
Moving Expenses / 83
Remote Work Locations, Special Work Sites, and Northern
  Residents Deductions / 84
    Remote Work Location Deduction / 84
    Special Work Site Deduction / 84
    Northern Residents Deduction / 85
Deduction Available for Imputed Interest / 85

PLANNING OPPORTUNITIES / 86
Benefits from Employee Loans / 86
Common Income Deferral Strategies / 87
    Deferred Income Plans / 87
    Employee Stock Options / 87
    Retiring Allowances / 87
    Contributions to Deferred Profit Sharing Plans (DPSPs) / 89
    Proceeds from DPSPs / 89
    Salary Deferral Arrangements (SDAs) / 90
    Retirement Compensation Arrangements (RCAs) / 91

>   Employee Benefit Plans (EBPs) / 92
>   Unpaid Remuneration / 92
> Shareholder Loans / 93
>
> DO YOU QUALIFY FOR A GST REBATE? / 95
> Who May Claim a Rebate? / 95
> What Expenses are Eligible? / 96
> Filing an Application / 96

For Canadians who earn income solely from employment sources, the best tax planning advice is that you must ensure that you use all credits, deductions, and tax deferral options available to you. For the most part, Canadian employees have limited opportunities for tax planning because they do not control the timing of their income.

EMPLOYMENT INCOME—WHAT IS INCLUDED?

Your taxable employment income in most cases will include almost all benefits you receive by virtue of that employment. These amounts are measured by your employer and reported to you and to the government on your T4 (Relevé 1 in Quebec) each year.

Fringe Benefits

Included in your taxable employment income are such things as personal use of an employer's auto, certain premiums paid by your employer under provincial hospitalization and medical care plans, prizes and incentive awards, financial counselling, travel benefits, and the total cost of group life insurance. Non-taxable benefits include such things as subsidized meals, uniforms or special clothing required for the job, recreational facilities provided at your work location, discounts on merchandise you purchase from your employer for personal use, retirement or re-employment counselling, mental or physical health counselling, and private health and income insurance plans.

> **Planning Opportunity:** Since 1997, if your employer either pays or reimburses you for the costs of taking a course, the Canada Customs and Revenue Agency (CCRA) may not consider the payment a taxable employment benefit. The course taken must be primarily for the benefit of your employer and not you, even if the course will lead to a degree, diploma, or certificate and even if you must take time off work to complete the program. In the latter case, it must be reasonable to assume that you will return to work after completing the course. In addition to tuition, reasonable costs for fees, meals, travel, and accommodation will be allowed. Other general employment-related courses will also qualify, including stress management, first aid, language skills, and in-house training.

Although there is less planning flexibility with employment income when it is compared with other sources of income, various compensation alternatives may be available to you through your employer. The following outlines these alternatives and their tax implications.

> **Caution:** If you use frequent flyer points accumulated while travelling on employer-paid business trips, you must include the fair market value of the air travel credits enjoyed for personal use in your income. If an employer does not control the credits accumulated in a frequent flyer program by employees flying on employer-paid business trips, it is the employee's responsibility to determine and include in income the fair market value of the benefits received.

Employee Loans

The term "employee loan" is something of a misnomer, since it applies to more than a simple loan between an employer and an employee. It describes any situation in which the employee is indebted in some way to the employer. The employee is taxed on any imputed interest benefit resulting from this indebtedness.

The benefit rules apply not only to loans, but also to any other form of debt incurred by virtue of the previous, current, or future office or employment of an individual. It is not necessary that the employee be the debtor, nor is there any requirement that the employer be the creditor. For example, the imputed interest rules will apply if your employer makes a loan to your child to help support your child's university education, or if you obtain a bank loan at a below-market interest rate as a result of your employer's involvement. Regardless of the actual debtor, any imputed interest benefit will be taxable in your hands. The rules also apply to third-party loans where the employer is financing part or all of the cost of the loan.

> **Caution:** The amount of the taxable benefit included in income is generally calculated as the difference between interest that would be paid using the prevailing prescribed interest rate, set by the government each quarter, and interest actually paid within the year or 30 days after the end of the calendar year.

For example, if you borrow $10,000 from your employer at 2 per cent and the prescribed rate is 5 per cent all year, you must include $300 in income as a taxable benefit (5 per cent minus 2 per cent times $10,000), assuming the loan is outstanding for the entire year.

Commercial Rate Rule Exception. The taxable benefit rules do not apply to an employee loan on which interest is charged at a rate equal to or above the commercial lending rate at the time the loan was made. This exception may be restricted, depending on all the terms and conditions of the loan.

Home Purchase Loans. A qualifying home purchase loan can be made to an employee or a related person for the purpose of acquiring a dwelling or to refinance a mortgage on such a dwelling. The borrower or the related person must live in the dwelling. The definition of a "home purchase loan" includes a loan used to acquire a share of a cooperative housing corporation entitling the purchaser or a related person to inhabit a dwelling unit in the cooperative.

The taxable benefit on home purchase loans arises if the interest charged on the loan by the employer is less than the prescribed rate. The prescribed rate (for purposes of home purchase loans only) is the lesser of the prescribed rate on the date the loan was made and the prescribed rate for a given date. In effect, the taxable benefit may decrease, but cannot increase, during the term of the loan. The prescribed rate for this purpose for 2003 was 4 per cent for the third quarter and 3 per cent for the other three quarters. All home purchase loans are considered to have a term not exceeding five years. On each fifth anniversary date of the loan, a new loan is deemed to be received, and the prescribed rate of interest at that time is compared to the prescribed rates for the next five-year period.

> **Planning Opportunity:** Because of the way the prescribed rate is calculated, we know in advance what the rate will be in the following quarter. If you as an employee arrange a loan from your employer to acquire (or to repay a loan that had been used to acquire) a home, you should request a short-term loan initially (i.e., less than three months). If the prescribed rate for the next quarter is lower than (or the same as) the current quarter, another short-term loan can be arranged. If the prescribed rate is showing a tendency to rise over an extended period, a long-term (e.g., five-year) loan could be finalized in the current quarter.

Home Relocation Loans. A deduction is available to employees who relocate or take up a new position, provided they are eligible to claim moving expenses (discussed on page 83) and have received a low-interest or interest-free loan to assist with the acquisition of a home at the new location. The deduction is made from any taxable benefit relating to this home purchase loan when taxable income is calculated. The deduction is equal to the lesser of the actual benefit included in income and the benefit from a $25,000 interest-free employee loan. There is a time limit: this deduction will be available for the lesser of five years or the length of time that the home purchase loan (or a replacement loan for it) is outstanding.

The *Hoefele* case (Federal Court of Appeal, 95 DTC 5602 and cited in *Siwik* v. *The Queen*, Federal Court of Appeal, 96 DTC 1678) sets out the test for determining when an amount, in this case an amount related to a home relocation, received from an employer is taxable as a "benefit." According to the court, "a receipt must confer an economic benefit, i.e., it must increase the recipient's net worth." In *Hoefele*, employees received mortgage interest subsidies from their employer to cover the higher market prices of Toronto. The court concluded that "the assistance received by the taxpayer was not a colourable attempt to increase his remuneration; it was merely a reimbursement for an expense incurred by virtue of employment."

Subsequent changes to the *Income Tax Act* restrict the tax exemption of employers' mortgage interest subsidy payments paid to relocated employees. Additionally, benefits paid by employers to relocating employees to reimburse them for losses incurred on the sale of the former residence are no longer tax-exempt unless they total less than $15,000. Half of any amount in excess of $15,000 will be included in the taxable income of the employee.

CREDITS AND DEDUCTIONS

CPP/QPP and Employment Insurance Credit

The federal CPP/QPP and EI tax credit is calculated as 16 per cent of CPP/QPP and EI payments for the year.

For 2003, the EI premium rate for employees is $2.10 per $100 of income up to a maximum of $39,000 of income. Maximum EI contributions are $819 for employees and

$1,146.60 for employers. The ceiling for 2003 earnings under CPP is $39,900. The maximum CPP payment is $1,801.80 by each of the employer and employee, based on a contribution rate of 4.95 per cent.

A self-employed person is not eligible for EI benefits, and therefore does not have to make contributions. Self-employed individuals must make CPP contributions, however, and the maximum contribution is $3,603.60 for 2003, based on a contribution rate of 9.9 per cent.

Insurable earnings for Employment Insurance (EI) do not include payments to employees for:

- board, lodging, and transportation at special work sites and remote locations;
- disability-related employment benefits;
- premiums under a private health services plan;
- subsidized school services; or
- transportation to a job.

Expenses Connected with Employment—The General Rules

Generally, employees are not entitled to claim deductions for expenditures they incur as a result of their employment, unless these deductions are specifically authorized in the *Income Tax Act*.

Deductible Expenses

Employment expenses that may be deductible include:

- union or professional dues (not including the initiation fee). In Quebec, these dues are eligible for a tax credit, excluding the amount corresponding to professional liability insurance, which is a deduction;
- up to $250 contributed by a teacher to a teachers' exchange fund;
- automobile expenses—if you use your own automobile for your employer's business, or in your own business, you may be entitled to deduct automobile expenses (see also Chapter 14);

- contributions made to a registered pension plan;
- moving expenses (discussed opposite);
- travelling expenses that are incurred in the course of employment, provided that you are ordinarily required to carry out your duties away from your employer's place of business or in different places, and you do not receive a tax-free allowance for travelling expenses;
- supplies consumed in the performance of your duties, if you are required by contract to pay for them (the courts have interpreted "supplies consumed in the performance of your duties" quite narrowly); and
- legal expenses incurred to collect or establish a right to a salary or other amount owing by an employer, or to collect or establish a right to a retiring allowance (which includes awards for wrongful dismissal) or pension benefit, may also be deductible. The deduction is limited to the amounts received that are not transferred to an RRSP or RPP. Excess amounts can be carried forward for deduction in any of the seven following years. Any reimbursement of these fees must be included in income.

You are also allowed to deduct the costs of care provided by an attendant, who is not the individual's spouse or a person under age 18, for an individual certified as having a severe and prolonged impairment. There is no maximum amount that may be deducted; however, it is limited to two-thirds of eligible income, which includes income from employment or self-employment, or a grant for research or similar work (net of expenses). This deduction is in addition to the personal tax credit (mental or physical impairment) that may be claimed by such a certified person.

Special expense deduction provisions are provided for clergy, travelling salespeople, musicians, artists, and certain railway and transport employees. If you qualify, be sure you have the appropriate prescribed forms signed by your employer.

Moving Expenses

Moving expenses are deductible if you meet certain conditions and your employer does not reimburse your expenses. Moving expenses must be incurred in connection with beginning a business, employment, or full-time post-secondary education at a new location. The distance between your old residence and your new work or school location must be at least 40 kilometres greater than the distance between your new residence and your new work or school location.

Qualifying expenditures include the travelling costs to move you, your family, and your household goods, as well as meals and lodging en route; disposal costs with respect to your old residence; and legal services with respect to the purchase of the new residence, provided that you or your spouse sold your old residence. You also may deduct storage costs incurred in the course of the move for your household goods. Since 1998, moving expenses have included specified expenses in connection with maintaining a vacant former residence, including interest, property taxes, and insurance premiums, subject to certain maximum amounts. Finally, eligible expenses also include the costs of revising legal documents to reflect your new address, including replacing a driver's licence, as well as the cost of disconnecting and connecting utilities.

Non-qualifying expenses include: fees paid for work done to make your former home more marketable; any loss from the sale of your home; expenses for house-hunting trips before the move; the value of items movers refused to take, for example, plants or paint; expenses for job-hunting in another city; expenses of replacing personal-use items, for example, a tool shed, firewood, drapes, or carpets; and mail-forwarding costs.

There are limits on the total amount that will be deductible, depending on the particular circumstances of your move. Remember that you must be earning taxable income in your new location to claim the deduction. Taxpayers may use either a detailed or a simplified method for calculating moving expenses. The detailed method requires that you keep your receipts on file although you do not have to file them with your return. Under the simplified method, receipts are not required and set deduction rates are provided. For example, for claiming meal expenses, you may claim a flat rate of $11 per meal, to a maximum of $33 per day per person, without receipts.

Remote Work Locations, Special Work Sites, and Northern Residents Deductions

These three items are closely related, particularly in the employment context, but each has specific qualification criteria. A tax benefit only arises with respect to remote work locations and special work sites if your employer pays your actual living expenses or pays you an allowance (not exceeding a reasonable amount) with respect to either of these work areas.

Remote Work Location Deduction. Two categories of criteria must be satisfied before this deduction can be claimed. To qualify as "remote," a work location must be 30 kilometres or more from the nearest community of at least 40,000 people and lack essential services (medical and educational facilities, housing, and food shopping). The employee must be working in the remote work location for longer than 36 hours because of work commitments. Overall, the conditions must render it unreasonable to expect the employee to set up and maintain a self-contained dwelling unit.

When employees are eligible for benefits for remote work locations, they can exclude from their income allowances for (or the value of) free or subsidized housing, board, and certain transportation.

Special Work Site Deduction. If an employee is undertaking temporary work for an employer far enough away from his or her principal residence that it is not reasonable to expect the employee to commute daily, the employee may qualify under this deduction. The 36-hour requirement also applies here and the benefits to the employee are the same as for the remote site deduction. Employees and their employers must complete a Declaration of Exemption—Employment at Special Work Sites form before the employers can exclude the relevant benefits or allowances from the employees' income.

Northern Residents Deduction. If an individual resides on a permanent basis for at least six months within a northern Canadian area designated by the Canada Customs and Revenue Agency (CCRA), he or she may qualify to claim the northern residents deduction. This deduction consists of two deductions: a residency deduction and a deduction for travel benefits received from an employer in the designated area. The CCRA has set the residency deduction at a ceiling based on the lesser of two amounts: 20 per cent of net income for the year, or a $7.50 per day basic residency amount for every day the individual lived in the designated area and an additional $7.50 per day for each day the individual maintained a self-contained dwelling unit and no other occupant of the dwelling claimed the basic deduction. The maximum amount that may be claimed is $5,475 per year. The deduction for travel relates to the value of two employer-provided trips per year and unlimited amounts for travel for medical reasons.

If an individual resides in an area designated by the CCRA as a "prescribed intermediate zone," the taxpayer may qualify to claim one-half of the northern residents deduction.

An individual may be entitled to claim the northern residents deduction even if he or she also qualifies for the exclusion from income available with respect to either a remote work location or a special work site.

Deduction Available for Imputed Interest
Employees may claim an offsetting deduction for any imputed interest included in income as a taxable benefit arising from an

employee loan, provided that the interest would otherwise be deductible if it had been actually paid. For example, low-interest or interest-free loans used for investment purposes (including investment in shares of an employer corporation) or for the purchase of an automobile or aircraft used in the business of the employer would qualify. (You will want to consider the tax treatment of automobiles used for business purposes, discussed in Chapter 14.)

Any potential deduction is available only to the debtor, even though the interest benefit may be included in another taxpayer's (i.e., the employee's) income. Where there is a potential interest deduction, it is recommended that the employee be the debtor; otherwise, the employee will have the taxable benefit but not the offsetting deduction. Where the debtor is in a higher tax bracket than the employee, however, the debtor should claim the deduction.

PLANNING OPPORTUNITIES

Benefits from Employee Loans

Interest-free or low-interest loans can produce a worthwhile benefit even if interest is imputed as a taxable benefit, because the tax on the imputed interest would always be less than the interest paid in the marketplace. If you borrow $25,000 from your employer at 3 per cent and otherwise would have to borrow at 5 per cent, you will save $500 each year in interest charges. No taxable benefit arises because the rate of interest you pay is higher than or equal to the prescribed rate (assuming that the prescribed rate does not exceed 3 per cent). Note that you must pay the interest by January 30 of the following year or it will not reduce the imputed benefit.

Of course, the benefits are even greater if the employee loan is interest-free. Let's assume that your marginal rate of tax is 44 per cent and you borrow $25,000 interest-free. Your cost of the loan is the tax paid on the imputed benefit of $750

($25,000 at 3 per cent), which is $330 (assuming the prescribed rate is 3 per cent throughout the year and the loan is outstanding for a full year). This works out to an effective interest charge of 1.32 per cent and a saving of $920, compared to the 5 per cent loan ($1,250 minus $330). If the loan is used to earn investment income, the imputed interest of $750 is deductible and no cost is associated with the loan, whereas your after-tax cost on a conventional loan would be $700 ($1,250 less tax saving at 44 per cent).

Common Income Deferral Strategies

Deferred Income Plans. Employers frequently offer such plans, many of which relate to retirement planning. Whether tax is deferred on employment income depends on the nature of your particular plan.

Employee Stock Options. The tax rules relating to stock options are extremely complex. To avoid any nasty tax surprises, obtain professional advice on this subject. As a general rule, the benefit derived by an employee when shares of an employer are purchased at less than fair market value is taxable as income from employment. The rules for stock option benefits have been expanded to include the purchase of mutual fund units as well as shares of the employer.

Retiring Allowances. To a certain extent, a retiring allowance can be considered a means of deferring income. It must not take the form of a deferred salary, however, which would be the case if an employee accepted a relatively low salary in exchange for a generous so-called "retiring allowance."

A retiring allowance is an amount (other than a superannuation or pension benefit or an amount received as a consequence of the death of an employee) received by the employee on or after retirement in recognition of long service. It includes early retirement incentives or any payment received with respect to a loss of employment, whether or not received as a termination payment or damages from loss of office. Termination payments are fully taxable, although tax may be deferred by transferring eligible amounts to an RRSP.

After your death, a retiring allowance may be received by your dependant or relative or by your estate, and tax may also be deferred by transferring eligible amounts to an RRSP.

As an employee, you can transfer only those retiring allowance payments that relate to years of service before 1996 to your RRSP. The maximum amount of a retiring allowance that can be transferred on a tax-free basis to a registered pension plan or RRSP is $2,000 for each partial or full calendar year before 1996 that the employee was employed by the employer paying the amount, or by a related employer (for this purpose, a related employer has an extended meaning). If the employee was not a member of the employer's pension plan or deferred profit sharing plan (DPSP), or the contributions made on his or her behalf did not become vested in the employee, an additional $1,500 may be transferred to a registered pension plan or an RRSP for each year that the employee was employed by the employer prior to 1988. Eligible amounts may still be transferred after 1995, but the years after 1995 cannot be included in the calculation.

Any amount of a retiring allowance not transferred to either a registered pension plan or RRSP must be included in income in the year it is received and will be taxed at your marginal rate. As noted before, the Alternative Minimum Tax no longer applies to amounts paid into an RRSP, including retiring allowances that are transferred. This change is retroactive to 1994.

For Quebec tax purposes, since 1997, the retiring allowance transferred to an RRSP is not taken into consideration in calculating the Quebec Alternative Minimum Tax.

A retiring allowance cannot be transferred to a spousal RRSP.

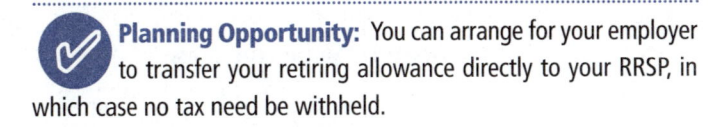

> **Planning Opportunity:** You can arrange for your employer to transfer your retiring allowance directly to your RRSP, in which case no tax need be withheld.

If you receive the amount directly from your employer and then make the transfer, your employer must withhold tax. You can then claim the tax as tax withheld during the year in your next return, and it will increase your refund or decrease your balance of tax owing.

Contributions to Deferred Profit Sharing Plans (DPSPs). Your employer may be making deductible contributions to a DPSP on your behalf. The maximum employer contribution for 2003 is limited to the lesser of 18 per cent of the employee's remuneration and $7,750. This amount will increase to $8,250 in 2004 and $9,000 in 2005.

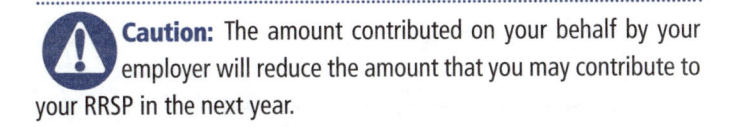

> **Caution:** The amount contributed on your behalf by your employer will reduce the amount that you may contribute to your RRSP in the next year.

Beginning in 2006, the maximum figure will be indexed according to the average increase in salaries. DPSPs must provide that the employer make a contribution based on company profits, but no contribution need be made in a loss year. A DPSP does not permit any type of past-service or employee contribution.

Proceeds from DPSPs. Amounts received from DPSPs must be included in income, except for capital amounts contributed by the employee for the years in which such contributions were permitted by law. Most plans allow for payment of taxable amounts to be spread over a maximum of 10 years. Otherwise, it is possible to purchase an annuity for life before reaching age 69, although, if there are guaranteed terms, they cannot exceed 15 years. Employee contributions may be withdrawn at any time. DPSP proceeds can also be deferred by transferring them into a registered pension plan, an RRSP, or another eligible DPSP. This must be done by the time the taxpayer turns 69. If the DPSP was previously an employee profit sharing plan at any time in the past, you may exclude an additional amount from income.

Salary Deferral Arrangements (SDAs). The rules concerning SDAs were introduced to curb abuses associated with employee benefit plans.

An SDA is defined as a funded or unfunded plan involving both an employee and employer where it is reasonable to consider that one of the purposes of the existence of the plan is to postpone the receipt of his or her remuneration beyond the end of a year. The rules restrict the ability of employees to defer the tax payable on salary earned by them in the year or a preceding year.

A variety of plans are excluded from the definition, including:

- registered pension plans and other registered plans;
- certain benefit plans, such as group sickness or accident insurance plans;
- plans to defer the salary of certain professional athletes;
- plans to provide funds for the education of workers;
- three-year bonus plans; and
- self-funded leave-of-absence plans.

In limited circumstances, the rules regarding SDAs do not apply to plans that existed before February 26, 1986.

Under the SDA rules, a right to receive deferred amounts, whether funded or not, must be recognized for tax purposes as it is accrued. This means that it must be included in the employment income of the employee in the year the amount is earned, even if not yet received. The employer will receive a deduction for the amount paid in that year. Interest or other amounts paid by the employer with respect to the deferred salary will be treated as employment income in the year earned and not necessarily in the year it is received. If a person other than the employee has a right to receive the deferred salary, these rules still apply.

Retirement Compensation Arrangements (RCAs). An RCA is any plan or arrangement established after October 8, 1986, under which a taxpayer's employer or former employer (or related person) makes payments to a custodian for the taxpayer. These payments must relate to benefits that will be provided to the taxpayer or others on the retirement, loss of office, etc., of the taxpayer. Certain arrangements are specifically excluded from the definition, including:

- registered pension plans;
- employee profit sharing plans and DPSPs;
- RRSPs;
- group sickness and accident insurance plans;
- certain plans established for professional athletes and officials; and
- SDAs.

Contributions to an RCA are deductible by the employer when made, but are subject to a refundable 50 per cent withholding tax (except for Quebec tax purposes). This tax is refunded when payments are made from the RCA and included in the recipient's income. Income earned in the RCA on the contributions is also subject to a 50 per cent tax that is refundable when payments are made to beneficiaries. Any income from an RCA is not taxable to the recipient until it is actually received. An employee may make contributions to an RCA, which are deductible by him or her, but these contributions are also subject to the 50 per cent refundable tax.

Employee Benefit Plans (EBPs). In the unlikely event that a deferral plan does not fall within the definition of an SDA or an RCA, the plan likely is an EBP. In this case, the employer will not receive a deduction for amounts deferred. Prior to the introduction of the SDA rules, EBPs were frequently used to defer the salary of employees who worked for non-taxable employers, such as government, non-profit organizations, or companies in a loss position.

Under an EBP, a portion of the employee's salary is placed with a custodian. The employer receives no deduction for amounts directed to the custodian, and the employee is not taxed on these amounts until they are actually received. Investment income earned on the deferred amounts is taxed in the hands of the plan, or in the hands of the employee or employer.

In a self-funded leave-of-absence arrangement, under which an employee may defer up to one-third of his or her salary each year for up to six years, the deferred amount must be included in the employee's income for tax purposes in the seventh year. The total deferred amount must be included to the extent that it has not previously been received and included in income.

Unpaid Remuneration. Deferring remuneration provides only a limited benefit. An employer is not allowed a deduction for remuneration expense incurred in the year if the amount remains unpaid to the employee for more than 180 days after the year-end of the employer. The employer will receive the deduction in the year the remuneration is actually paid. This provision applies regardless of whether the employer and employee are related. Remuneration expense does not include reasonable amounts for vacation or holiday pay, or deferred amounts under an SDA.

The SDA rules do not affect remuneration amounts paid within the 180-day limit. Thus, for the year the remuneration is earned, employees will not have to include a benefit in income for tax purposes equal to the unpaid amount.

Shareholder Loans

If you are a shareholder as well as an employee, be aware of the special rules regarding loans or advances from your company. Although many of the rules for low-interest and interest-free loans are the same, there are greater tax implications regarding the granting of shareholder loans.

If a shareholder or a relative of the shareholder receives a loan or incurs any type of indebtedness from the shareholder's corporation or a related corporation, and the amount is not repaid by the end of the lender's following taxation year, the amount of the loan is included in the debtor's income in the year the loan was made. Depending on the corporation's year-end in relation to the taxpayer's year-end (the calendar year), the taxpayer may be required to amend his or her income tax return. If the amount is included in income and is repaid at a later date, it is deductible from income in the year of repayment. A repayment that is a part of a series of loans and repayments would not qualify for the deduction.

In the year of repayment, you should ensure that you have sufficient income to absorb any deduction resulting from the repayment of such a loan. This is necessary because, if the amount of the repayment exceeds other income, the excess will be a non-capital loss that can be carried back.

There are four other exceptions to the rules requiring a loan to be included in income:

- when the creditor lends the money as part of its ordinary business;
- when loans are made to employees of the creditor or their spouses, enabling the employee or spouse to purchase a dwelling for their own habitation;
- when loans are made to employees of the creditor, enabling the employee to purchase an automobile for employment purposes; and

- when a corporate creditor loans funds to employees, enabling the employees to purchase, from the corporation or a related corporation, fully paid treasury shares of the corporation for their own benefit.

This last provision does not provide for the employee to purchase shares from any other shareholder; rather, they must be purchased directly from the corporation. In each of the four cases above, *bona fide* arrangements for repayment of the loan or indebtedness within a reasonable period must be in place at the time the loan is made.

A loan made to an employee who is a shareholder must be made to him or her as an employee, and not as a shareholder, in order for the exemptions to apply. Accordingly, the loan must be available to all employees. One of the effects of this requirement is that the exclusion is denied to loans made by a company in which all the employees are also shareholders.

The taxable benefit rules regarding imputed interest on low-interest or interest-free employee loans apply for the most part to all types of shareholder loans and indebtedness (see above). The home purchase and home relocation loan rules do not apply to shareholder loans unless the shareholder is an employee and the loan was received because of the borrower's status as an employee.

Advances to shareholders during the year in anticipation of dividend payments are considered to be indebtedness, and the imputed interest taxable benefit rules apply.

The governing corporate law statute under which a corporation was formed may contain restrictions on lending money to employees, officers, directors, and shareholders of the corporation. Reference should be made to the relevant act before any such loan is made.

DO YOU QUALIFY FOR A GST REBATE?

To receive a rebate of any GST/HST and QST paid, you must be a registrant. An exception to this general rule applies to certain employees and members of a partnership. Under specific conditions, these individuals may qualify for a rebate of the GST/HST and QST paid, even if they are not registrants. These individuals may obtain this rebate by filing a special form with their income tax return. They will receive a rebate only for those expenses that are deductible when calculating income for income tax purposes. A rebate factor of 7/107 (15/115 in the HST provinces) is used to calculate the qualifying portion of net expenses (7.5/107.5 for the QST rebate).

Taxpayers must include the GST/HST (or QST) rebate in the computation of their income for the taxation year in which the rebate is received. For example, a rebate claimed in the 2002 income tax return, but received in 2003, must be included in the taxpayer's 2003 income.

Who May Claim a Rebate?

Only the employees of a registrant employer and the members of a registered partnership may claim the rebate, provided the registrants are not otherwise entitled to a rebate of the GST/HST and QST on the same eligible expense. For example, an employee of a non-profit organization is entitled to claim the rebate only if the organization is a registrant.

Commissioned and other salespeople, and employees and partners who have expenses related to a motor vehicle are the most common claimants for GST/HST and QST rebates.

> **Caution:** An employee cannot claim the GST rebate if his or her employer is a listed financial institution. However, he or she may be entitled to the QST rebate.

This restriction means that a salesperson who works on commission at a brokerage firm or an insurance company is not eligible for the GST/HST rebate on the expenses that he or she deducts when calculating income. This restriction does not apply to the QST rebate.

What Expenses Are Eligible?

The rebate is available solely for expenses deducted for income tax purposes in the computation of a taxpayer's employment income, or income from a partnership.

Entertainment expenses (50 per cent of the amount), advertising costs, professional membership dues, office expenses, leasing costs, various supplies, automobile expenses, and capital cost allowance (CCA) on a motor vehicle, a musical instrument, or an aircraft generally qualify for a GST rebate. If the rebate is with respect to the capital cost of property, the rebate reduces the capital cost of the property at the time the rebate is received (usually the following year), rather than being included in income.

If an employer pays a reasonable allowance to cover expenses, the employee will not be eligible for a tax rebate. An employee or partner can, however, claim a GST/HST (or a QST) rebate if the allowance received was unreasonable (i.e., one that must be included in the employee's or partner's income). In such cases, the employee or partner must obtain a statement from the employer or partnership to the effect that it has claimed no input tax credit for the allowance.

Filing an Application

In general, a rebate application (form GST-370 for the GST/HST, and form VD-358 for the QST) is filed with the income tax return for the calendar year in which the expenses are incurred, although a claim can be made retroactively within four years after that calendar year.

The example on page 97 illustrates how the GST and QST rebates are calculated.

Based on this example, the salesperson is entitled to a GST rebate of $144 (7/107 of $2,200) and a QST rebate of $153 (7.5/107.5 of $2,200).

If You Are an Employee ▶ 97

Computing the Rebate

	Salesperson's Expenses	GST Rebate Computed on	QST Rebate Computed on
Entertainment	$ 800	$ 400	$ 400
Office expenses:			
Electricity	400	400	400
Property taxes	200	—	—
Insurance	300	—	—
Suppliers	100	100	100
Automobile expenses:			
CCA	1,000	1,000	1,000
Interest	200	—	—
Insurance	400	—	—
Operating costs	150	150	150
Repairs and maintenance	150	150	150
	$3,700	$2,200	$2,200

Since property taxes, insurance and interest are not subject to GST, no rebate is allowed. In Quebec, there is a tax on insurance premiums, but there is no entitlement to a rebate.

Note that the capital cost allowance (CCA) on the car is eligible for the QST rebate if the car was purchased after July 31, 1995. In our example, the car was purchased in 2001.

The portion of the GST and QST rebates that relates to the expenses ($79 and $84, respectively) must be included in the income of the employee for income tax purposes the following year, whereas another portion (CCA on automobile) equal to $65 and $61, respectively, reduces the capital cost on which the CCA is based at the beginning of the following year.

CHAPTER SEVEN

If You Are a Business Owner

IF YOU ARE A SOLE PROPRIETOR OR IN A PARTNERSHIP / 99
Income from a Business Defined / 99
Taxation of Income from a Business / 100
Taxation Year / 101

DEDUCTIONS / 102
Home Office Expenses / 102
Conventions / 103
Deductible Interest / 103
Golf and Entertainment Expenses / 103
Deduction for Private Health Service Plan Contributions / 104
CPP/QPP Deduction for Self-Employed Individuals / 105

PLANNING OPPORTUNITY / 105
Hiring Your Spouse and Children / 105

IF YOU HAVE AN INCORPORATED BUSINESS / 105
Corporation Defined / 106
Corporate Taxation: The Basics / 106
Canadian-Controlled Private Corporations (CCPCs) / 107
Large Corporations / 109
Inherent Tax Deferral / 109
Setting Up the Corporation / 110
Taxation of Distributions from the Corporation / 110
Integration / 111
Advantages and Disadvantages of Incorporating
  Your Business / 114

PLANNING OPPORTUNITIES / 117
Payment of Investment Income / 117
Spousal Salaries / 118
Salary/Dividend Trade-Offs / 118
Selling Your Business / 120
 Purification / 121
 Increasing Your Capital Gain / 121
 Buyer's Interest versus Vendor's Interest / 121
Corporate Planning and Your Family / 122

IF YOU ARE A SOLE PROPRIETOR OR IN A PARTNERSHIP

Income from a Business Defined

The category of business income is fairly broad. If an activity is a business, you are taxed on the "profit" from that business. Profit results when you deduct the expenses incurred in generating revenue from total revenue. As a sole proprietor, you declare your profit in your personal tax return. If you realize a loss in a business other than "hobby" farming, this loss may offset income from other sources, including employment and investment income. There are special rules for "hobby" farm losses that may restrict taxpayers from using them to fully offset other types of income, including income from other businesses.

If the income or a portion of it is derived from the sale or transfer of property, it could be characterized by the Canada Customs and Revenue Agency (CCRA) either as business income or income from property. If it is characterized as business income, it will be fully included in calculating taxable income. If it is considered income from property, the proceeds of the sale or transfer will be a capital gain (or loss) and eligible for a partial exclusion (application against other capital gains).

The economic reality of the activity should control its tax treatment. However, it is absolutely critical that you have detailed documentation of your activity. For example, if you are starting a new business while you remain employed, you must maintain detailed records to demonstrate that you have a reasonable expectation of profit from the business and that you are approaching the business in a professional manner. This includes obtaining business advice, if necessary, and demonstrating that you either have abilities in the field or are seeking guidance.

If you cannot demonstrate an expectation of profit and a businesslike approach to the activity, you may be treated as having a hobby. If so, your tax deductions will be restricted to the income generated from the activity. If the activity generates a loss, you will not be able to offset the loss against other income. Further, if your activity generates losses for a number of years, the CCRA may view it as a hobby rather than a business. Maintaining accurate and detailed records is particularly important for any activity, including part-time farming, and will assist you if you decide to challenge the CCRA if it views your business as a hobby.

If you have entered into the activity as an investment, hoping to use the property acquired to generate income, it is equally important that you document this intent and provide evidence that it is reasonable to expect that the property will give rise to investment income. For example, if you buy a piece of land, expecting to build an office building or some other income-generating asset, the land may be a capital asset eligible for capital gains treatment on disposition. On the other hand, if you invest in land with the intention of holding it to generate income from its rise in value, this action would probably be considered an adventure in the nature of trade, or a business (depending on the volume of similar activity), and any profit would probably be fully taxable as income. The CCRA is more inclined to treat increases in value as ordinary income and decreases in value as capital than they are to treat increases as capital and decreases as ordinary income.

Taxation of Income from a Business

Because of the different tax rules and income calculations that apply to business income, there are numerous opportunities for tax planning if you are self-employed or own a business. Taxation of business income will differ depending on whether the business is operated in corporate or unincorporated form. The second part of this chapter discusses the advantages and disadvantages of incorporation, as well as aspects of tax planning for small incorporated businesses. If you are considering incorporating your small business, you can transfer assets from an unincorporated business to a partnership or a corporation on a tax-deferred basis, subject to certain restrictions.

If you own and operate an unincorporated business, you will be taxed on the "profit" regardless of how much you withdraw from the business. Profit is measured by deducting from the gross income of the business the various expenses that are allowed as deductions. These expenses must be reasonable in amount and must be incurred for the purpose of generating income. Common deductions include the cost of merchandise sold, expenditures for salaries paid to your employees, supplies, rent, advertising, and so forth. The amounts spent for items such as furniture or equipment are capital in nature and are not deductible, but you may claim an annual capital cost allowance (depreciation) for such acquisitions.

With the exception of farming and fishing, profit is determined on an accrual basis, rather than on a cash basis. Under the accrual method, income is calculated as it accrues, instead of when it is actually paid, as under the cash method.

Taxation Year

Unincorporated businesses are required to operate with a December 31 fiscal year-end for tax purposes. With the exception of certain professional partnerships, an unincorporated business may choose any year-end for accounting purposes, but it must adjust its income from the business to a calendar year for calculating and reporting taxable income. Individuals and eligible partnerships that initially adopt an off-calendar fiscal year-end are permitted to change to a December 31 fiscal year-end for a taxation year. They are required, though, to provide notification of the change before the filing deadline for the individual's or partners' income tax returns for the year of the change. Once the business owned by an individual or eligible partnership has adopted a December 31 fiscal year-end, it cannot subsequently change to an off-calendar fiscal year-end.

DEDUCTIONS

Home Office Expenses

If you are self-employed, or run your own sideline business and have an office in your home, you may be able to deduct expenses relating to that office.

> **Caution:** For home office expenses to be deductible, the office must either be (a) your principal place of business, or (b) used exclusively to earn business income and on a regular and continuous basis for meeting clients, customers, or patients.

The amount deducted cannot exceed the income from the business for the year, after other expenses are deducted. Any excess amount may be carried forward for future deduction in years when the business generates income.

In Quebec, home office expenses are limited to 50 per cent of the amount that would otherwise be deductible. This deduction limit does not apply to expenses directly related to the use of the office for business purposes, such as electricity and heating.

You may deduct all expenses directly associated with your office, such as filing cabinets, computers and software, advertising costs, and telephone costs for the office line. General, or common, expenses such as utilities and rent payments must be apportioned to what can be directly attributable to the costs of running your office (usually based on a square-footage allocation).

Conventions

The *Income Tax Act* allows you to deduct convention expenses relating to not more than two conventions per year held by a business or professional organization, at a location consistent with the territorial scope of the organization. This restriction places a reasonableness limit on your claimed expenses. For example, if the organization hosting the conference has no clear connection with Hawaii, you will not be able to claim expenses associated with a convention there. To claim convention expenses as a business expense, you must establish that you are attending for the purpose of earning income in your business. If the convention is primarily educational in purpose, your expenses cannot be applied against income.

Deductible Interest

If you borrow funds to earn income, see "Deductible Interest" in Chapter 8.

Golf and Entertainment Expenses

Expenses incurred for the use of a golf course are not deductible, but meals will qualify for a 50 per cent deduction, provided that certain restrictions are satisfied. Federal legislation precludes claims for both annual club membership dues and green fees, even in cases where belonging to a golf club and organizing golf tournaments with clients, suppliers, or staff are justified for business reasons. Meals and beverages consumed at a golf course or club's dining room, banquet hall, conference room, and lounge are deductible as entertainment expenses, provided there is a genuine business purpose to the use of the facilities. Meal and beverage expenses must be clearly itemized to qualify for the deduction. If the purpose of the golf club expenses relates to a charity fundraiser or an office golf day, the expenses are 100 per cent deductible. The Quebec government has adopted a similar position.

Other business entertainment expenses, such as taking clients to a hockey game, are subject to the same 50 per cent deduction limitation as meal expenses.

> **Planning Opportunity:** In spite of the restrictions, as an employer you can generally provide an employee golf day, and up to a total of six employee sporting or social events annually, and be entitled to deduct the expenses for income tax purposes. All green fees remain non-deductible, however. The costs for such events must be "reasonable" and the events are to be made available to all employees at a particular place of business.
>
> From your employees' perspective, if the cost of the event is "reasonable," the event will not be considered a taxable benefit. As a guideline, a per-person cost of up to $100 is reasonable. Parties and events costing more will likely be viewed as exceeding the privilege point and will be a taxable benefit to the employee.

Deduction for Private Health Service Plan Contributions

If you are self-employed, you are eligible to deduct premiums and contributions to private health service plans from your business income. Eligible plans, covering medical and dental services, may be for the benefit of you and your immediate family.

A self-employed individual is defined as an individual actively engaged in business alone or with a partner. Your business must be your primary source of income or your income from other sources must not exceed $10,000 for the year.

The maximum amount deductible is $1,500 for each of you and your spouse and $750 for each of your children. If you claim a deduction as an expense, you cannot also claim the personal medical expenses credit on your tax return for the same expenditure.

However, if you hire full-time employees for your business, you must offer equivalent coverage to all of them to claim the deduction. The deduction limits will not apply if more than one-half of your full-time employees are covered under the plan.

CPP/QPP Deduction for Self-Employed Individuals

Self-employed individuals may deduct the portion (one-half) of Canada Pension Plan and Quebec Pension Plan contributions that represents the employer's share and may claim a tax credit in respect of the other half.

PLANNING OPPORTUNITY

Hiring Your Spouse and Children

Provided you can establish that your spouse and/or children earn income for the business in some fashion, you can pay them a salary. The salary must be reasonable in light of the duties performed.

> **Caution:** Depending on the structure of your business, the recent introduction of the income splitting tax may restrict your ability to split income from a business with minor children. Any distributions from a business to minor children will be taxed at the top marginal rates, and parents who are actively involved in the business will be liable for their children's tax on this income. Consult a professional tax advisor.

IF YOU HAVE AN INCORPORATED BUSINESS

If you own your own business, you may wonder whether to incorporate. Traditionally, the Canadian income tax system has favoured incorporated Canadian small businesses. While the calculations for income and deductions remain essentially the same as for an unincorporated business, there are some differences in the structure of corporate taxation and in planning opportunities through corporations. Tax planning for your business may provide opportunities for income splitting, tax deferral, increasing your capital gains exemption, estate planning, and retirement planning. Because these are complex tasks involving tax, corporate, and family law issues, consult your professional tax advisor for personalized planning in this area.

Corporation Defined

A corporation is a completely separate legal entity from the shareholders or incorporators based on the following principles:

- As a separate legal entity, it has an ongoing existence and the ability to enter into contracts (i.e., buy, sell, employ, borrow, loan, and own property).
- It must act through individuals.
- Ownership is represented by shareholders who may also be employees.
- Profits are distributed by dividends, which are taxed in the hands of the shareholders.
- It is a separate taxable entity and must file income tax returns and pay taxes.

Corporate Taxation: The Basics

If you run your business as a sole proprietorship, you include the income from the business on your personal tax return. A corporation, on the other hand, is a separate taxable entity. The corporation must file its own tax return and pay its own tax. You include income from the corporation on your personal tax return only when you receive distributions from your corporation in the form of salary, dividends, interest, or some other payment.

Similar to the individual rate structure, the corporate structure varies based on the province where the corporate income is generated. In addition, the tax rate also varies depending on the type and amount of income.

The basic federal income tax rate for corporations is 38 per cent. When calculating corporate tax liability, the rate is reduced by 10 per cent to accommodate provincial and territorial taxation.

A further deduction from the basic tax rate is available for income generated from manufacturing and processing (M&P) activities performed in Canada. The M&P deduction also applies to corporations that produce electrical energy or steam for sale. The M&P deduction is 7 per cent, reducing the federal corporate rate to 21 per cent.

The federal government is reducing the basic corporate tax rate by 7 per cent over five years: 1 per cent in 2001, 3 per cent in 2002, 5 per cent in 2003, and 7 per cent in 2004 and subsequent years. Corporations that earn income that is already taxed preferentially (such as manufacturing and processing or small business income), or corporations that are investment holding corporations, mortgage investment corporations, mutual fund corporations, or non-resident-owned investment corporations will not qualify for the reduced rate.

There is also a federal surtax of 4 per cent of the net federal rate, which, for 2001, increased the federal tax rate for income earned in a province from 27 per cent to 28.12 per cent without the M&P deduction, and to 22.12 per cent with the M&P deduction.

Canadian-Controlled Private Corporations (CCPCs)

A CCPC is a resident Canadian corporation not controlled by non-residents of Canada or public corporations. Generally, control for this purpose will exist if Canadian residents hold 50 per cent or more of the voting rights in the company.

The 50 per cent rule is not always the deciding factor, however. When a person has any direct or indirect influence that, if exercised, would result in control of the corporation in fact, he or she is considered to have *de facto* control of the corporation. For example, a person who holds 49 per cent of the votes of a corporation may be considered to control it in the following circumstances:

- where the balance of the votes is widely dispersed among employees of the corporation; or

- the minority shareholder effectively controls the actions of the majority shareholder(s).

A CCPC is eligible for a federal tax rate reduction, the small business deduction (SBD), on its annual "business limit" (defined below). If the corporation's tax year is less than 12 months, this limit must be prorated.

The federal SBD of 16 per cent applies to the CCPC's annual business limit of $200,000 in 2002, $225,000 in 2003, $250,000 in 2004, $275,000 in 2005, and $300,000 after 2005.

The 7 per cent reduction in the federal tax rate noted in the previous section, which will be fully in effect by 2004, applies to active business income between $200,000 and $300,000. To qualify, the corporation must be eligible for the SBD. This reduction does not apply where the income of the corporation is already taxed preferentially (i.e., is eligible for the manufacturing and processing rate reduction and refundable dividend tax treatment).

The 16 per cent SBD is phased out when the taxable capital of the corporation and its associated corporations for the previous year exceeds $10 million. The benefit is eliminated when taxable capital exceeds $15 million.

The annual business limit must be shared by "associated corporations." This prevents taxpayers from abusing the SBD by forming several corporations and claiming the annual business limit for each of them. Generally, associated corporations are corporations controlled by the same person or group of persons.

There is no M&P deduction for income eligible for the SBD. Therefore, if your company is a CCPC generating income from an active business in Canada, the federal corporate tax rate will be 12 per cent on the amount of the annual business limit. When you include the 4 per cent federal surtax (calculated on 28 per cent), the federal income tax rate is 13.12 per cent. The regular tax rate applies on income in excess of the annual business limit.

In addition to the federal corporate tax, all provinces impose an income tax. The provincial tax rates vary from nil to 17 per cent, depending on the province, and on whether there is an M&P deduction, an SBD, and/or a tax holiday (often for new corporations). Combined federal and provincial corporate income tax rates therefore vary considerably.

Large Corporations

A federal tax is imposed at a rate of 0.225 per cent on a large corporation's capital in excess of $10 million employed in Canada. Starting in 2004, this tax will be reduced progressively until it is eliminated in 2008 (0.2 per cent in 2004, 0.175 per cent in 2005, 0.125 per cent in 2006, and 0.0625 per cent in 2007). In addition, the $10-million threshold will increase to $50 million in 2004. With such a large threshold, most small businesses are not subject to this large corporations tax (LCT). Additionally, the 4 per cent surtax that corporations are required to pay can be used to offset LCT liability. The LCT cannot be deducted in computing income subject to income tax.

Inherent Tax Deferral

For small companies, the combined federal-provincial corporate tax rate is between 16.12 and 22.05 per cent, depending on the province. If you compare these rates to those for individuals (see Chapter 19), you'll notice that the small company rates are significantly lower.

If you operate your business in an unincorporated form, you will include the income from the business in your personal tax return as it is earned (the accrual method). Thus, you will pay tax on your business income at your personal marginal tax rate.

> **Planning Opportunity:** If you incorporate your business, you initially pay only the corporate tax rate. You will not pay individual tax on the corporate earnings unless you receive dividend distributions. You are therefore able to defer the personal tax on the portion of taxed earnings retained in the business.

For example, if you earned $1,000 of income in Quebec, you would pay about $482 in personal income tax at the highest tax rate, leaving $518 for reinvestment in the business. If the $1,000 were generated by a Quebec corporation eligible for the SBD, the maximum corporate tax rate would be about $220, leaving $780 for reinvestment. No individual tax would be due until earnings were distributed to shareholders. In comparing the two, as much as $262 ($482 minus $220) of tax could be deferred.

Setting Up the Corporation

Administrative costs are associated with incorporating a business, resulting largely from the legal requirements of preparing and filing the appropriate documents with the government. Unlike other transfers of property, however, you can transfer your business assets to a corporation without any tax consequences, subject to certain restrictions. In return, the corporation must issue shares to you. You may choose to have part of your investment in the corporation in the form of debt rather than shares. By holding some debt, you have the opportunity to draw earnings out of the corporation as interest, which is tax-deductible to the company, as well as drawing earnings out as dividends.

Taxation of Distributions from the Corporation

When you receive payments from the corporation, the tax treatment depends on the nature of the payment. Salary you receive as an employee of your corporation is included in your income in the year of receipt. If you have financed your company by loaning the company money, any interest income is fully included in your income. If you have leased assets to the corporation, lease payments paid to you would be included in your income when received, and so forth.

These types of payments from the company to you are deductible in calculating the corporation's income. Deferring the tax on these payments is possible if you can obtain a tax deduction for the corporation before you must pay the individual tax on the payments. There are some restrictions on deferring income that limit your ability to delay accrued payables.

It may be possible to achieve limited deferral through the payment of salaries or bonuses. In such cases, for the corporation to obtain a deduction in the year that the salaries or bonuses accrue, these amounts must be paid within 180 days after the corporation's year-end. When they are paid, you include them in your taxable income. However, if the corporate year-end is after July, the amounts can be paid in the following calendar year, but within 180 days after the corporation's year-end. This delay provides about six months of tax deferral benefit. Tax should be withheld on bonuses paid to avoid a large tax payable when you file your tax return.

Integration

Although you may own most or all of the shares of a corporation, you and the corporation are separate taxpayers. The corporation pays its own income tax when it earns a profit. When the after-tax profits are distributed from the corporation as dividends, they are included in your income and the corporation does not receive a deduction. Consequently, profits generated through a corporation are taxed twice—once when earned by the corporation and again when distributed as dividends to the shareholders.

To alleviate this double taxation of income earned through a corporation, the corporate and individual tax systems are integrated. This integration is accomplished by grossing up the dividend received by the shareholder to approximate the amount earned before tax at the corporate level. A tax credit is then granted in an amount designed to reflect the amount of tax already paid by the corporation.

Accordingly, when you calculate your total dividend income from the corporation, you gross up (increase) the dividend by 25 per cent of the dividend to calculate your total dividend income amount. After you apply your federal income tax on the grossed-up amount, you take a dividend tax credit equal to two-thirds of the grossed-up portion of the dividend. For Quebec taxes, the dividend tax credit is 54 per cent of the dividend gross-up.

For example:

Dividend received	$100
Dividend gross-up (25% × $100)	25
Taxable income	$125
Federal tax at 29% (maximum)	$ 36.25
Dividend tax credit (⅔ × $25)	(16.67)
Federal tax	$ 19.58
Provincial tax (Ontario)	11.16
Total individual tax on dividend	$ 30.74

The integration system is rough justice designed to approximate an individual receiving dividends from a corporation that has already enjoyed the small business deduction. To achieve perfect integration, the federal and provincial combined corporate rate must be 20 per cent, with no surtaxes, and the individual must have, effectively, a provincial tax rate of 50 per cent. Under these conditions, there will be no difference between earning business income through a corporation or directly, as demonstrated in the following example (assuming the taxpayer is in the highest tax bracket).

How Tax Integration Works for Individuals in the Highest Tax Bracket

	Income Earned Directly	Income Earned Through a Corporation
Corporate income		$100
Corporate tax		20
After-tax profits		$ 80
Individual income:		
Business profits	$100	
Dividend		$ 80
Dividend gross-up		
(25% × $80)		20
Taxable income	$100	$100
Federal tax at 29%	$ 29	$ 29
Dividend tax credit		
($2/3$ × $20)	0	(13.33)
Provincial tax at 50%	14.50	7.83
Total individual tax	43.50	23.50
Corporate tax	0	20.00
Total tax on $100 income	$ 43.50	$ 43.50

To the extent that the tax rates differ from these hypothetical rates, there will be differences in total taxes paid depending on whether the income is earned directly by an individual or through a corporation. If the corporate tax rate and/or individual tax rates are lower than these hypothetical rates, the total tax paid on income earned through the corporate structure is likely to be less than the total tax that would be paid if the income were earned directly by the individual. To the extent that the corporate tax rates are higher than for a small business corporation, there will be a proportionate decrease in the amount of relief from double taxation.

Advantages and Disadvantages of Incorporating Your Business

To a great extent, the trade-offs between the corporate and unincorporated structures depend on the nature of your activities and the income generated. Either mode favours a range of activity type and scale. Compare the corporate and individual tax rates for the province in which you do business to determine how much of a tax difference exists between the two rates. In many cases there will be a tax advantage to having a corporate structure.

Generally, the tax and non-tax advantages to incorporating your business include:

- *Limited Liability.* Because the corporation is a separate legal entity, individual shareholders are not responsible for corporate debts or other liabilities. This may not apply to a small business because it is common for lending institutions to request personal guarantees on small business loans. Your liability remains limited for such things as lawsuits, however, unless you are personally negligent.
- *Tax Savings or Deferral.* As mentioned above, there may be tax-saving and tax deferral opportunities. The saving or deferral opportunities are of particular value to a business that will be investing to expand. The extent of these opportunities depends on the comparative corporate and individual tax rates in the particular circumstances, as well as on the nature of the income earned.
- *Income Splitting and Estate Planning.* Some income splitting and estate planning opportunities are only available through a corporate structure. The major advantage from an estate planning perspective is that a corporation can continue in existence beyond the life of its incorporators. This distinction is significant when you are developing a succession plan for your business. In either a sole proprietorship or an incorporated business, you can shift management control

by hiring your children. In an incorporated business, you can shift ownership control by transferring shares, as opposed to assets.
- *Level Income.* It is possible to achieve a levelling of personal income through control of salary and dividends to avoid high- and low-income periods, particularly in a business where profits fluctuate from year to year.
- *Pension Plans.* A shareholder who is also an employee of the corporation may participate in the company's registered pension plan (RPP). A sole proprietor may not participate in an RPP. There also are other types of fringe benefits, such as group term life insurance plans and group sickness or accident insurance plans, which may be available to you as an employee of your company but are not available if your business is unincorporated.
- *Capital Gains Exemption.* The corporate structure permits access to the capital gains exemption on the sale of shares of the corporation running the business. The $500,000 capital gains exemption is available to holders of shares of a small business corporation, but not for assets of an unincorporated business. This exemption includes the regular $100,000 capital gains exemption on other capital properties, which was abolished on February 22, 1994.

To qualify for the $500,000 exemption, the corporation must be a small business corporation at the time of the sale and the shares must not have been held by anyone other than the seller, or related persons, within the 24 months preceding the sale. In addition, throughout the 24-month period, more than 50 per cent of the fair market value of the assets of the corporation must be used in an active business carried on primarily in Canada. A "small business corporation" is a CCPC provided that it uses all or substantially all (90 per cent or more, expressed in terms of fair market value, according to the *Income Tax Act*) of the fair market value of its assets in an active business carried on primarily in

Canada. The shares of a Canadian holding company also qualify if substantially all of its assets are shares or debt of other small business corporations.

Disadvantages of the corporate structure include:

- *Losses.* A corporation is unable to use losses to offset income generated by the individual. If you generate losses through an unincorporated business, you may use these losses to offset income from other activities. Because the corporation is a separate entity, neither the income nor the losses flow directly to your individual tax return. As a result, you cannot use these losses to offset other types of income. If the corporation generates income in other years, the losses may offset such other income of the corporation. Specifically, business losses of the corporation for a given year may be carried back three years and forward seven years to offset other income of the corporation. If your corporation is generating a loss, you can adjust a reported loss by reducing your salary payments and substituting dividends.
- *Costs of Incorporating.* There are additional costs to setting up and maintaining a corporation that do not apply to an unincorporated business. Such costs include the initial expenses of preparing the legal documents, as well as added taxes such as provincial capital taxes. Ongoing costs include those associated with filing forms such as tax returns, holding directors' meetings, maintaining corporate records, and so forth.
- *Capital Taxes.* In 1989, the federal government introduced a special tax similar to the capital tax system that has existed in some provinces for years. Because this tax is payable only when the capital used in Canada by the corporation exceeds $10 million ($50 million starting in 2004), the federal capital tax liability is usually eliminated or substantially reduced for small corporations.

The Quebec capital tax rate is 0.6 per cent in 2003. The government has announced its intention to provide a deduction in calculating the amount of capital subject to the tax ($250,000 in 2003 and $600,000 starting in 2004). An exemption is available for the first five taxation years of a newly incorporated business with paid-up capital less than $2.25 million ($3 million before June 13, 2003).

For taxation years ending after March 14, 2000, and before March 15, 2003, any corporation carrying on a business and having an establishment in Quebec was required to make a contribution equal to 1.6 per cent of its income tax payable to the Youth Fund. Corporations that pay the capital tax applicable to financial institutions had to contribute up to 1.6 per cent of the capital tax payable.

PLANNING OPPORTUNITIES

In addition to tax planning opportunities, it is also important to keep in mind non-tax factors when developing your plan for your business. You must consider your cash needs and the cash needs of the company. In addition, you must review all other sources of income and your position regarding investment income, capital gains, and investment losses. All of these factors should be considered when you are reviewing your tax planning for your company.

Payment of Investment Income

One aspect you may want to review is your position under the cumulative net investment loss (CNIL) rules (see also Chapter 8). In short, these rules apply if you have not earned sufficient investment income to cover your claimed investment expenses or losses. An outstanding CNIL will prevent you from claiming the $500,000 capital gains exemption on the proceeds of sale of otherwise qualifying capital property.

If you have outstanding CNILs, one common strategy for reducing them is to receive payments in the form of interest or dividend income from your corporation. This income would be netted against any investment losses to reduce the amount of your CNIL, thereby regaining room to claim any available capital gains exemption once your CNIL amount reaches zero.

Spousal Salaries

As with an unincorporated business, you can pay a salary to your spouse or other family members. It is necessary that the person actually perform some services for the company, that there be a *bona fide* employer-employee relationship, and that you be able to support the salary as reasonable. A salary generally will be considered reasonable if a reasonable businessperson would have paid the salary under similar circumstances and the amount is commensurate with the value of the responsibilities assumed and the services performed.

Under these conditions, the corporation will obtain a deduction for the salary payment, and you will have achieved additional income splitting. This salary payment also may create an opportunity for increased contributions to retirement savings plans for that family member. By earning income, your spouse will create more room for contributions to a registered retirement savings plan (RRSP).

Salary/Dividend Trade-Offs

One of the interesting areas of planning for the owner-managed corporation is the determination of the appropriate split between salary and dividend payments for the owner-manager.

Salary reduces corporate income tax payable, but the salary is subject to personal tax. Although a dividend does not reduce corporate tax, the dividend tax credit means less personal tax is paid than on salary income. In theory, it is not supposed to matter whether you draw a salary or a dividend, provided the company's taxable income (and that of all associated companies, prorated for any tax years less than 12 months) is not more than the company's annual business limit.

As with integration, this theory is effective only when the combined federal and provincial corporate rate is 20 per cent, there are no surtaxes, and the individual is in a 29 per cent federal tax bracket in a province imposing tax at effectively 50 per cent of the federal rate. In such a case, if 100 per cent of after-tax corporate income were distributed, the total tax would be identical whether it is distributed as salary or dividends. (For every $100 of corporate income, the numbers would be identical to the previous example.)

The theory is fine, but the system does not work exactly as it was intended. In some provinces, and for certain business activities, drawing a dividend may be preferable to drawing a salary and maximizing RRSP contributions.

> **Planning Opportunity:** As the main corporate owner, your best plan is to withdraw from the company an amount up to or equal to the level at which the net amount of tax you pay is equal to the tax the company would have paid had you not withdrawn the funds.

Depending on your particular circumstances, the most feasible way to do this may be taking all salary or a combination of salary and dividends. If cash flow for the corporation is an issue, you can lend funds back to the company, and at any time in the future the company can repay the loan to you on a tax-free basis. Structuring your income using salary and dividends works if the corporation (and all associated companies, etc.) generates active business income that does not exceed its annual business limit, making its income eligible for the small business deduction (SBD).

If there is taxable income in the corporation in excess of its annual business limit, the SBD will not apply to this excess, and the corporate tax rate will be considerably higher. To avoid a higher tax rate, it is advisable to keep the taxable income of the corporation at or below the annual business limit. If the income of your corporation or corporate group is near the threshold, the most common way of achieving this goal is through salary or bonus payments to you as the owner-manager.

Remember that this salary will be included in your taxable income in the year of receipt. Depending on the timing of salary payments, the corporation might receive a deduction for your salary in the year before you actually receive it. There may be a slight deferral advantage to leaving income in the corporation, but the total tax is likely to be higher than if salaries were paid.

From a personal tax perspective, it is important to maximize the amounts that you can contribute under the Canada/Quebec Pension Plan and RRSPs. These plans have contribution limits based on your earned income for the year. As a result, even though the corporate income may be less than the annual business limit without additional salaries or bonuses, you may want to pay enough salary to yourself to maximize your contributions to such plans, providing you have not fully used your pension amount in a company pension plan.

The contribution limit for RRSPs for a given year is based on the income earned in the preceding year. Consequently, your earned income in the preceding year (2002) must be at least $80,556 to contribute the maximum amount ($14,500) to your RRSP for 2003. This $14,500 maximum will increase gradually over the next few years (see Chapter 13).

For salaries to be deductible by the corporation, they must be "reasonable." What constitutes a reasonable salary is generally a question of fact. As a rule, however, the CCRA will not question the payment of a salary or bonus to a shareholder manager provided payroll tax withholdings are paid.

Selling Your Business

If your business is unincorporated, and you are contemplating its sale, you can in most cases transfer the assets to a corporation and then immediately sell the shares of the corporation to take advantage of the $500,000 capital gains exemption.

Purification. If your business is already incorporated, but does not qualify as a small business corporation, it may be possible to "purify" the corporation (i.e., ensure that it qualifies) by removing non-qualified assets from the company. With careful planning, removal of assets can be carried out on a tax-free basis. The purification process should begin long before a sale is being contemplated. The *Income Tax Act* contains provisions that may deny the transfer of such non-qualified assets on a tax-free basis when the transfer occurs as part of the sale process.

Increasing Your Capital Gain. If you are expecting to sell the shares of your company, you could consider accumulating income in the company to increase the gain. This must be done carefully because, to maintain the small business corporation status, substantially all (90 per cent or more, according to the CCRA) of the assets, expressed in terms of fair market value, must be used in carrying on the corporation's business. As a result, you cannot accumulate earnings in the corporation and use those earnings to buy passive investments if such investments constitute more than 10 per cent of the total fair market value of the corporate assets at the time of sale (or more than 50 per cent for the preceding 24 months). Consider using the earnings to reduce the corporation's debts and other liabilities.

Buyer's Interest versus Vendor's Interest. When you are negotiating the sale of your business, the buyer may prefer to buy the assets of the company, rather than your shares. This provides the buyer with tax write-offs that would be unavailable if the buyer purchased the shares. On the vendor's part, the preference will be for a sale of the shares. Profit on a sale of shares can be reduced by the capital gains exemption. In addition, if you previously have organized the share structure to permit ownership by your spouse and children, the exemption can also be claimed by them.

There is room for negotiation. If the disposition qualifies for the $500,000 capital gains exemption, negotiate a deal with a purchaser that permits both of you to share the tax benefits from your expanded capital gains exemption.

Corporate Planning and Your Family

It may be possible to reorganize the capital structure of your company to permit ownership by your spouse and children. A reorganization of the capital structure may provide both income splitting and estate planning opportunities if it is properly planned. Arranging for share ownership by a spouse and children also could provide for a reduction in tax if the company is sold. Specifically, with a small business corporation, each family member would be entitled to the $500,000 capital gains exemption if the company were sold.

Reorganizing share capital does have its pitfalls and you should not proceed without proper advice.

CHAPTER EIGHT

If You Own Investments

INCOME FROM CAPITAL PROPERTY / 124
The Basics / 124
Capital Gains Exemptions / 125
  Your Exempt Capital Gains Balance / 125
The $500,000 Exemption / 125
  Qualified Small Business Corporation Shares / 126
  Qualified Farm Property / 127
  Cumulative Net Investment Losses (CNILs) / 129
Other Rules / 132
  Rules for Losses / 132
  Restriction on Deduction of Loss / 132
  Denial of Deduction of Loss / 132
  Settlement Date / 133
  Superficial Loss / 133
  Identical Properties / 133
  Allowable Business Investment Losses / 134
  Special Cases—Reserves for Proceeds Not Yet Due / 135

INCOME IN THE FORM OF INTEREST / 136
Planning Around the Accrual Rules / 136

INCOME FROM DIVIDENDS / 138
The Taxation of Canadian Dividends / 138

CREDITS AND DEDUCTIONS RELATED TO INVESTMENTS / 139
Investment Deductions / 139
Deductible Interest / 139
Rental Expenses / 140

INCOME FROM CAPITAL PROPERTY

The Basics

Income from capital property comes in the form of interest, dividends, and capital gains. Interest and dividends are covered later in this chapter and we begin with capital gains.

A capital gain or loss will occur when, upon the disposition (i.e., sale or transfer) of capital property, there is a difference between the owner's cost base of the property and the proceeds of disposition. Capital property is a broad category, but can generally be described as property that can appreciate (or depreciate, as the case may be) and that is generally held for the purpose of earning income.

The *Income Tax Act* creates numerous classes of capital property, including "non-depreciable property," "personal-use property," "listed personal property," "qualified small business corporation [generally CCPC] shares," "eligible capital property," "flow-through entities," and "other" depreciable properties in both tangible and intangible forms. These are defined terms in the Act and there are special rules regarding their disposition, valuation, and exemption claims for accrued gains. While we discuss some issues related to these specific classes of capital property, we focus on the category of "other" capital property. This "catch-all" class includes publicly traded shares, a common capital investment for Canadians. We recommend that you consult your tax planning professional for issues relating to the other forms of capital property.

Capital gains first became taxable after December 31, 1971. That date is commonly referred to as the valuation date for all capital property. If you have owned capital property since a point in time before 1972 and plan to sell it, you must obtain the value of that property as of that date. The December 31, 1971, value will act as your cost base for the property for tax purposes.

If a sale of capital property results in the owner recognizing a gain, he or she must include a portion of that gain in taxable income for that year. If the owner loses money, a portion of the loss can be applied against current-year capital gains. If losses of other capital property exceed capital gains for a given year, the losses can be carried back three years and forward indefinitely and applied against capital gains.

Capital Gains Exemptions
Your Exempt Capital Gains Balance. The $100,000 capital gains exemption was abolished as of February 22, 1994, and the late filing provisions expired in 1997. If you made an election to realize capital gains on units of mutual funds, however, you have until December 31, 2004, to utilize any remaining exempt capital gains balance for the fund. This balance offsets any gains that you realize if you sell units of the fund or when you receive a capital gains distribution from the fund. As of January 1, 2005, the amount remaining in your exempt capital gains balance will automatically be added to the adjusted cost base of your mutual fund units.

The $500,000 Exemption
As a result of the discontinuation of the $100,000 capital gains exemption, the $500,000 lifetime capital gains exemption is the only remaining capital gains exemption. The lifetime exemption may be applied to gains on the disposition of qualified farm property, qualified small business corporation shares, or eligible fishing property in Quebec. The deduction permitted in computing your taxable income for a year for qualified farm property, qualified small business corporation shares, or eligible fishing property in Quebec is the least of the three following amounts:
- the unused portion of your maximum capital gains exemption;
- the annual gains limit for the year; or
- the cumulative gains limit at the end of the year.

The unused portion of the maximum capital gains exemption corresponds to the amount of exemption available over your lifetime, less the portion used in previous years (including any portion of the $100,000 personal capital gains exemption previously claimed). The annual gains limit for the year equals the amount of the capital gain for the year from the disposition of qualified small business corporation shares, qualified farm property, or eligible fishing property in Quebec, less deferred capital losses and allowable business investment losses (defined in what follows).

This annual gains limit must be calculated on an annual as well as a cumulative basis. The result is that, for a particular taxation year, the cumulative results of previous years must be taken into account.

Qualified Small Business Corporation Shares. The $500,000 lifetime capital gains exemption can be used to shelter gains arising from the disposition of qualifying shares. The shares must, at the time of disposition, be owned by you (or a person or partnership related to you) and be shares of the capital stock of a small business corporation.

A "small business corporation" is a Canadian-controlled private corporation (CCPC) of which all or substantially all of the fair market value of the assets is used principally in an active business carried on primarily in Canada (other than a specified investment business and a personal services business). The "active business" requirement translates into 90 per cent or more of the fair market value of the assets, according to the Canada Customs and Revenue Agency (CCRA). The assets also may be shares in one or more small business corporations connected with the corporation, or a bond, debenture, or similar obligation issued by such a connected corporation.

In addition, the shares must satisfy both a holding period and an active business asset requirement. First, you or a person or partnership related to you must have been the only owner of the shares throughout the 24-month period immediately preceding the disposition. Treasury shares will qualify under certain conditions.

As for the active business asset requirement, more than 50 per cent of the fair market value of the corporation's assets must have been used in an active business throughout the 24-month holding period. This is in addition to the 90 per cent business use requirement applicable at the time of disposition. Active business assets consist of:

- assets used principally in an active business carried on primarily in Canada by the corporation or a related (associated through common share ownership) corporation; and
- certain shares or debt of connected corporations that are small business corporations.

Qualified Farm Property. The disposition of qualified farm property (or eligible fishing property in Quebec—see Chapter 18) also entitles an individual to the $500,000 lifetime capital gains exemption (see also Chapter 12 for details on transferring farm property to your child).

> **Caution:** This exemption does not create an additional $500,000 exemption for an individual. These deductions can be used at the same time, provided that the total capital gain exempted does not exceed $500,000.

To claim the exemption, you, your spouse, or a qualifying partnership must own the qualified farm property. A partnership only qualifies if it is an interest in a family farm partnership of you or your spouse. This last rule enables you or your spouse to qualify for the exemption in situations where the family farm partnership owned the disposed property.

Qualified farm property can be:

- real property (land or building) used in the course of carrying on the business of farming in Canada;
- a share of the capital stock of a family farm corporation of the individual, the individual's spouse, or any of the individual's children;

- an interest in a family farm partnership of the individual, the individual's spouse, or any of the individual's children; and
- eligible capital property (usually intangible, in the form of goodwill or government rights) used in a farming business, to the extent that the disposition of this property creates a qualifying capital gain under the *Income Tax Act*.

The terms "family farm partnership" and "family farm corporation" both refer to an entity that carries on the business of farming in Canada. Specifically, more than 50 per cent of the fair market value of all of the farm's property must be used in the business, and the farmer, the farmer's spouse, or the farmer's child must be actively engaged in the business on a regular and continuous basis.

In addition, the property must be used in the course of carrying on the business of farming in Canada by:

- the individual;
- a beneficiary of a trust who is related to the person from whom the trust acquired the property;
- the spouse, a child, or the mother or father of the individual; or
- a partnership or a family farm corporation in which any one of the above three classes of individuals has an interest.

Additionally, to qualify for the exemption, the real property must have been owned by one of the persons mentioned above for at least 24 months before the transfer, and:

- for at least two years, the gross revenue from the farming business earned by any one person mentioned above must have exceeded the individual's net income from all other sources; or
- throughout the 24-month period, the real property must have been used by a partnership or a family farm corporation in the course of carrying on the business of farming in Canada.

In both cases, one of the persons mentioned above must have also been actively engaged on a regular and continuous basis in the farming business.

> **Caution:** These two requirements restrict the $500,000 exemption only to individuals for whom farming (or, in Quebec, fishing) is their main activity.

Relief is provided if the real property was acquired before June 18, 1987, and the property otherwise meets the pre-June 18, 1987, requirements, even if the current requirements do not. Specifically, the property must have been used for farming in the year of disposition or in at least five prior years (not necessarily consecutive) under the ownership of any person mentioned above.

Cumulative Net Investment Losses (CNILs). Since 1988, net capital gains eligible for the capital gains exemption have been reduced by all CNILs deducted in computing income for taxation years after 1987. This reduction prevents you from using your capital gains exemption to offset capital gains while, in the same year, offsetting your other income with investment losses. Your CNIL at the end of a year is the amount by which your accumulated investment expenses exceed your accumulated investment income.

Your investment expenses consist of the following items that have been deducted in computing your income for the 1988 and subsequent taxation years:

- Deductions claimed on property that will yield interest, dividends, rent, or other income from property. Such deductions include interest, safe-deposit box rental, other carrying charges, and capital cost allowance.
- Carrying charges, including interest, with respect to an interest in, or a contribution to, a limited partnership

(unless you are the general partner) or any other partnership where you are not actively engaged in the business of the partnership (unless you carry on a similar business).
- Your share of a loss (except allowable capital losses) of any partnership described above.
- Fifty per cent of your share of deductions attributed to a resource flow-through share or related to Canadian exploration and other resource expenses of a partnership where you are not actively engaged in the business.
- Any loss for the year from property, or from renting or leasing real property owned by you or a partnership, not otherwise included in the investment expenses listed above.
- The amount by which net taxable capital gains that are not eligible for the capital gains exemption are offset by net capital losses of other years that are deducted by you in the year. These ineligible amounts include capital gains realized between March 1, 1992, and February 22, 1994, as a result of the disposition of a vacation or investment property you own in addition to your principal residence.

Your investment income for a year essentially consists of the following items that are included in computing income for the year:

- Interest, taxable dividends, rent, and other income from property (including recaptured depreciation on items generating income from property).
- Your share of the income (including recaptured depreciation but not including taxable capital gains) from most limited partnerships or other partnerships where you are not actively engaged in the business of the partnership (unless you carry on a similar business).
- Income (including recaptured depreciation) that is not otherwise included for the year from property or from the renting or leasing of real property owned by you or a partnership.

If You Own Investments ▶ 131

- Fifty per cent of recovered exploration and development expenses included in income.
- The income portion of certain annuity payments, other than those from an income-averaging annuity contract or an annuity purchased pursuant to a deferred profit sharing plan.
- Net taxable capital gains realized on non-qualifying real property, which are not eligible for the capital gains exemption. As defined opposite, these ineligible gains include a portion of gains that accrued between March 1, 1992, and February 22, 1994, and were realized on the disposition of a vacation or investment property you own in addition to your principal residence.

Whether your capital gains qualify for the capital gains exemption or not, you can still deduct the interest paid on funds you borrow for investment purposes.

Recaptured depreciation arises when a depreciable capital property is sold for more than the amount not yet claimed for depreciation, or the "undepreciated" amount. The amount of the sale proceeds, up to the original capital cost over the undepreciated amount, will be added back into income.

The interest expense on funds you use to carry on an unincorporated business or profession does not enter into the CNIL calculation.

Your net investment loss is not calculated on an investment-by-investment basis, nor on an annual basis, but rather on a cumulative and pooled basis after 1987 for all of your investment assets. Carrying charges associated with one security may therefore reduce your capital gains exemption available to offset a taxable capital gain realized on the sale of another security. The CNIL rules do not erode your capital gains exemption, but they can delay your use of all or part of it until your cumulative investment income exceeds your cumulative investment expenses.

If you intend to use your exemption in 2003, your CNIL balance at December 31, 2003, will be taken into consideration.

If you have a positive CNIL balance, you may wish to take steps to eliminate it.

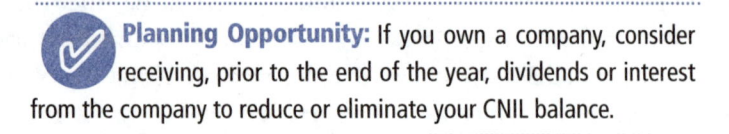

> **Planning Opportunity:** If you own a company, consider receiving, prior to the end of the year, dividends or interest from the company to reduce or eliminate your CNIL balance.

Since there are a number of factors to consider, consult your professional tax advisor.

Other Rules

The following applies to taxpayers who will be taxable on their capital gains or who have incurred capital losses from the disposition of other property.

Rules for Losses. Allowable capital losses, other than "business investment losses" (see page 134), offset taxable capital gains that are realized in a given year. Any unused allowable capital losses can be carried back to the three preceding years, or carried forward indefinitely to offset taxable capital gains in future years. You may choose the amount of loss carryovers to use and the year in which you use them.

Restriction on Deduction of Loss. A loss on transfer of property to a corporation controlled by you, your spouse, or a corporation controlled by you or certain other affiliated persons must be deferred until you are no longer affiliated with the corporation or the corporation sells the property that was transferred.

Denial of Deduction of Loss. A loss on transfer of property to your RRSP, your RRIF, or your spouse's RRSP is denied completely.

> **Planning Opportunity:** Consider selling the property to realize the loss, and then transferring or reinvesting the proceeds, taking care to avoid the superficial loss rules (see below).

Settlement Date. Remember that a disposition of shares through a stock exchange is deemed to take place at "settlement date." For Canadian exchanges, the settlement date is three business days after the trading date. This means the last trading date in 2003 is December 24. If the transaction is a cash sale (payment made and share certificates delivered on the trade date), you have until December 31, 2003, to make the trade.

Superficial Loss. You cannot claim a capital loss when you sell an asset that you, in fact, intend to continue to hold. This rule also applies if your spouse, a corporation controlled by you, or certain other affiliated persons acquire the assets. The rule applies when property is sold at a loss and the same asset or "identical" assets are purchased within 30 days before or after the disposition, and the repurchased asset is still held at the end of the 30th day following the original disposition. The person acquiring the replacement asset adds the loss to his or her cost base and the seller of the asset is denied the loss.

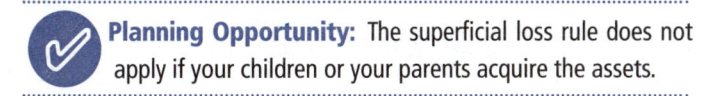

> **Planning Opportunity:** The superficial loss rule does not apply if your children or your parents acquire the assets.

Identical Properties. Capital properties of a similar kind are subject to special rules covering "identical properties." Stocks of the same class, or bonds of identical characteristics of the same corporation, are "identical properties." For tax purposes, these assets are "pooled" and lose their specific identities.

For example, if 200 shares of a stock are purchased for $8 per share and, subsequently, 100 shares are purchased for $11 per share, the tax cost of the shares is considered to be $9 per share ($2,700 / 300). If the 100 shares purchased for $11 are sold the next day at the same price, you will have a capital gain of $2 per share, and $100 ($1/2$ of $200) will be included in your taxable income.

Effective for certain securities acquired after February 27, 2000, the identical properties rule referred to above may not apply. Securities acquired after February 27, 2000, under an employee stock option plan and disposed of within 30 days after the acquisition may be deemed not to be identical property to other securities held by the taxpayer.

Provided the taxpayer follows certain reporting rules, there will be no requirement to pool the cost base of the securities acquired through the exercise of stock options with other identical securities owned at the time of exercise. This will be an advantage, for example, for a taxpayer who holds shares of an employer corporation ("old shares") with a low cost base and who exercises and sells shares of the employer ("new shares") at a value higher than the amount paid for the "old shares." With this new provision, the taxpayer will not realize a capital gain on the disposition of the "new shares" as the result of having to pool the cost bases of the "old" and the "new" shares.

Allowable Business Investment Losses. A business investment loss can occur on the disposition of shares in, or the debt obligations of, a small business corporation (defined in "Qualified Small Business Corporation Shares" on page 126).

> **Planning Opportunity:** Business investment losses can be used to reduce income from other sources.

To qualify as a business investment loss, the shares or debt must be transferred in an arm's-length transaction. This precludes intra-family transfers, except in the case of shares of a bankrupt corporation (or one that has ceased operation, in limited cases). In addition to traditional methods, debt that is unrecoverable will qualify.

An allowable business investment loss (ABIL) is defined as one-half of the total business investment loss. Allowable business investment losses are treated in the same manner as non-capital losses, including business losses. You must deduct the allowable portion from all sources of income in the current taxation year first. Any unused losses can be carried back three years and forward seven years.

> **Caution:** Because income in the loss year must be reduced to zero before ABILs can be carried backward or forward, you will be unable to claim your personal tax credits for that year.

You can choose how much of a loss carryover you want to claim in a carryover year. After the seven-year carryforward period, unused ABILs become ordinary capital losses and may be carried forward indefinitely. For example, if you had an ABIL in 1995 that became a non-capital loss and you were not able to deduct it in the three years before or the seven years after 1995, you can now use the loss to reduce your taxable capital gains in 2003 or any year after.

To the extent that lifetime capital gains exemptions were claimed in previous years, a taxpayer's business investment loss for a taxation year after 1985 is treated as an ordinary capital loss. Similarly, any recognized capital gain is not eligible for the capital gains exemption to the extent of any previous business investment losses realized by the taxpayer after 1984.

Special Cases—Reserves for Proceeds Not Yet Due. If a capital asset is sold, resulting in a capital gain, and the full amount of the proceeds is not due by the end of the year, a part of the capital gain may be deferred by claiming a reserve for the proceeds not yet due. The reserve is recalculated each year, depending on the amount of proceeds outstanding at the end of the year. Although you may claim less than the maximum available reserve in any year, you cannot claim a larger reserve in the next year.

The *Income Tax Act* requires that the reserve be brought into income and taxed over a maximum period of five years, including the year of disposition.

> **Planning Opportunity:** A 10-year (including the year of disposition) reserve is allowed on the transfer of farm property, shares in a family farm corporation, or shares in a small business corporation to your child, grandchild, or great-grandchild (resident in Canada).

INCOME IN THE FORM OF INTEREST

Debt securities provide income to investors in the form of interest payments. Interest income is added directly to taxable income and taxed at the taxpayer's top marginal rate. Interest is generally taxed in the year you receive it. However, if you buy a debt instrument where the interest is compounded and paid at maturity, you will have to recognize the income annually. Compound-interest Canada Savings Bonds and guaranteed investment certificates are examples of investments that are subject to annual income accrual rules. The Bank of Canada and other issuers of investments subject to the annual accrual rules provide annual information slips to the holders of the instruments showing the amount of interest accrued to each anniversary date of the investment.

Planning Around the Accrual Rules

Before investing in deferred income securities or annuities, take maximum advantage of deferred income plans for which you are not required to report income on an annual basis: registered retirement savings plans (RRSPs) and registered pension plans (RPPs).

The earnings inside these plans are completely sheltered from tax until you withdraw funds. RRSP and RPP contributions are generally deductible from income in the current year and payments from a plan can be postponed well into your retirement. Because you have some measure of control over how and when you will withdraw payments from RRSPs and RPPs, you can plan now to optimize your tax position when you eventually withdraw the funds.

For example, assume that you have the option of contributing $5,000 to an RRSP from which you will begin receiving a retirement income in 20 years. Your marginal tax rate now is 40 per cent, and in the table below it is assumed that your marginal rate in 20 years will be either 30 per cent or 40 per cent. To keep the example simple, it is assumed you will pay tax on the RRSP amount in a lump sum in the 20th year, which of course would probably not be the case. The RRSP earns interest at the rate of 5 per cent over the 20 years.

Sheltering Effect of RRSPs on $5,000 Invested Now and Held for 20 Years

Future Marginal Tax Rate	After-Tax Amount Available
30%	$9,287
40%	$7,960

If you did not make the RRSP contribution and paid tax at 40 per cent on the $5,000, you would have $3,000 left to invest. Assuming your annual after-tax return is 3 per cent (after paying tax at the rate of 40 per cent on 5 per cent earnings), you will accumulate $5,418 in 20 years. This accumulation is $2,542 less than you would accumulate by contributing to the RRSP, even after paying 40 per cent tax in 20 years on the income.

The advantage is that the before-tax amounts in the RRSP accumulate interest on a tax-free basis. Investments made with your after-tax earnings outside an RRSP are taxed each year, leaving you a smaller amount available for reinvestment. In addition, through the RRSP you are able to pay your taxes in the future with inflated dollars that are worth much less than today's dollars.

For a more comprehensive analysis of the retirement saving rules related to RRSPs, see Chapter 13.

Planning Opportunity: Your financial and tax-savings strategy evolves in response to your current needs and your future plans. Consequently, your investment choices will change. Individuals in higher marginal tax brackets will benefit from diversifying their investments. If you currently hold only interest-earning investments, consider the possibility of deferring tax by acquiring capital property. The accrual rules do not apply to unrealized capital gains, and you will not have to recognize tax until you sell the property.

INCOME FROM DIVIDENDS

Both preferred and common shares can provide income to shareholders in the form of dividends. We limit our discussion to Canadian-source dividend income.

The Taxation of Canadian Dividends

Dividends from Canadian corporations qualify for the dividend tax credit. To calculate the credit, dividends are grossed up by 25 per cent, and the dividend tax credit of 16.67 per cent of the cash amount of dividends received is applied against the total. The following example shows how a top-bracket taxpayer is taxed on a $1,000 dividend received in 2003.

Taxation of $1,000 Dividend at the Highest Marginal Rate

Cash dividend	$1,000
Gross-up	250
	1,250
Federal tax (29%)	363
Dividend tax credit	(167)
	196
Provincial tax (Ontario)	112
Total tax	$ 308
Amount retained after tax	$ 692

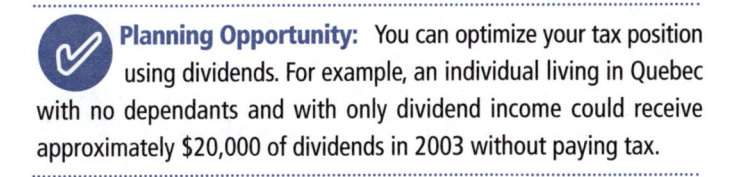

> **✓ Planning Opportunity:** You can optimize your tax position using dividends. For example, an individual living in Quebec with no dependants and with only dividend income could receive approximately $20,000 of dividends in 2003 without paying tax.

CREDITS AND DEDUCTIONS RELATED TO INVESTMENTS

Investment Deductions

Fees for investment counselling, portfolio management, and safekeeping are deductible from income earned through your investments. Similar fees charged for self-directed RRSPs are not deductible.

Deductible Interest

If you borrow funds to earn income, any interest expense incurred is deductible from income, with certain exceptions. Earning income does not necessarily mean that you have to earn a profit immediately, but you must demonstrate that you have a reasonable expectation of profit. Incurring a loss does not prejudice the deductibility of the interest expense, although the CCRA may disallow the portion of the interest expense that exceeds the return on your investment. If it were reasonably foreseeable, at the time the loan was taken out, that the interest rate would exceed the rate of return in the future, your claim for an interest deduction could be disallowed.

Before 1994, interest expense was deductible only if you continued to own the related investment throughout the period that the funds were borrowed. Since 1994, you may deduct interest expenses after selling the investment, but only on that portion of the loan represented by the loss realized on the sale of the investment.

You are never allowed to deduct the interest on funds borrowed for personal expenditures, such as interest on money borrowed to finance a vacation or purchase a home.

> **Planning Opportunity:** Borrow only for investment or business purposes and pay for personal expenditures out of your savings. You can deduct interest, however, when a personal asset (such as your home) has been used as collateral for a loan to finance an investment.

Rental Expenses

Although not discussed as a separate category, rent can be characterized either as income from property or business income. The CCRA will accept that you are earning income from property if you rent space and provide basic services only. Basic services include heat, light, parking, and laundry facilities. If you provide additional services to tenants, such as cleaning, security, and meals, the CCRA will more likely characterize your services as a business. Generally speaking, the more services you provide, the greater the chance that your rental operation is a business. In that case, you will be required to calculate your income as a business owner (see Chapter 7).

If you earn rental income from an investment property, you may deduct all the current expenses you incur with respect to the rental property and claim capital cost allowance (CCA) on the property itself. Capital cost allowance applies to depreciable property and allows a deduction of the costs of the property against rental income over a certain period.

> **Caution:** Capital cost allowance cannot be used to create or increase a loss with respect to rental property. It can only offset the net rental income on that or other property that arose prior to the CCA claim.

Current expenses include the cost of advertising for tenants, heat, electricity, property taxes, water rates, insurance, and labour and material for routine repairs and maintenance. Capital expenditures such as major additions or renovations are not deductible, but can usually be added to the capital cost of the property and then claimed over time as CCA.

If you rent out part of your principal residence, the same basic rules apply for current expenses and CCA may be claimed for the rented portion. Expenses fully attributable to the rented portion are fully deductible. Common expenses such as heat, electricity, and property taxes must be prorated so that only the portion that relates to the rented part of the principal residence is deducted from rental income. Before you claim any CCA, note that any CCA claimed will erode a proportionate amount of your principal residence exemption. As a result, you could open yourself to a future taxable gain when you sell your house.

You cannot claim CCA if you designate your house as a principal residence for years during which you are not occupying it.

CHAPTER NINE

If You Invest in Tax Shelters or Offshore

HOW CAN YOU PROTECT YOURSELF? / 143

LIMITED PARTNERSHIPS / 143

MINERAL EXPLORATION AND OIL AND GAS SHELTERS / 144

MULTIPLE-UNIT RESIDENTIAL BUILDINGS (MURBS) / 144

CANADIAN FILMS / 145

FARMING AS A TAX SHELTER / 145

PROVINCIAL TAX SHELTERS / 146

GENERAL RULES FOR OFFSHORE INVESTMENT REPORTING / 146
Form T1135 / 146

Many upper-income Canadians have discovered too late that the quality of a tax shelter investment, as opposed to the promise of tax savings, is by far the most important element when making an investment decision. Security for your money should outweigh all other considerations. Receiving a deduction for the money you put into a tax shelter is no consolation if you ultimately lose your money because you made a poor investment. If you are considering investing in a tax shelter, read the entire prospectus offering and obtain professional advice before committing your funds and future state of mind to these high-risk investments.

HOW CAN YOU PROTECT YOURSELF?

Because a tax shelter identification number carries no guarantee that the Canada Customs and Revenue Agency (CCRA) will authorize any tax benefits on your investment, you must take action to protect yourself. The following provides a starting checklist:

- Ask for the prospectus or any other documentation relevant to the tax shelter, and read it carefully.
- Consider closely any statements or opinions in the documentation explaining the income tax consequences of the investments.
- Get any and all verbal assurances concerning the shelter in writing.
- Ask the promoter for a copy of any advance income tax rulings provided by the CCRA with respect to the investment.
- Seek professional advice before signing any documents.

LIMITED PARTNERSHIPS

Investment tax credits and losses claimed by limited partners are limited to the extent that their investment in the partnership is at risk. Exceptions to these "at-risk rules" are limited to certain partnerships that pre-date February 25, 1986, or prospectuses filed before June 12, 1986. The amount at risk for the first purchaser is generally the adjusted cost base (the purchase cost net of expenses incurred in the purchase) of his or her partnership interest at the end of the year plus his or her share of the current year's income of the partnership. This amount is reduced by any amount owing to the partnership and any guarantee or indemnity provided to protect the limited partner against the loss of his or her investment. If allocating losses of a partnership or withdrawing funds results in a negative cost base, the negative amount is a capital gain of the partner in the year it becomes negative. In spite of the strict rules, limited partnerships frequently offer a good way of arranging financing and limiting risk.

For more information about purchasing units in a limited partnership, consult your securities broker.

> **Planning Opportunity:** Since 1998, units of certain limited partnerships have not been considered foreign property and thus are not subject to the 30 per cent ceiling when held in an RRSP. See Chapter 13.

MINERAL EXPLORATION AND OIL AND GAS SHELTERS

With flow-through shares, the various deductions and tax credits associated with oil and gas drilling and mineral exploration flow through directly to the unitholders.

As with limited partnership units, consult your securities broker for information about investing in mineral and gas exploration opportunities.

MULTIPLE-UNIT RESIDENTIAL BUILDINGS (MURBS)

MURBs lost their special tax treatment in 1994. The CCRA now treats them the same as other rental properties owned by persons not actively engaged in the real estate business. For this reason, tax shelter opportunities are limited. Capital cost allowance (CCA) can be used only to reduce rental income to zero, but not to create or increase a loss deductible against other income. Recall that CCA is the portion of the cost amount of a depreciable property that you can use to offset income on an annual basis. CCA is depreciation for tax purposes.

CANADIAN FILMS

The benefits of investing in Canadian films have been severely curtailed over the years. The CCA claim rules have been replaced by a system of refundable credits to Canadian film producers with no possible flow-out to investors. This system applies to films produced after February 29, 1996.

FARMING AS A TAX SHELTER

Depending on the crop or product raised and the market for it, farming may be a viable tax shelter. Several rules in the tax law, however, including a mandatory inventory adjustment, make it more difficult to create losses from farming to offset income from other sources. Most taxpayers will also be subject to the restricted farm loss rules, which currently limit deductible losses in a year to $8,750. To claim even the restricted farm loss amount, your farm operation must have some reasonable expectation of profit and you, as an operator, must establish that you are running the farm as a business.

There are numerous cases on horse- and other livestock-breeding operations where the Minister of National Revenue has argued successfully that the individual owning the operation did not qualify as a farmer, or only qualified for the restricted farming loss. Ensure that you obtain expert advice before embarking on a farming venture, particularly if you are looking for business losses.

In spite of the obstacles, farming (and in Quebec fishing) may still be an attractive tax shelter because of the $500,000 capital gains exemption available for gains on qualifying farm property. Again, to claim the exemption, the farm must be a viable Canadian farming business. If that is the case, you do not necessarily have to be a full-time farmer to take advantage of this exemption.

PROVINCIAL TAX SHELTERS

Many provinces provide incentives to encourage investment in certain areas or industries. For example, some provinces have stock savings plans that provide for tax credits. Others have venture-capital plans to encourage investment in small to medium-sized companies. Consult a tax professional in your province to determine which provincial plan suits you.

GENERAL RULES FOR OFFSHORE INVESTMENT REPORTING

Numerous Canadians hold offshore investments to reduce their exposure to the unstable Canadian dollar, to take advantage of the rules of lower-tax regimes, or to invest in vehicles that are not available in Canada, among many other reasons. The Canadian government does not discourage its residents from investing offshore, but it does not look kindly upon its residents not paying their full complement of Canadian taxes. The basic rule is that all Canadian residents must declare their worldwide income to the CCRA in their annual personal tax return.

Since 1998, all Canadian resident taxpayers have been required to report specified foreign assets over $100,000. The information here is presented only as an overview of the foreign asset reporting requirements. Consult your tax professional to determine how your investments will be directly affected.

Form T1135

Individuals, corporations, trusts, and partnerships that own specified foreign property with a total cost of more than $100,000 any time during the year must file a T1135, Foreign Income Verification Statement, and report those assets. According to the CCRA, foreign bank accounts, other indebtedness, shares of foreign corporations, real and tangible property, and intangible property situated outside Canada will trigger the reporting rules. Property used exclusively for the purpose of carrying on an active business, funds in registered pension plans, personal-use property, and shares in foreign affiliates are exempt from the reporting rules.

Remember that even if the cost of your foreign assets does not exceed $100,000, you must still report any income that you earn on these assets. If you own units of foreign mutual fund trusts, you must report them on another form related to trust holdings, Form T1142, even if their cost base is less than $100,000.

Along with the reporting rules, there are substantial penalties for delayed reporting, under-reporting, and non-reporting of foreign income. Penalties will apply in the case of intentional non-filing for more than 24 months, as well as for under-reporting. The penalty will equal the greater amount of $24,000 or 5 per cent of the cost of the under- or non-reported asset.

To encourage compliance with the reporting rules, the CCRA introduced Form T1135 in a "check-the-box" format. Taxpayers are not required to provide a detailed listing of foreign holdings, but must check the box that most closely corresponds with the type, location, and range of investment levels. In addition to reporting income from the reported property, remember to include Form T1135 with your annual tax return.

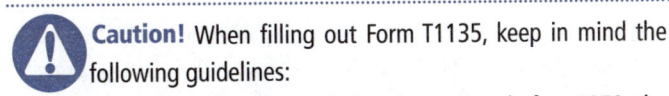

> **Caution!** When filling out Form T1135, keep in mind the following guidelines:
> - If you have owned foreign capital property since before 1972, the Canadian valuation rules for capital property apply. Your cost amount is the fair market value of the property as of December 31, 1971.
> - If you own Canadian shares that are exchangeable for foreign shares, under certain conditions you are required to report those shares as foreign property.
> - If you recently became a resident of Canada, the foreign property that you still hold must be reported, but its cost amount is calculated as its fair market value on the day you became a resident of Canada.

> **✓ Planning Opportunity:** Here are some ways to plan around the reporting rules:
> - Your best and easiest method for not having to report is to not hold foreign assets that cost more than $100,000 in total. Dividend reinvestment, for example, will increase the cost base of your foreign investment, while interest payment reinvestment will not.
> - Because investment in an active foreign business will not trigger the reporting rules, you might consider this investment option. However, caution must be exercised if you choose this option. The standard for determining whether a business is active is defined by the Canadian *Income Tax Act*. In addition, just as in Canada, investing in an active foreign business often carries higher risk than investing in a foreign bank account or mutual fund.
> - Invest offshore in assets that qualify as personal-use property. Personal-use property is a broad category and includes capital and non-capital property that is owned for personal use or enjoyment. Under the Canadian rules, the cost base of personal-use capital property is $1,000. If you buy and sell an asset under $1,000, you will not attract any capital gains and need not report any income. Recall also that you can claim a principal residence exemption on a home located outside of Canada. Investing in personal-use property might limit your investment options, but it could be a means of maintaining your cost base of other foreign assets below $100,000 (e.g., diverting your dividends to purchase qualifying personal-use property). In addition, you will not necessarily tie up your foreign investments if you purchase personal-use property that is also a liquid investment.

Investing offshore is still an attractive option for many Canadians, but you should be aware of the risks involved, both at home, in terms of increased tax vigilance, and abroad, because of the inherent investment risks. Consult a professional investment advisor before taking your money outside of

Canada. Furthermore, on October 11, 2002, the federal government proposed substantial changes to the taxation of non-resident trusts and offshore investments. The intent of the changes was to expand the CCRA's ability to tax offshore transactions. Once they are enacted, the new rules will apply from 2003 onwards.

CHAPTER TEN

If You Own Your Own Home

PRINCIPAL RESIDENCE EXEMPTION / 150
Post-1981 Principal Residence Rules—The Details / 151
Determining the Taxable Portion / 152
Designating a Property as a Principal Residence / 152
Second Homes / 152

PLANNING OPPORTUNITIES / 153
The Home Buyers' Plan / 153
Home Office Expenses / 154
Income Splitting / 155
To Sell or Not to Sell / 155

The single biggest tax advantage to owning your own home is that, with a few exceptions, any capital gain that arises on the sale or transfer of your principal residence is exempt from capital gains tax.

PRINCIPAL RESIDENCE EXEMPTION

To qualify for the exemption, you must satisfy the following principal residence exemption rules:

- Only one home can be designated as your principal residence for a particular year.
- You can make the designation only for the years you are resident in Canada.
- Since 1982, only one principal residence per family unit per year is allowed.

- Your residence must be a house, condominium, mobile home, trailer, houseboat, or a share in a cooperative housing corporation.
- The dwelling can be owned outright or jointly with one or more other individuals.
- Although your home does not have to be located in Canada to qualify, the Canadian rule does not exempt you from foreign property or income tax that may arise upon disposition of the property.
- For the home to be your principal residence, you, your spouse, or your child must be ordinarily resident in the home during the designated year. Usually the family home is the designated property, but a part-time residence, such as a summer cottage, can also qualify.

> **Caution:** If you have more than one family home, deciding which home to designate and for how many years can be a complex decision with significant tax consequences. We recommend consulting your professional advisor prior to the sale.

Post-1981 Principal Residence Rules—The Details

As of 1982, a family unit can designate only one home under the principal residence rules with respect to each year. In any particular year, a family unit consists of you, your spouse (provided you had a spouse throughout the year and were not living apart and legally separated), and children who, throughout the year, were unmarried and under 18 years of age. This means that if you and your spouse each own a home, you will be liable for tax on all or a portion of the capital gain accruing on one of the homes beginning January 1, 1982.

When a couple marries after 1981 and both people own homes, each may designate his or her home for the year of marriage and prior years, but only one home may be designated after the year of marriage. Same-sex or opposite-sex common-law partners are treated the same as married couples for tax purposes.

Determining the Taxable Portion

The taxable portion of the gain on the sale of a principal residence is calculated by subtracting the exempt portion from the total gain. The remainder, if any, is subject to the normal capital gains rules (see Chapter 8).

The exempt portion is based on the number of years that the property was a principal residence compared to the number of years of ownership. Although the actual rules are complicated, if you can designate the property as your principal residence for all years of ownership, or all years except one, the total gain is generally exempt.

Special transitional rules apply where a property owned on December 31, 1981, is subsequently sold. The rules provide that the non-exempt portion of the gain is the lesser of two amounts. One amount is calculated using the normal method to determine the gain, i.e., by viewing the total years of ownership as one period. The second amount is calculated by separating the years of ownership into two periods, one pre-1982 and one post-1981. To do this latter calculation, you must determine the fair market value of the property on December 31, 1981.

Designating a Property as a Principal Residence

If you dispose of a property that you wish to claim as your principal residence, and you recognize a gain, you have two filing options. If a portion of the gain is subject to tax, you must file a prescribed form with your tax return for that year and designate your property as your principal residence for specified years.

Second Homes

If your family currently has, or intends to acquire, a second home, record all capital costs associated with both homes.

Capital costs include the costs of adding a pool, finishing the basement, or adding an extra room. These costs will increase the cost base of each home. Unless a record is kept of such expenditures, you may have to compute any ultimate gain using only the original purchase price as the cost base, and you will lose the value of your investments in the property.

PLANNING OPPORTUNITIES

The Home Buyers' Plan

The HBP allows individuals to withdraw up to $20,000 from their RRSPs to buy a home without having to pay tax on the withdrawal. A couple can contribute up to $40,000 from two RRSPs. A qualifying home must be acquired before October 1 of the calendar year following the year of the withdrawal.

The Home Buyers' Plan (HBP) is no longer a one-time offer. Since 1999, you can participate in the HBP more than once in your lifetime, provided that you qualify as a first-time home buyer and you have a nil HBP balance at the beginning of the calendar year when you withdraw funds from your RRSP. To be a first-time home buyer, neither you nor your spouse can have owned a home and lived in it as a principal residence in any of the four calendar years beginning before the time of the withdrawal.

A disabled person or a supporting individual may withdraw funds from an RRSP under the HBP even if he or she currently owns a home. To qualify, the funds must be used to purchase a home that is more accessible or better suited to the individual's personal needs. The disabled individual must qualify for the disability tax credit to be eligible.

Except in the case where a supporting individual purchases a home for a disabled individual, the withdrawals must be repaid to the home buyer's RRSP. Payments can be in instalments over a maximum period of 15 years. For example, if you withdraw $15,000 from an RRSP under the HBP, your scheduled annual repayment would be $1,000 per year ($15,000 divided by 15 years). The 15-year repayment period begins in the second year following the year in which you make the withdrawal. Repayments made in the first 60 days of a year can be treated as having been made in the preceding year (similar to the regular RRSP rules). If, in any year, you decide not to repay the scheduled amount, or decide to repay only part of it, the amount that is not repaid will be included in your income for the year and, consequently, will be subject to tax.

> **Caution:** In addition to your normal RRSP contributions every year, you should restore the funds withdrawn from your RRSP as quickly as possible to maximize your retirement income.

You may repay more than the scheduled annual repayment in any year. Increased payments result in a lower outstanding balance and lower scheduled annual repayments for the remainder of the pay-back period.

A special rule denies a tax deduction for contributions to an RRSP that are withdrawn within 90 days under the HBP. Your contributions within the 90-day period will not be allowed as a deduction unless your RRSP balance after the withdrawals is more than or equal to the amount of the contributions.

Home Office Expenses

Certain home office expenses can be deductible, provided that you use your office as your principal place of business, or you use it exclusively to earn business income and to meet clients, customers, or patients on a regular and continuous basis. The amount deducted cannot exceed the income from the business for the year, after other expenses are deducted. You can carry forward any excess amount and deduct it in years when the business generates income. Refer also to the discussion of "Home Office Expenses" in Chapter 7.

Income Splitting

If your family has only one house, consider selling ownership of the personal residence to the lower-income spouse at fair market value. This strategy will ensure that any potential taxable gains that may arise when the house is sold will be taxed in the tax bracket of the lower-income spouse. A taxable gain could arise if the house is used for something other than a principal residence (i.e., to earn rental or business income). To ensure that the CCRA will not attribute the taxable gain to the high-income spouse, the high-income spouse must elect in his or her tax return that the sale took place at fair market value and the low-income spouse must actually pay fair value consideration.

To Sell or Not to Sell

Consider retaining your residence whether you plan on leaving it for either an indefinite or temporary period. During your absence, you may rent your home and still retain your ability to designate it as your principal residence for the years in which you were living in it and, provided certain conditions are met, for up to four years after that.

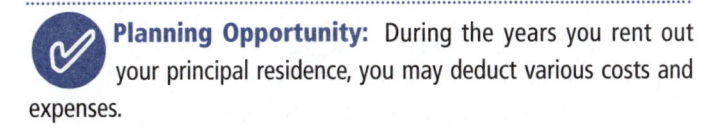

> **Planning Opportunity:** During the years you rent out your principal residence, you may deduct various costs and expenses.

If you sell the residence instead of reoccupying it, the gain that accrued during the years in which you designate the home as a principal residence will be tax-free. The gain that accrued during the years when the residence was rented may not be taxable if it was rented for less than five years.

Special rules will extend the four-year maximum period if you have moved because your employer or your spouse's employer required that you or your spouse relocate. Certain conditions must be met to take advantage of this extension.

CHAPTER ELEVEN

If You Have a Spouse

DEFINITION OF SPOUSE / 157

CREDITS AND DEDUCTIONS / 157
Spouse Credit / 157
Pooling of Credits / 157

PLANNING OPPORTUNITIES / 158
Income Splitting / 158
   Business Income / 158
   Interest on Interest / 159
   Spousal Registered Retirement Savings Plans / 160
   Pay Your Spouse's Taxes / 161
   Who Pays the Family Expenses? / 161
   Pay Your Spouse a Salary / 161
   Spousal Business Partnerships / 162
   Transfers at Fair Market Value / 162
   Gift Interest Expenses to Your Spouse / 163
   Using Transferred Funds for Leverage / 163
   Locking in the Best Rate on Spousal Loans / 163
   Professional Management Companies / 164
Situations to Avoid—Application of the Attribution Rules / 165
   No Attribution Occurs / 165
   Transfers to Your Spouse or Minor Child / 166
   Attribution Rules and Trusts / 167
   Substituted Property / 168
   Property Loans to a Non-Arm's-Length Party / 168
   Corporate Attribution Rules / 169

CONSEQUENCES OF MARRIAGE OR COMMON-LAW RELATIONSHIP BREAKDOWN / 170

DEFINITION OF SPOUSE

The definition of "spouse" includes married, common-law, and same-sex partners. Same-sex couples will be referred to as "common-law partners," which is defined as two persons, regardless of sex, who cohabit in a conjugal relationship and have done so for a continuous period of at least 12 months.

CREDITS AND DEDUCTIONS

Spouse Credit

In 2003, the maximum amount of the spousal credit you can claim depends on the income of your spouse. If your spouse's net income is $659 or less, you may claim the full federal spouse credit of $1,054. The credit is reduced by 16 per cent of your spouse's net income in excess of $659. No credit is available if your spouse's net income is more than $7,245 for 2003.

If you live apart from your spouse at the end of the year by reason of marriage breakdown, use your spouse's income for the portion of the year while you were living together as spouses to calculate the credit.

You may claim the credit for only one person. If you divorce and remarry in the same year, you cannot double the credit. The federal spouse tax credit is now fully indexed along with the rest of the personal tax credits.

Pooling of Credits

> **Planning Opportunity:** If you and your spouse are taxed in different brackets, pooling tax credits provides a simple opportunity for income splitting. For example the higher-income spouse pays all the expenses and taxes for the family, while the lower-income spouse invests all available savings. Income from the investments will be taxed in the hands of the lower-income spouse at a lower rate while the higher-income spouse can claim all available credits.

The following can be transferred between spouses:

- medical expenses (see Chapter 5);
- mental or physical impairment credit (see Chapter 12);
- tuition fee credit (see Chapter 12);
- age 65 and over credit (see Chapter 15);
- pension income credit (see Chapter 15); and
- charitable donation credit (see Chapter 17).

PLANNING OPPORTUNITIES

Income Splitting

There will be overlap between the income splitting strategies discussed in this chapter and those covered in Chapter 12. More detailed descriptions of the strategies appear in this chapter. Although the options are similar, refer to Chapter 3 and the discussion of the income splitting tax and its effects on certain investments held by minor children or trusts for their benefit.

Remember that successful income splitting requires that, as a starting position, you and your spouse (or children, as the case may be) pay tax at different rates. Shifting income between two individuals in the same tax bracket will not achieve any tax savings. In addition, the more complex the plan, the more important it is that you consult your tax planning advisor to ensure that the attribution rules will not reverse any tax savings. The attribution rules are the biggest barrier between you and successful income splitting with your spouse (or children, as the case may be).

Business Income. If your spouse earns income from funds that you lend or transfer to him or her, the attribution rules generally apply, and you will be taxed on the income. To get around these rules, ensure that your spouse personally runs the business or invests in a partnership in which he or she actively participates. Alternatively, the attribution rules should not apply if you and your spouse operate a business as a *bona fide* partnership. Capital gains that arise on disposition of the business by your spouse will be attributed to you, however.

If you lend or transfer property that is an interest in a partnership to your spouse (or your child), your spouse's share of the business income of the partnership may be considered income from property and not income from business. The *Income Tax Act* makes a distinction between the loaning of money and the loaning of property. As a result, the attribution rules may apply, and the partnership income may be attributed back to you. This provision will apply where your spouse is a "specified member" of the partnership. According to the *Income Tax Act*, a specified member is someone who is:

- a limited partner of the partnership during the fiscal period in which the income arose; and
- neither actively engaged in the activities of the partnership, nor carries on a business similar to that of the partnership (other than as a member of the partnership) on a regular, continuous, and substantial basis throughout the period.

For example, if you lend your spouse $100,000 that is used to acquire an interest in a limited partnership, the attribution rules may apply because your spouse is only a passive investor. If your spouse's share of the partnership income is $10,000 for a given year, that $10,000 will be added to your income for the year.

Interest on Interest. Attribution rules do not mean that you should abandon the idea of giving or loaning your spouse funds to earn investment income. Interest on interest is generally not subject to attribution rules, and amounts earned this way can be significant in the long run. For example, assume that you give your spouse $20,000 and it is invested to earn 8 per cent annually over the next 10 years, and the annual interest payments are reinvested at this same rate. Over the 10 years, only the simple interest of $16,000 (8% of $20,000 = $1,600 × 10 years) will be attributed to you. Interest on interest of $7,178, over and above the simple interest of $16,000, will be earned over the 10-year period if the annual interest of $1,600 is reinvested at 8 per cent. This interest on interest will be taxed in your spouse's hands, not in yours.

There is no attribution of income earned on attributed income, such as interest on interest, unless the attributed income is a stock dividend.

> **Planning Opportunity:** Although the income or gain is attributed for tax purposes, these amounts still legally belong to your spouse. For this reason, this type of income is considered almost creditor-proof, meaning that your creditors are largely unable to access these funds.

Spousal Registered Retirement Savings Plans. Details on spousal RRSPs are contained in Chapter 13.

Overall, spousal RRSPs are an effective method of achieving future income splitting because the attribution rules will generally not apply when your spouse begins withdrawing from the plan. The RRSP, annuity, or registered retirement income fund (RRIF) payments that will provide retirement income for your spouse are taxable only in the hands of your spouse.

If you foresee the need to withdraw RRSP funds from the spousal plan in the near future, stop contributing to a spousal RRSP for at least two years. Any funds withdrawn from the spousal RRSP can be attributed to you if you contributed to any spousal RRSP during the year or during the two years preceding the withdrawal. If your spouse will be withdrawing funds from an RRSP, the funds should be withdrawn from his or her own RRSP and not a spousal RRSP.

Remember that amounts contributed to a spousal RRSP belong to your spouse. Because of this, a spousal RRSP is another way of creditor-proofing your money to some degree. If you contribute to your spouse's RRSP, make the payment directly to the trustee and have a receipt created in your name so that you can prove you made the payment.

Pay Your Spouse's Taxes. From a tax perspective, paying your spouse's tax is treated the same as making a gift. Of course, no income would be earned on the amount, since it is used to pay taxes and therefore there would be no attribution. Your spouse could then invest the funds that otherwise would have gone to pay his or her taxes, and any income earned on these funds would not be attributed back to you. This arrangement is not possible if your spouse's employer deducts tax at source.

Who Pays the Family Expenses? As explained above, if both spouses are earning income but one spouse will continually pay tax at a higher rate than the other, the higher-income spouse should pay all or most of the family expenses while the lower-income spouse invests all or most of his or her earnings. The income generated from these investments will be taxed at a lower rate and is not attributable.

Pay Your Spouse a Salary. You may pay your spouse a salary for work performed in your unincorporated business, and deduct the salary in calculating your income from the business. The salary will be taxed in your spouse's hands. The salary or wages paid must be reasonable in relation to the duties performed. Your spouse can then contribute to the Canada Pension Plan and will also earn income that should result in increased RRSP contribution limits and thereby allow for contributions to an RRSP.

> **Planning Opportunity:** If you are operating a sideline business that has a reasonable expectation of medium-term profit, and you pay your spouse a reasonable salary, you could create a loss in the business for a given year. This may be useful if you can apply the loss to other sources of income.

Spousal Business Partnerships. Even though you may pay a salary to your spouse, for business and tax reasons you may want to characterize the business as a partnership. As a partner, your spouse is entitled to a share of partnership profits, as well as a proportionate share of the liabilities. This situation is common in farm operations, but can also apply to any type of business.

> **Caution:** Draft a properly documented partnership agreement that details the profit sharing arrangements and ownership of assets of the business.

If the Canada Customs and Revenue Agency (CCRA) considers the allocation of the partnership income to be unreasonable, it will change it to an allocation that it considers reasonable in the circumstances.

If the spouse's capital contribution to the business is significant, a spousal partnership will be more advantageous than paying the spouse a salary. This could permit a larger share of the business profits to be recognized by the spouse than if the spouse were paid a reasonable salary for duties performed.

> **Planning Opportunity:** If you cannot establish a spousal partnership, consider incorporating the business. Your spouse could participate by owning shares acquired with his or her own funds.

Transfers at Fair Market Value. You can elect to transfer property to your spouse and receive fair market value consideration for it. The attribution rules will not apply (if certain conditions are satisfied), and future income and capital gains will be taxed in your spouse's hands. With capital property transfers, you must recognize any accrued capital gains or losses at the time of the transfer. If you transfer property with unrealized capital losses at fair market value, the superficial loss rules (see Chapter 8) come into play, and you will be denied the capital loss if the property is still owned by your spouse 31 days after the transfer.

Gift Interest Expenses to Your Spouse. Because the attribution rules apply only where there is income or a capital gain earned on transferred funds, give your spouse funds to pay the interest on a loan made by you to your spouse to earn income. No attribution will arise on the amount gifted for the interest expense, or on the net income earned by the spouse from the loaned funds.

The loan must be a *bona fide* loan, interest must be charged at the lesser of the prescribed rate for tax purposes and commercial rates, and the interest must be paid within 30 days of the year-end.

While you must include the interest paid to you by your spouse in your income for tax purposes, your spouse's investment income will compound much more quickly because it is not depleted annually by an interest payment on the loan.

Using Transferred Funds for Leverage. Attribution will not arise on income or capital gains earned on funds borrowed commercially by your spouse, provided there is no guarantee by you. As a result, if you are considering borrowing for investment purposes, transfer funds to your spouse to enable him or her to borrow. For example, if you give your spouse $25,000 to facilitate a loan of $75,000, your spouse can then buy $100,000 worth of securities, which would be lodged as collateral with the lending institution in lieu of your guarantee. In this situation, only 25 per cent of any net income or capital gains earned ($25,000 / $100,000) would be attributed to you.

Locking in the Best Rate on Spousal Loans. If you intend to lend funds to your spouse, charge interest at the rate prescribed by the CCRA. This rate likely will be lower than commercial lending rates. The prescribed rate is set each quarter based on 90-day Treasury Bill yields of the first month of the preceding quarter. As a result, you know two months in advance what the rate will be for any quarter. Before locking in the interest rate on a spousal loan for longer than three months, check the direction the prescribed rate will move in the next quarter. If the rate is expected to increase, and you do not expect rates to fall again, consider setting the term of the loan for an extended period. If the rate is expected to decline, keep the loan on a variable-rate basis.

Professional Management Companies. Professional management companies are popular because the attribution rules do not apply to small business corporations. Professionals, such as doctors or dentists, set up professional management companies, which are owned by the spouse and/or children of the professional. The company provides services to the professional and charges a fee, usually 15 per cent, above the cost of the services. Such services could include the rental of equipment and facilities, the services of assistants, and bookkeeping, secretarial, and administrative services. Seek professional advice to ensure that the company will not be considered a personal services business. The *Income Tax Act* applies limits on expenses and charges a higher rate of tax on a personal services business.

If it is incorporated, a professional management company is considered a small business corporation, and no attribution of income will occur if the professional loans or sells assets to a small business corporation and the professional's spouse or children are shareholders. If the management business is unincorporated, which is generally not advisable, and assets are transferred to the spouse and used to earn business income, no attribution would occur.

Depending on the nature of services provided, fees billed for these services may be subject to GST/HST and, in Quebec, Quebec Sales Tax (QST). Some activities, such as most health care services, do not qualify for a reimbursement of the

GST/HST and QST paid. In such cases, this additional cost must be considered in determining if a professional management company provides any advantage.

Situations to Avoid—Application of the Attribution Rules

No Attribution Occurs. Clearly defined guidelines determine when the attribution rules will only partially apply or not apply at all. Any event outside these guidelines will trigger the rules.

Subject to the income splitting tax, if you have transferred income or property to a related minor, attribution of income ceases the year the child turns 18 (for exceptions, see "Property Loans to a Non-Arm's-Length Party" on page 168). In the case of a spouse, attribution ceases upon divorce or when the spouses are living separate and apart by reason of marriage or relationship breakdown. The transferor/lender spouse must file an election jointly with the transferee/borrower spouse to prevent the attribution of capital gains after the breakdown of a marriage and before divorce. Attribution also ends when a lender or transferor dies or ceases to be resident in Canada.

Income from certain loans or transfers is not subject to attribution if:

- interest is charged on the loan at a reasonable rate or at the rate prescribed for income tax purposes at the time the loan was made; and
- the interest payable for each year is paid within 30 days after the end of that year.

In the case of a transfer, there is no attribution if:

- the fair market value (FMV) of the transferred property does not exceed the FMV of the consideration received by the transferor on the transfer;
- in the case where the consideration received includes debt, the conditions listed above for an exempt loan are met; and
- in a transfer to a spouse, the transferor elects not to have the tax-deferred rollover provisions apply.

The following are situations where the attribution rules always apply and, consequently, where tax savings are nearly impossible to achieve. We discuss the rules in relation to spouses and children. The rules regarding transfers to minor children are subject to the income splitting tax (refer to Chapter 3).

Transfers to Your Spouse or Minor Child. The attribution rules apply if an individual lends or transfers property to, or for the benefit of, a spouse (or future spouse) or certain minors, or a trust established for such a person. The attribution rules apply to minors (under age 18) who are the individual's child, grandchild, brother, sister, brother-in-law, sister-in-law, niece, or nephew.

Rules similar to the attribution rules apply where property is lent to any non-arm's-length person, such as an adult child, and one of the main reasons for the loan is to reduce the tax of the lender by including the income in the child's tax return. Property includes money, shares, bonds, a right of any kind, a home, land, etc.

The word "transfer" has been interpreted very broadly and can include a gift or a sale at fair market value.

If the attribution rules apply, income (or losses) from lent or transferred property, or from property substituted for it, is not taxed in the hands of the recipient, but is included in the income of the individual who made the loan or transfer. In most cases, it is the net income or loss from the property that is attributed to the lender or transferor.

The attribution rules also apply to capital gains and losses realized by a spouse on lent or transferred property or substituted property. There is no attribution of capital gains or losses realized by a minor (under age 18 throughout the taxation year), unless it involves certain farm property that has previously received preferential tax treatment.

Capital gains are only attributable to the transferor for transfers occurring after 1971. While a capital gain arising from property transferred before 1972 is not attributable, any income earned on that property, such as dividends, is attributable to the transferor.

> **Caution:** Attributed income retains its character (except in corporate attribution situations; see page 169). If you lend funds to your spouse, who then invests the funds in preferred shares, any dividends, capital gains, or capital losses on the preferred shares will be attributed back to you. You will then be taxed on the attributed amounts as dividends, capital gains, or capital losses.

Attribution Rules and Trusts. For there to be attribution of income (or loss), the spouse or minor child must earn income from the transferred assets (except in certain corporate situations; see "Corporate Attribution Rules" on page 169). Consequently, if property is transferred to a trust for the benefit of minor children and the income from the property is taxed in the trust, there is no attribution of income. All of the income of an *inter vivos* trust (a trust created during your lifetime) is taxed at the highest personal tax rate to the trust and no advantage would be gained, however.

If the income is paid or payable to the children from the trust, the paid or accrued income constitutes income to the child and the attribution rules will apply. On the other hand, a net loss suffered by a trust cannot be allocated to beneficiaries, with the result that there can never be attribution of trust losses.

If the attributed income is earned through a trust, special rules apply to determine the amount of trust income of a designated beneficiary (i.e., the spouse, minor child, minor niece or nephew) that will be attributed. These rules will produce different results depending on whether all or only a portion of the income earned by the trust is from "lent or transferred property," or whether there is more than one designated beneficiary.

> **Caution:** If you and your spouse each decide to contribute funds to the same trust, which includes your minor child as a beneficiary, the income of that minor could be attributed to both you and your spouse, leading to double taxation.

To avoid this, each parent should create a separate trust. The income of only one trust would then be attributed back to the parent who created it.

If you are involved in trusts, review your situation with a professional and ensure that you do not inadvertently stumble into unfortunate tax complications.

Substituted Property. Attribution rules apply not only to lent or transferred property, but also to property that is substituted for the lent or transferred property. If you lend funds to your spouse, who then uses the funds to acquire preferred shares, the shares are considered substituted property and the attribution rules will apply to the income from, and the capital gains or losses on, the shares. If the preferred shares are sold and the funds are used to acquire bonds, the bonds are considered substituted property to which the attribution rules would apply.

Stock dividends received on a share will be considered property substituted for that share. Attribution rules will apply to any income earned (and in the case of a spouse, any gains realized) on a stock dividend that was received as income on lent, transferred, or substituted property.

Property Loans to a Non-Arm's-Length Party. Attribution rules may apply if you lend property to any individual with whom you do not deal at arm's length. If it is reasonable to consider that one of the main reasons for the loan is to reduce or avoid your tax liability on income from the property (or property substituted for it), the loan will trigger the attribution rules.

The outright transfer of property (e.g., by gift or sale at fair market value) to a non-arm's-length individual does not create adverse tax consequences.

A non-arm's-length party is an individual who is related to you by blood (both forebears and descendants), marriage, or adoption. Parents, spouses, and even adult children are affected. The typical situation covered by the non-arm's-length rule is a low-interest or no-interest loan made to your adult child. While commercial rate loans are exempted, if the rate of interest is less than both the prescribed interest rate for income tax purposes (announced quarterly) and the rate that arm's-length parties would have otherwise agreed to, income attribution will apply. It will also apply if the interest on the loan is not paid within 30 days after the end of each year. If the debtor spends the funds for a non-investment purpose (e.g., paying tuition fees), there is no income to attribute.

Corporate Attribution Rules. These rules apply to loans (including transfers) between individuals that are routed through certain corporations. There will be deemed attribution of interest income to the transferor if it can be determined that one of the main purposes of the loan is to reduce the transferor's income and to benefit a "designated person." If the transferor receives (as a minimum) an annual prescribed return on the debt or shares in return for the loan or transfer of property, there will be no attribution. A designated person is a spouse or certain minors if they own at least 10 per cent of any class of shares of the corporation.

The corporate attribution rules do not apply to small business corporations (SBCs) that also qualify as Canadian-controlled private corporations (CCPCs) and carry on an active business in Canada. Both public corporations and CCPCs that hold portfolio investments or real estate are excluded from this exception.

Potential problems for intra-corporate loans include:

- Attribution can occur if the shareholders of the corporation that receives the loan include the individual's spouse, certain minors, or a partnership or trust in which the spouse or a minor is, respectively, a member or a beneficiary.
- Unlike the normal attribution rules, the spouse or a minor need not actually receive income for the corporate attribution rules to apply.

Corporate attribution rules do not apply when the shares of the corporation are held in trust, and under the terms of the trust the individual may not receive any of the capital or income of the trust while he or she is a designated person (spouse, related minor, niece, or nephew who is under 18 years of age).

CONSEQUENCES OF MARRIAGE OR COMMON-LAW RELATIONSHIP BREAKDOWN

Marriage breakdown, or the dissolution of a common-law union, creates numerous legal consequences, but our discussion is limited to the tax issues. The following tax principles or strategies will be affected by marriage breakdown. Because this is not an exhaustive list, ensure that your professional advisors are aware of your situation.

- The good news is that the attribution rules no longer apply.
- Opportunities exist for settlements to be transferred to your ex-spouse's tax-deferred investment vehicle.

    You will no longer be able to claim a deduction for contributing to a spousal RRSP, but the money already deposited will continue to be your spouse's property. The rules discouraging the collapsing of spousal RRSPs do not apply on the breakdown of a marriage or common-law relationship.

    Settlement funds may be transferred from one spouse's RRSP or RRIF to the ex-spouse's RRSP, RRIF, or RPP on a tax-

deferred basis. The attribution rules are not triggered by this kind of RRSP transfer. In order not to be taxed, payments made from your RRSP to your ex-spouse's RRSP must be pursuant to a decree, order, or judgment of a competent tribunal or a written separation agreement.
- There are tax issues related to alimony and maintenance payments.

  If you are divorced or separated, you may be receiving (or paying) amounts of alimony and/or maintenance. These payments are included in your income in the year of receipt (and are deductible for the payer in the same year). These payments are very different from child support payments, which are no longer included in the income of the recipient or deductible from the income of the payer. The general rule is that if a payment is taxable income to one party, it is an allowable deduction to the other.

  Alimony or maintenance must be:
  – periodic;
  – pursuant to a decree, judgment, or written agreement; and
  – made for the maintenance of the recipient and/or children.

  In addition, the parties to the agreement must be living apart pursuant to a divorce, judicial separation, or written separation agreement, from the time of the payment until the end of the year. The issues are further complicated if there is a question of whether the payments are periodic alimony or maintenance versus instalments of lump-sum obligations, and whether payments made to third parties qualify as alimony or maintenance. A third-party payment includes home mortgage payments or rental payments to a landlord. If a payer is making both alimony and child support payments, unless a third-party payment is clearly delineated as a payment for spousal support, it will be considered child support under the new rules. Voluntary additional payments that are not part of the agreement will not qualify as either alimony or maintenance.

> **Caution:** Ensure that you receive competent legal and tax advice regarding payment arrangements under separation and/or divorce agreements. The federal child support guidelines came into effect May 1, 1997.

Frequently, alimony and maintenance agreements result in income shifting from a higher-income individual to a lower-income individual. As a result, there are tax benefits inherent in the payments because the higher-income individual obtains a deduction that saves a greater amount of tax than the corresponding tax cost to the recipient of the payment. Because of the shifting aspects of these payments, many separation or divorce agreements are negotiated on an after-tax basis.

- There are also tax consequences related to child support payments.

Child support paid pursuant to a written agreement or court order made on or after May 1, 1997 are neither deductible by the payer, nor included in the income of the recipient for tax purposes. Existing child support orders will remain unaffected unless varied after April 30, 1997, to change the amount of the child support.

After May 1, 1997, where the payer and the recipient of child support agree and file a joint election with the CCRA, the new rules apply for payments after May 1, 1997, even if their agreement is not varied. Agreements entered into or court orders after March 5, 1996, can provide that the new rules apply for payments made after May 1, 1997.

These tax changes do not apply to spousal support. Periodic payments of spousal support pursuant to a written agreement or order will be tax-deductible to the payer and taxable to the recipient.

> **Caution:** If an agreement or order does not clearly distinguish the amount of spousal support from child support, the entire amount will be deemed to be child support.

For this reason, expenses paid to third parties will be treated as child support unless they are clearly identified in the agreement or order as being solely for the benefit of the recipient spouse. As well, if only a partial payment is made, it will be deemed to be child support before it is allocated as spousal support.

CHAPTER TWELVE

If You Have Children

COMMON-LAW AND SAME-SEX COUPLES / 175

**IF YOU HAVE CHILDREN OR GRANDCHILDREN UNDER 18:
   CREDITS AND DEDUCTIONS / 175**
Eligible Dependant / 175
Canada Child Tax Benefit / 175
Child Care Expenses / 176

PLANNING OPPORTUNITIES / 177
Income Splitting / 177
Transferring the Canada Child Tax Benefit (CCTB) / 177
Transferring Capital Property / 177
Exception: Farm Property Transfers to a Child / 178
Testamentary Planning for Your Grandchildren / 179

**IF YOUR CHILDREN ATTEND POST-SECONDARY SCHOOL
   AND/OR ARE OVER 18: CREDITS AND DEDUCTIONS / 179**
Tuition Fees / 179
Education Amount / 180
Unused Tuition and Education Amounts / 181
The Student Loan Interest Credit / 182

PLANNING OPPORTUNITIES / 182
Maintaining a Dependant's Status / 182
Registered Education Savings Plans (RESPs) / 182
Canada Education Savings Grant (CESG) / 183

IF YOUR CHILD HAS SPECIAL NEEDS: CREDITS AND
    DEDUCTIONS / 183
Dependent by Infirmity / 183
Disability Amount and Disability Supplement Amount / 183

COMMON-LAW AND SAME-SEX COUPLES

For 2001 and later taxation years, the federal government enacted new definitions of "common-law partner" and "common-law partnership" to afford common-law and same-sex couples the same tax treatment as married heterosexual couples (see Chapter 11). As a result, all references in this chapter to "spouse" should be read as "spouse or common-law partner," and references to "marriage" as "marriage or common-law partnership."

IF YOU HAVE CHILDREN OR GRANDCHILDREN UNDER 18: CREDITS AND DEDUCTIONS

Eligible Dependant

If you do not claim the spousal amount (see Chapter 11) and you support a related person, you may be able to claim the eligible dependant credit (formerly called the equivalent-to-spouse credit) of $1,054 in 2003. To qualify for the credit, you must be unmarried or living apart from your spouse and neither supporting nor being supported by your spouse. The credit is reduced if the dependant's income exceeds $659 and is nil if the dependant's income is $7,245 or more for 2003. This credit is fully indexed annually according to increases in the consumer price index.

Canada Child Tax Benefit

Canadians may qualify for basic benefits payable under the Canada Child Tax Benefit (CCTB) for children under the age of 18. As of July 2003, the basic monthly benefits are $97.41 for each of the first two children and $104.24 for each additional child.

The CCTB is supplemented by the National Child Benefit Supplement (NCBS). If the parents earn $21,529 or less, the family will qualify for the full NCBS. As of July 2003, the program provides up to $121.91 per month for the first child, $104.50 per month for the second child, and $98 per month for each additional child. The phase-out of the NCBS begins for families with net incomes above $21,529.

Finally, since July 2003, parents with children who have a severe and prolonged mental or physical impairment have been entitled to an additional supplement to the CCTB, known as the Child Disability Benefit (CDB). The first payment of the CDB will be made in March 2004.

The Canada Customs and Revenue Agency (CCRA) also administers many provincial and territorial child benefit and credit programs, using information provided for the CCTB to determine your eligibility for these programs. If you live in Ontario or Quebec, the CCRA will automatically send the information needed to determine your eligibility for related programs in these provinces.

Child Care Expenses

The child care expense deduction limits for 2003 are:

- $4,000 per child if the child is between the ages of seven and 15 at any time during the year.
- $7,000 per child under seven years of age at the end of the year.
- $10,000 if the child qualifies for the disability tax credit, regardless of age.

For federal tax purposes, the deduction is restricted to two-thirds of earned income and must be claimed by the lower-income spouse. In Quebec it is a refundable tax credit, based on net family income (see Chapter 18). Generally, this credit is limited to the full amount of earned income of the lower-income spouse.

If you are a student in a qualifying program with children under the age of 16, or caring for a dependant with a mental or physical infirmity, you may be eligible to deduct child care expenses incurred while you take courses.

> **Planning Opportunity:** Certain day camp and day sport school costs will qualify for the child care expense deduction. The program must provide a sufficient level of child care services. Qualification of a program will depend on the age of the children involved, the qualifications of the instructors, and the types of facilities used. Consult with your tax advisor to determine if your child's summer program qualifies.

PLANNING OPPORTUNITIES

Income Splitting
Subject to the attribution rules (discussed in Chapters 3 and 11), there are opportunities to split your income with your minor children. For details on these arrangements, refer to Chapter 11. Pay particular attention to the section on "Situations to Avoid—Application of the Attribution Rules."

The following income splitting strategies can be applied specifically to your children.

Transferring the Canada Child Tax Benefit (CCTB)
Transferring the CCTB is the most common method of generating income that is taxable in the hands of a child. Even though the cheque is issued in the name of a parent, the benefit is considered to be the child's income. Therefore, the funds may be invested in the child's own investment vehicle, such as a savings account, mutual fund, bond, or investment certificate, and the income earned on these funds will not be attributed back to the parent.

Transferring Capital Property
Although income earned on property transferred to your child will be attributed back to you, capital gains will not. This fact opens up many possibilities for transferring property, particularly property that will not qualify for the $500,000 capital

gains exemption. Non-qualifying property includes shares of public and some private corporations and units in growth equity mutual funds that provide capital gains income. Ensure that any arrangements you make comply with the attribution rules (see Chapter 11).

Exception: Farm Property Transfers to a Child

During your lifetime, you can transfer farm property to a child, grandchild, or great-grandchild. You may choose the value for the transfer of the property at any amount between your adjusted cost base (the cost of the property plus the costs incurred to purchase it) of the farming property and its fair market value. A commercial woodlot that meets criteria contained in a prescribed forest management plan is also eligible to be transferred. The child assumes a tax cost equal to the transfer value and becomes liable for any tax on capital gains on a future disposition.

> **Caution:** If the child sells the farm property, including farming assets, before the year he or she turns 18, and the property was transferred to the child at less than fair market value, any resulting capital gain will be attributed to you.

To qualify, the farm property assets must be used principally in the business of farming and must be located in Canada. The transferor, the transferor's spouse, or any of the transferor's children must actively farm the property on a regular and continuous basis immediately before the transfer, and the child must be a Canadian resident. This type of tax-deferred transfer is also allowed for an interest in a qualifying family farm partnership and shares of family farm corporations.

A lifetime capital gains exemption of $500,000 is available to you on the disposition of qualified farm property (see Chapter 8). The $500,000 exemption is reduced by any amount you claimed under the $100,000 exemption (available until February 22, 1994).

Unless you expect to fully use your exemption in the future, your children will benefit (i.e., will have a smaller gain to realize in the future) if you transfer the farm property at a value above your cost, such that the resulting gain would be offset by an equal deduction under your $500,000 lifetime capital gains exemption.

Testamentary Planning for Your Grandchildren

Because estate planning is an ongoing process, you should continually update your will and adapt it to your most current situation. If your children are now grown and have their own minor children, consider bequeathing funds in your will in trust to your grandchildren rather than to your adult children. On your death, the funds can go in trust, with your children as trustees, to the minor grandchildren. There is no attribution because the attribution rules cease to apply on your death. Your grandchildren can earn income on the bequeathed funds and be taxed at a much lower rate than if their parents (your children) had earned the income. As trustees, the parents could direct the trust to use the funds and income for the benefit of your grandchildren (e.g., education costs).

IF YOUR CHILDREN ATTEND POST-SECONDARY SCHOOL AND/OR ARE OVER 18: CREDITS AND DEDUCTIONS

Tuition Fees

The federal tuition tax credit is 16 per cent of eligible tuition fees paid in respect of a calendar year. Tuition must be paid to a qualified institution for courses at the post-secondary school level, or to an institution certified by the Minister of Employment and Immigration (for courses intended to provide occupational skills to a student who is at least age 16 at the end of the year). An occupational skills course must demand a fee of at least $100. Special rules extend the tax credit to eligible tuition fees paid by a full-time student enrolled at a university outside Canada. The credit also covers fees in excess of $100 paid by a Canadian resident who is enrolled in and commutes to an educational institution providing courses at the post-secondary level in the United States.

For the purpose of the credit, the following fees qualify as tuition fees:

- admission, examination, application, and academic fees;
- charges for the use of library or laboratory facilities;
- charges for a certificate, diploma, or degree;
- mandatory computer service fees;
- the cost of any books that are included in the total fees for a correspondence course; and
- supplementary fees, such as athletic and health services fees, provided that all students are required to pay them.

Fees levied by student bodies for non-educational purposes are not included in eligible tuition fees.

Only tuition fees paid for programs held during the tax year are eligible to determine the tuition tax credit for that year. If tuition fees cover the cost for an academic session extending beyond the year, the portion covering the excess period is eligible in determining the tuition tax credit for the next year. For example, if the session covered by the tuition fees extends from September of one year to April of the next year, the tuition tax credit is computed for each of those years as one-half of the total tuition fees paid multiplied by 16 per cent.

If the tuition fee is paid by a non-related third party and the amount is not included in the student's income, the student cannot claim the tuition credit.

Education Amount

The federal education tax credit is $64 ($400 × 16%) for each month in the year during which the student was a full-time student in a qualifying program at a designated educational institution. Qualifying programs include regular and cooperative university and college programs as well as certified occupational skills development courses. Cooperative students can only claim the credit when they attend school. To be considered full-time, the program must continue for at least three weeks and must entail at least 10 hours per week of instruction or work, excluding homework. Students who are unable to register full-time for a qualifying program because of a mental or physical impairment, as certified by a doctor, or who are entitled to claim the disability tax credit, can also qualify for the $64 per month credit.

The tax credit for a part-time student is $19.20 ($120 × 16%) per month. To qualify, the student must also be registered in a qualifying program at a designated educational institution that continues for at least three consecutive weeks and requires at least 12 hours of instruction per month. As mentioned above, students are eligible to deduct child care expenses incurred while they take courses.

If the student receives an allowance or reimbursement for the program, or received employment income while taking the course in connection with the student's duties of employment, the credit cannot be claimed.

Although the student is not required to file the certificate issued by the education institution with his or her return, the certificate should be retained.

Unused Tuition and Education Amounts

Students who do not need to fully use the tuition or education amount credit to reduce their federal taxes payable to zero may carry forward any unused tuition fee credit or education tax credit to a later year.

Alternatively, the student may transfer any unused portion (up to $800, or 16% of $5,000) of the tuition tax credit and the education tax credit to his or her spouse. Tuition fees are not transferable in Quebec, however. If the spouse did not claim the student as a dependant, and did not claim any of the student's unused tax credits that could have been transferred to the spouse, the student's supporting parent or grandparent may claim the student's unused tuition fee and education tax credits (to a maximum of $800, or 16% of $5,000). The parent or grandparent making the claim is not required to file the certificate issued by the education institution, but it should be completed and signed by the student and retained by the parent or grandparent.

The Student Loan Interest Credit

The Student loan interest credit is 16 per cent of interest paid by the individual or a person related to the individual on eligible student loans. Eligible loans include those that are issued under the *Canada Student Loans Act* or an equivalent provincial statute. Note that interest on student loans obtained outside of the government student loan program, such as those offered by most major banks, will not qualify for this tax credit. The student can choose to claim this credit in the year the interest is paid or in any of the subsequent five years.

PLANNING OPPORTUNITIES

Maintaining a Dependant's Status

If your child has generated RRSP contribution room by earning qualifying "earned income," you may want to contribute to an RRSP on behalf of the child. Your child will be able to lower his or her taxable income by claiming the contribution on his or her tax return for the year the contribution is made or any subsequent year. If the child's taxable income is lowered sufficiently, you may then claim a portion of the child's tuition fee and education tax credits, if applicable.

Registered Education Savings Plans (RESPs)

Although a parent who contributes to an RESP will not receive a tax deduction for the contributions, there is a long-term tax advantage to these plans. Contributions will grow tax-free until your child becomes entitled to the savings or the plan is otherwise dismantled. When your child receives the income, it will be taxed in his or her hands, and will not be attributed back to you. In this way, RESPs provide another opportunity, to some degree, for income splitting.

The annual limit for contributions is $4,000 per child to a lifetime maximum of $42,000 per child.

If your child does not attend post-secondary school, up to $50,000 of RESP funds may be transferred on a tax-deferred basis to your own RRSP. Any excess income withdrawn from an RESP is subject to a tax of 20 per cent in addition to any normal taxes payable. To take advantage of the $50,000 transfer limit:

- you must have sufficient contribution room available in your RRSP;
- the RESP must have been in existence for at least 10 years; and
- your child must be at least age 21.

RESPs can also be used to fund the cost of distance education, provided it is equivalent to a full-time course load.

Canada Education Savings Grant (CESG)

Contributions to an RESP are eligible for a CESG of 20 per cent for the first $2,000 contributed. Catch-up contributions in excess of the $2,000 limit made in later years will also qualify for the CESG.

IF YOUR CHILD HAS SPECIAL NEEDS: CREDITS AND DEDUCTIONS

Dependent by Infirmity

If a person is dependent on you by reason of mental or physical infirmity and is 18 years of age or older at any time in the year, you may claim a dependant tax credit of $586 ($3,663 × 16%) in 2003. The credit is eroded if the dependant's income exceeds $5,197, and is reduced to nil if the dependant's income is $8,860 or more for 2003. The credit is fully indexed annually according to increases in the Consumer Price Index. The CCRA requires that a doctor must provide a statement supporting the infirmity before allowing a taxpayer to claim this credit.

The "eligible dependant" credit can also be claimed for children with special needs. However, you must choose between claiming either the dependant credit or the eligible dependant credit for any one dependant. You may claim both credits if you have two dependants who qualify for the respective tax credits.

If more than one individual is entitled to claim a dependant tax credit for the same dependant, the total claimed by the individuals must not exceed the maximum allowed if only one individual had made the claim. The CCRA is permitted to allocate the total tax credit to the supporting individuals if they cannot agree on an allocation.

Disability Amount and Disability Supplement Amount

Persons with a severe and prolonged mental or physical impairment that has been certified by a medical doctor, optometrist, audiologist, occupational therapist, or psychologist may claim a federal tax credit in 2003 of $1,005 ($6,279 × 16%). This federal credit is fully indexed annually according to increases in the Consumer Price Index.

Any unused portion of the credit may, under certain circumstances, be transferred to a spouse or to another person who supported the individual.

The disability tax credit extends to individuals who must undergo therapy in order to maintain mental or physical ability. Certain conditions apply to the type, frequency and duration of the therapy.

A supplement to the disability tax credit of up to $586 ($3,663 × 16%) is available for children under the age of 18 with severe disabilities. The supplement is reduced by expenses claimed for child care and attendant care in excess of $2,145.

CHAPTER THIRTEEN

If You Have an RRSP

MAKING AN RRSP WORK FOR YOU / 187

CONTRIBUTION RULES AND RRSP MECHANICS / 188
Who Can Contribute? / 188
Contribution Limits / 189
    For Individuals Who Are Not Members of RPPs or DPSPs / 189
    For Members of DPSPs or Money Purchase RPPs / 190
    For Members of Defined Benefit RPPs / 190
Pension Adjustment for a Year / 191
Earned Income Defined / 192
Carryforward Rule / 193
    Withdrawals from an RRSP—Including the Lifelong
      Learning Plan / 193
Spousal RRSPs / 195
    Withdrawals from a Spousal RRSP / 196
Locked-In RRSPs / 198
Types of Contributions / 198
Should You Borrow for Your RRSP Contribution? / 199
Transfers to and from an RRSP / 199
Penalties, Special Taxes, and Deregistration / 200
    Excess Contributions / 200
    Foreign Investments / 201
    Non-Qualified Investments / 201
    Borrowing Money or Carrying on Business / 202
    RRSP as Collateral for a Loan / 202
    Deregistration / 202

RRSP INVESTMENTS / 203
Plan Your Investments: Interest, Dividends, or Capital Gains in Your RRSP / 203
Canada Deposit Insurance / 204
Types of RRSPs / 205
Self-Directed RRSPs / 205

SPECIAL SITUATIONS / 206
RRSPs and Non-Residents / 206
Creditor Access to Your RRSP / 207
RRSPs on Death / 208

MATURING YOUR RRSP / 209
Maturity Options / 209
Consequence of Early Maturity / 211
RRSP Annuities / 211
Registered Retirement Income Funds (RRIFs) / 212
Collapsing Your RRSP / 215

The registered retirement savings plan (RRSP) program is the best tax deferral opportunity for average Canadians. An RRSP will allow you to invest pre-tax employment, self-employment, or any other form of "earned" income within specific limits. Any income earned in the RRSP is not taxed until withdrawn. Eventually, the accumulated amount in your plan is paid back to you as retirement income from your RRSP or a post-RRSP plan, such as a registered retirement income fund (RRIF). Tax is payable only when you withdraw funds or begin to receive a retirement income from the RRSP or the chosen post-RRSP plan.

RRSPs may also be used effectively for saving for a down payment on a home, returning to school full-time, or taking a year's sabbatical from your job. Withdrawing RRSP funds for these purposes should be done only as a last resort. The more you withdraw from your RRSP, the less likely you will be able to accumulate an adequate retirement income.

MAKING AN RRSP WORK FOR YOU

Because your RRSP contribution allows you to claim a deduction on your income tax return, you save the tax that you otherwise would have had to pay on the amount of the contribution. The saving gives you more money to invest within the RRSP than you would have if you paid the tax and used after-tax dollars to invest outside an RRSP. As the time value of money principle demonstrates, if you pay the tax now, those dollars are gone forever. If you contribute to an RRSP, you can use those tax dollars as part of your investment program and, depending on your age, you may enjoy the tax deferral for a very long time. Optimizing the time value of your money now can give you a powerful boost toward a financially worry-free retirement.

The longer the funds remain in your RRSP, the greater their growth when compared with funds invested outside the RRSP. Begin making RRSP contributions as early in your working life as possible.

> **Planning Opportunity:** The earlier you begin contributing to an RRSP, the more you contribute each year, and the earlier you contribute each year, the more funds you will have available in the RRSP for retirement income.

If you fail to contribute or to maximize your contributions as early as possible, you will have less RRSP money available to provide your retirement income.

In addition, the higher the earnings rate for your investments, the faster they will grow within an RRSP as compared to growth outside. Your RRSP contribution gives you a larger sum to invest than you would have if you paid tax and invested only after-tax dollars.

CONTRIBUTION RULES AND RRSP MECHANICS

Contributions can be made each year and are deductible from income for tax purposes, within specific limits, in the year they are made or a subsequent year.

> ✓ **Planning Opportunity:** Contributions made in the first 60 days of the year are deductible in that year or in the immediately preceding year. You can carry forward unused deduction room for a given year and use it in subsequent years.

Any income or capital gain arising in the RRSP is not immediately subject to tax, provided certain requirements are met. Capital gains and dividends lose their special tax status when earned within an RRSP and are fully taxed when withdrawn.

> ✓ **Planning Opportunity:** Although you must weigh this special tax status against the value of long-term tax deferral in your RRSP, capital gains and dividends may best be earned outside the RRSP.

You will be able to use the dividend tax credit, the preferential income inclusion rate for capital gains, or the $500,000 lifetime capital gains exemption where applicable. If these credits are not available, or are of limited value to you for your dividend or capital gain income, the RRSP remains an effective tax deferral mechanism (refer to "Plan Your Investments: Interest, Dividends, or Capital Gains in Your RRSP" on page 203, for further considerations).

Who Can Contribute?

Canadian residents and in certain circumstances non-residents with earned income (defined on page 192) can contribute to an RRSP. Since you must arrange to receive a retirement income from your RRSP by December 31 of the year you turn age 69, no further contributions to your own RRSP can be made past this date. If you are 69 or older, you can still contribute to a spousal RRSP if your spouse is under age 69 and you have contribution room. If you have not yet reached age 69, but you are receiving an RRSP retirement income, you may continue to contribute to your own RRSP, provided that you still have earned income.

Children under the age of 18 may contribute to an RRSP, assuming they have "earned income" and meet RRSP contribution rules. However, you may have trouble finding an issuer willing to enter into an RRSP contract with a minor. Some taxpayers have made contributions (for which no deduction is received) to their child's RRSP to split income with the child and reduce the family's overall tax bill. Depending on how long the funds are left in the RRSP and the child's tax rate at the time the funds are withdrawn, the tax deferral advantage may be sufficient to offset your increased tax cost. To avoid penalty taxes, the child must have deductible RRSP room. Moreover, there is no reduction of the penalty taxes for the $2,000 "excess contribution" limit unless the RRSP owner attained age 18 in a prior year.

Contribution Limits
For Individuals Who Are Not Members of RPPs or DPSPs.

The RRSP contribution limit for individuals who are not members of registered pension plans (RPPs) or deferred profit sharing plans (DPSPs) is 18 per cent of the prior year's earned income to a specific dollar maximum, which is $14,500 for 2003, $15,500 for 2004, $16,500 in 2005, and $18,000 in 2006. Starting in 2007, the $18,000 amount will be indexed according to the average increase in salaries. (Note that some participants in special plans, such as certain foreign retirement plans, may be treated as if they were participating in an RPP.)

For example, the maximum RRSP contribution for 2004 is 18 per cent of earned income in 2003 to a maximum of $15,500. To put it another way, if you want to contribute the maximum of $15,500 to your RRSP with respect to 2004, you need earned income in 2003 of at least $86,111.

For Members of DPSPs or Money Purchase RPPs. A different calculation applies to RRSP contributions for members of DPSPs or money purchase RPPs. Under a money purchase RPP, accumulated contributions and earnings in the plan are used at retirement to purchase the best possible pension. In these two cases, the RRSP contribution limit is 18 per cent of the previous year's earned income to the dollar maximum for the current year, minus the "pension adjustment" (PA). The PA for these individuals is simply the total of all employee and employer contributions (for RPPs) and employer contributions (for DPSPs) and reallocated forfeitures made in the previous calendar year to all money purchase RPPs and DPSPs.

For example, assume that in 2003 your employer contributes $1,800 to your money purchase RPP and you contribute $1,600 to the plan. Your earned income in 2003 is $50,000, which means that your maximum RRSP contribution for 2004 is $9,000 (the lesser of $15,500 and 18% of $50,000). From this you must deduct your PA from the previous year (2003) of $3,400 (RPP contributions of $1,800 and $1,600). Thus, your allowable RRSP contribution in 2004 is $5,600 ($9,000 − $3,400). If you withdraw from your DPSP or money purchase RPP before your benefits vest, you may be allocated a pension adjustment reversal. This reversal will increase your RRSP contribution room.

For Members of Defined Benefit RPPs. Individuals under a defined benefit RPP are guaranteed a specific pension through their RPP. Their RRSP contribution limit is also 18 per cent of the previous year's earned income to the dollar maximum for the current year, as noted above. However, the contribution limit is reduced by a PA that reflects the value of accrued benefits under the RPP for the previous year and any past-service pension adjustment (an amount that reflects retroactive enhancements to the plan) reported in the year, and increased by any pension adjustment reversals reported in the year. The pension adjustment reversal is reported if an individual ceases to participate in a registered plan and the amount received from the plan (other than retirement income or a deferred annuity) is less than the pension adjustments reported while the taxpayer participated in the plan. Pension adjustment reversals will be most common when a taxpayer leaves a defined benefit RPP, but also may arise when a member ceases to participate in a DPSP or money purchase RPP. If the individual is also a member of a DPSP or money purchase RPP, the PA will reflect the amount of any contributions and forfeitures under these plans.

> **Caution:** If you are a member of a defined benefit pension plan, remember that your total retirement benefit may be calculated to include pension benefits from CPP/QPP. Under an "integrated" plan, if you retire early, the pension your plan provides will likely be reduced once you turn 65 and begin to receive your government benefits.

Pension Adjustment for a Year

The PA for a calendar year is used to determine the RRSP deduction limit for the following year. The PA is designed to ensure that RPP (or DPSP) members in different plans, with similar incomes but different benefit rates, have equal access to tax assistance to help build their retirement income.

For example, a member of a pension plan that provides generous benefits will have a relatively high PA. A high PA will lessen the individual's ability to contribute to an RRSP. Many members of non-contributory defined benefit plans have found that they cannot contribute to an RRSP. Less generous pension plans will result in a smaller PA and larger allowable RRSP contributions.

Employers must calculate PAs for each employee and report them on the T4 issued by the last day of February each year. Once employees receive their T4 and consider the past-service pension adjustments and pension adjustment reversals reported in the year, they can determine precisely their RRSP contribution limit for the following year. The Canada Customs and Revenue Agency (CCRA) also advises taxpayers of their RRSP deduction limit on their income tax assessment for the preceding year.

Earned Income Defined

Your RRSP contribution limit is based on a percentage of your earned income. Earned income for a Canadian resident includes:

- salary or wages minus any allowable deductions from this income (other than RPP contributions, contributions to a retirement compensation arrangement (RCA), and deductions for a clergyman's residence);
- disability pensions paid under the Canada Pension Plan or Quebec Pension Plan, provided you were resident in Canada when you received the payments;
- income from royalties with respect to a work or invention of which the taxpayer was the author or inventor;
- income from carrying on a business, either alone or as a partner actively engaged in the business;
- net rental income, whether active or passive, from real property;
- payments from supplementary unemployment benefit plans;
- alimony or maintenance included in income for tax purposes (including that received by a common-law spouse), as well as taxable reimbursements received by you of alimony or maintenance payments you paid;
- taxable net research grants;

   less the following:

- losses from carrying on a business, either alone or as a partner actively engaged in the business;
- net rental losses from real property;
- deductible alimony or maintenance payments, as well as reimbursements paid by you of alimony or maintenance payments you received;

- certain negative cumulative eligible capital amounts that have been included in business income.

Non-residents use different rules to calculate earned income.

Carryforward Rule

If you contribute less than the maximum allowable amount to your RRSP in any particular year, the "unused RRSP deduction room" can be carried forward. This means that you can make contributions of more than the maximum amounts otherwise permitted in later years.

> **Caution:** Waiting until later years to make up deduction room carried forward may result in a tax cost and in many cases will result in a smaller accumulation in the RRSP by the time you retire.

There also appears to be little point in delaying your contribution to a later year when you expect your tax rate will be higher. Your tax saving may be offset by the cost of giving up the tax shelter advantage that you could have gained from earlier contributions. However, in some situations, it may be worthwhile to defer claiming the deduction. For example, if your earned income increases significantly for one year, claiming a larger RRSP contribution deduction for that year will benefit you.

Withdrawals from an RRSP—Including the Lifelong Learning Plan

You invest in an RRSP to save for your retirement, at which point you establish a retirement income program. There are no government restrictions against withdrawing funds from most RRSPs at any time, however. The amount withdrawn will be included in income for tax purposes, although if the withdrawal relates to a non-deductible excess RRSP contribution, an offsetting deduction may be available.

You may withdraw funds tax-free to be used for a down payment on a principal residence under the Home Buyers' Plan (for a detailed discussion, see Chapter 10).

Unless you qualify as a disabled individual or you support a disabled individual, you must be a first-time home buyer to participate in the Home Buyers' Plan. A first-time home buyer in 2003 is an individual who has never previously owned and occupied a home or has not owned and occupied a home since before January 1, 1997. Note that if you have resided with a spouse in a home owned by the spouse in the periods discussed above, you do not qualify as a first-time home buyer.

Under the Lifelong Learning Plan (LLP), you can make tax-free withdrawals from your RRSP to cover the costs of returning to school full-time in a qualifying program. Programs that require full-time attendance for periods of three months or longer will qualify. You are entitled to withdraw up to $10,000 per year to a maximum of $20,000 over four years. In general, the pay-back provisions require that you pay back the withdrawals in equal instalments over 10 years, beginning no later than 60 days after the fifth year following the year of the first withdrawal.

> **Caution:** As with the Home Buyers' Plan, before you make your withdrawal under the LLP, weigh the immediate cash benefit over the long-term effects on your retirement savings. Consider also how you will be able to pay back the withdrawals, as well as continue to make contributions to your plan.

Apart from these tax-free withdrawal programs, you may withdraw any amount from your RRSP for your own reasons, if your plan allows it. Some plans require you to provide up to one or two months' notice for withdrawal. For pre-1986 RRSPs, only the issuer can amend the plan to allow a partial withdrawal. The issuer of the RRSP is required to withhold tax at the following rates on any RRSP amount paid to you:

Withholding Tax Rates for RRSP Withdrawals

Amount	Canadian Residents Outside Quebec (%)	Inside Quebec (%)
$5,000 or less	10	23
$5,001 to $15,000	20	31.5
Over $15,000	30	36.5

> **Planning Opportunity:** If you plan to withdraw relatively large amounts from an RRSP or a RRIF, make several separate withdrawals to lessen the withholding rate, and perhaps make withdrawals over several years to avoid a significant increase in your marginal tax rate.

Spousal RRSPs

You can contribute any amount of your regular allowable RRSP contribution to a spousal RRSP, whether or not your spouse makes his or her own RRSP contributions. You are entitled to claim an RRSP contribution deduction for the amounts contributed to your plan and to the spousal plan. Under a spousal RRSP, your spouse is the only annuitant.

Make the contribution directly to the trustee of the plan and have a receipt made out in your name so that you can prove that you made the payment.

Spousal RRSP contributions are extremely valuable for splitting retirement income, particularly when your spouse has few or no other sources of pension income. If your spouse's marginal tax rate will be 25 per cent on retirement while yours will be 45 per cent, you and your spouse will have up to an extra 20 cents on every dollar of RRSP retirement income available if you contribute to a spousal plan. Expressed in percentage terms, your after-tax disposable income on the RRSP amounts after retiring could increase by over 36 per cent. In addition, your spouse will have income eligible for the tax credit on pension income when he or she reaches age 65.

> **Caution:** Contributions to a spousal RRSP reduce the amount that you can otherwise contribute to your own RRSP.

In other words, your contribution limit to both plans is your total available deduction room. You may not transfer amounts from your own RRSPs or RPPs to a spousal RRSP, except on marriage or relationship breakdown or death.

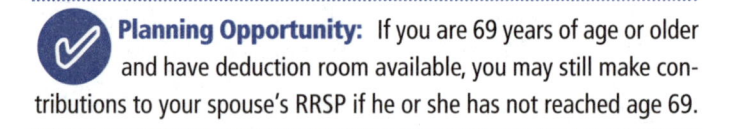

> **Planning Opportunity:** If you are 69 years of age or older and have deduction room available, you may still make contributions to your spouse's RRSP if he or she has not reached age 69.

Within 60 days of the end of the year in which a taxpayer dies, it is possible for the executor of an estate to make a contribution to a spousal RRSP if the spouse is under age 69. This creates a deduction equivalent to the contribution on the deceased's final return of income.

Withdrawals from a Spousal RRSP. If your spouse receives funds from any of his or her RRSPs after you have made a spousal contribution, you could be taxed on the withdrawn amounts. The same condition applies if your spouse receives funds from any commuted annuity from a spousal plan, or from any registered retirement income fund (RRIF) that received funds from a spousal plan in excess of the minimum amount required to be paid from the RRIF. The taxable amount to you will be equal to the lesser of:

(a) the amount received by your spouse; or
(b) the aggregate of your contributions to any spousal plans that were made in the same year your spouse receives the funds and the two preceding calendar years (excluding

amounts already added back to your income for those two years).

The excess, if any, of (a) over (b) is included in your spouse's income.

For example, assume you contribute the following amounts to a spousal RRSP:

Year	Amounts Contributed By You	By Spouse
1	$2,000	—
2	—	$4,000
3	$1,000	—

If your spouse removes $4,000 from the RRSP at the end of Year 3, $3,000 is included in your income and $1,000 is included in your spouse's income. If your spouse contributed the $4,000 to a separate, non-spousal plan in Year 2 and then withdrew the $4,000 in Year 3, the entire amount is included in your spouse's income, assuming you had not made a contribution to that particular plan.

This restriction on withdrawal applies regardless of the number of different RRSPs your spouse may have or whether funds have been transferred from a "spousal" RRSP to another RRSP to which no spousal contributions were made directly. If your spouse receives funds from his or her own RRSP, the amounts are not included in your income, even though you may have made spousal RRSP contributions to other plans within the prescribed period.

The withdrawal restriction does not apply on your death, or if you are divorced or separated and living apart from your spouse.

Locked-In RRSPs

Upon termination of employment, employees can either leave their pension entitlements with their former employer; transfer them to a pension plan with their new employer, if the new employer agrees; or transfer them to an RRSP.

The RRSPs usually employed in this situation are locked-in plans, which are more restrictive than ordinary RRSPs. They do not provide for withdrawals prior to retirement. In addition, the typical locked-in RRSP will provide that, upon your retirement, you must purchase an annuity, or a life income fund, using the plan funds. Certain provincial pension laws already require this treatment on transfers from RPPs to RRSPs.

Types of Contributions

You can contribute either cash or property to an RRSP, depending on the type of RRSP you have. Managed RRSPs generally allow only cash contributions, whereas self-directed RRSPs allow a much broader variety of contributions. Nevertheless, the value of your contribution of property is the fair market value of the property at the time of contribution. For tax purposes, a deemed disposition will occur upon the transfer to the plan, resulting in a capital gain or loss. Any gain must be included in your income for tax purposes.

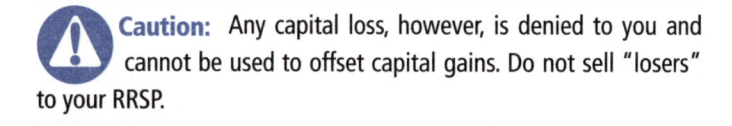

> **Caution:** Any capital loss, however, is denied to you and cannot be used to offset capital gains. Do not sell "losers" to your RRSP.

If you contribute a non-qualified investment (defined on page 201), the fair market value of that investment is included in computing your income for the year of contribution. Other penalties and taxes may also apply, as described later in this chapter.

Should You Borrow for Your RRSP Contribution?

Because any interest paid on funds borrowed to make an RRSP contribution is not deductible for tax purposes, try to limit your investment borrowing to non-RRSP investments. But it is better to borrow to make a contribution than to not contribute at all, and making a contribution now rather than waiting several years is also essential to building an RRSP. Before you borrow, try to ensure that your earnings inside your RRSP are growing at a higher rate than your interest payments.

Transfers to and from an RRSP

Tax-free transfers between plans, up to a prescribed maximum, are possible if the transfers are made directly and in lump sums. For example, tax-free transfers can be made directly from one RRSP to another RRSP, RRIF, or RPP. RRSP amounts can only be transferred by the issuer of the RRSP and must be done before the maturity of the plan. If you receive the amount directly, it will be included in your taxable income.

> **Planning Opportunity:** The tax-free rollover of a retiring allowance into an RRSP is still allowed, subject to certain limits.

A retiring allowance is a payment made in recognition of long years of services and as compensation for a loss of office or employment, including retirement. For the years of employment before 1996, the limit is $2,000 per year of service. Up to and including 1988, this may be increased by $1,500 for each year for which no employer contributions to a pension plan or DPSP are vested. The employer should make the transfer directly to the RRSP to avoid withholding taxes.

> **Planning Opportunity:** Provided that the general transfer conditions are satisfied, a retiring allowance can be an effective mechanism for a self-employed individual or small business owner to enhance his or her RRSP holdings. The key is to ensure that

the amount received as a retiring allowance will qualify as reasonable in the eyes of the CCRA. If the payment can be characterized as additional employment income, the tax-free transfer will not be allowed.

Annuity and RRIF payments are also transferable between RRSPs or other RRIFs. You are allowed to make direct transfers of commuted annuity amounts and payments from a RRIF in excess of the required minimum payment (see page 215) to an RRSP or another RRIF. You can also use these transferred funds to acquire any of the RRSP-type annuities. The purchased annuity must provide for equal annual or more frequent payments, starting no later than one year after the transfer.

A payment received by you as a spouse or dependent child or grandchild from the RRSP of a deceased person may also be transferred tax-free to your RRSP in some situations that are discussed later in this chapter. As well, the transfer reduces the taxable income of the deceased. Finally, a tax-free transfer of RRSP amounts to your spouse on marriage or relationship breakdown is also possible.

Penalties, Special Taxes, and Deregistration

Excess Contributions. When undeducted RRSP contributions exceed a certain limit at the end of a month, a 1 per cent penalty tax is imposed on the amount in excess of $2,000 until this amount is withdrawn. Transition rules are provided for taxpayers who had overcontributions on February 26, 1995, that did not exceed an $8,000 limit. These overcontributions can be retained in the RRSP without penalty and deducted as contributions for 1996 and subsequent years, until the limit is reduced to $2,000.

> **Caution:** You cannot claim a deduction for any new contributions until you have reduced your overcontribution.

> ✓ **Planning Opportunity:** Consider maxing out your overcontribution allowance in the year you turn 69 to maximize your RRSP holdings.

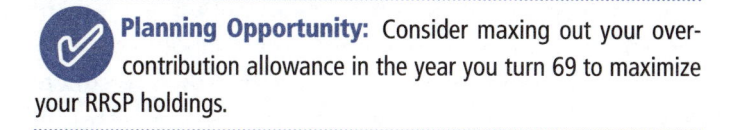

Foreign Investments. As the wavering world value of our Canadian dollar occasionally reminds us, more stable currencies are available in the global markets. For this reason, just as foreign investments will provide a stabilizing effect for your non-RRSP investments, so too will they benefit your RRSP investments.

The direct RRSP foreign investment limit has been 30 per cent since January 1, 2001. If you exceed the investment levels, your RRSP is subject to tax at the rate of 1 per cent per month on the excess amount invested in foreign securities for each month the excess remains in the RRSP.

> ✓ **Planning Opportunity:** You can exceed the 30 per cent limit, within certain limits, if you make investments in eligible small businesses or invest through certain trusts. You can also maximize your foreign holdings by investing in mutual funds that have a high percentage of foreign investments. Consult your tax advisor.

Non-Qualified Investments. If your RRSP acquires an investment that is not a qualified RRSP investment, the fair market value of the investment at the time of acquisition is included in your income in that year. In the year the RRSP disposes of the investment, you may deduct from your income the proceeds of disposition or the amount previously added to income, whichever is less.

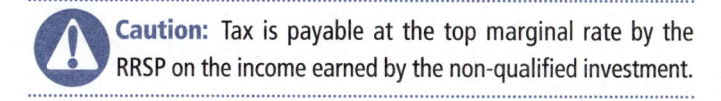

> ⚠ **Caution:** Tax is payable at the top marginal rate by the RRSP on the income earned by the non-qualified investment.

If a qualified investment in your RRSP becomes a non-qualified investment, the RRSP must pay a special tax. The tax is equal to 1 per cent of the fair market value of the investment at the time of acquisition and is applied for each month the investment retains its non-qualified status or until the investment is disposed of by the RRSP, assuming the value of the investment was not included in your income.

Borrowing Money or Carrying on Business. If your RRSP borrows money at any point in the year, tax is payable by the RRSP on all its income each year until the borrowed funds are repaid. An RRSP is a trust and is subject to tax at the maximum personal rate in your province of residence.

If the RRSP carries on a business at any time during the year, the resulting business income is subject to tax at regular trust rates.

RRSP as Collateral for a Loan. If any of your RRSP property is used as collateral for a loan, the fair market value of the property used as collateral is added to your income in that particular year. When the RRSP property ceases to be used as collateral, an amount equal to the amount previously added to income, less any losses suffered on the loan transaction, may be deducted from income. If the RRSP is a deposit plan, it will be subject to deregistration should any of the RRSP be pledged, assigned, etc. In that case, the entire amount in the plan is included in your income for tax purposes and there is no way that the plan can be subsequently reinstated.

Deregistration. RRSPs can be deregistered for a variety of reasons. The fair market value of all of the assets of the particular plan is included in your income for tax purposes in the year the plan is deregistered. Rest assured that most issuers structure an RRSP to prevent it from being deregistered in most circumstances. Specifically, the contract or arrangement you have with the issuer will prohibit actions that would result in deregistration.

An RRSP will automatically be deregistered if you do not arrange a retirement income to be paid by December 31 of the year you turn age 69. The plan is effectively deregistered on the first day of the following year and its full value is included in income in the year you turn age 70. Some plans provide for an automatic annuity purchase if no other retirement income is arranged, but an annuity may not suit your retirement income needs.

RRSP INVESTMENTS

Plan Your Investments: Interest, Dividends, or Capital Gains in Your RRSP

If all your investments are held inside an RRSP, your investment strategy should be to maximize your return over the long term. Remember that all amounts received from RRSPs are included in your taxable income and taxed at your marginal rate. As a result, capital gains and dividends earned in an RRSP lose their identity and are not eligible for preferential tax treatment.

If you have investments both inside and outside RRSPs, the rules of thumb are somewhat different. First, hold interest-bearing investments in the RRSP because interest income is taxed at full rates outside your RRSP. Second, hold dividend-paying preferred shares or common shares inside an RRSP if you anticipate realizing significant non-exempt capital gains on these investments in future. If the choice comes down to holding either equities or interest-earning investments in your RRSP, you should opt to retain the interest-earning investment within the plan. Capital investments that qualify for the $500,000 lifetime capital gains exemption should be held outside the plan to take full advantage of that benefit.

Your age also plays a factor when choosing the most appropriate investments for your RRSP. Generally, the younger you are, the more heavily you can weight your portfolio in favour of equities. Since you are investing for the long term, you can take advantage of the expected higher return over this period. You will be able to weather the ups and downs of the stock market. The closer you are to retirement, however, the more heavily your RRSP (and non-RRSP investments) should be weighted toward less risky investments, such as interest-bearing securities, to protect your accumulated capital.

Canada Deposit Insurance

Determine if the Canada Deposit Insurance Corporation (CDIC), or other comparable deposit insurance programs, insures your RRSP investments. The other insurance plans are established on a provincial basis for deposits made with credit unions and *caisses populaires*. CDIC-covered investments include savings and chequing accounts, and guaranteed investment certificates (GICs) and term deposits that are redeemable within five years. The insurance does not apply to foreign currency deposits (such as U.S. dollar savings accounts or U.S. dollar GICs) or mutual funds.

The maximum insurance coverage provided by CDIC is $60,000 per customer per member institution. The coverage available to members of credit unions and *caisses populaires* varies by province and is at least equal to the CDIC coverage.

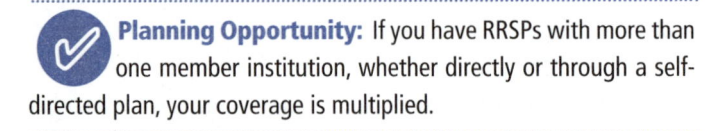

> **Planning Opportunity:** If you have RRSPs with more than one member institution, whether directly or through a self-directed plan, your coverage is multiplied.

Similarly, if you have a self-directed RRSP that holds investments from various member financial institutions, each of these investments will be covered separately. CDIC insurance on your RRSP is separate from CDIC insurance on investments you hold personally, which in effect doubles your maximum coverage at one institution to $120,000.

Types of RRSPs

There are three major categories of RRSP investment vehicles:

- insurance-type, where you contract to pay a certain amount, usually periodically, in return for a retirement income of a certain size, also paid periodically;
- deposit RRSPs, where your deposits are made directly with the issuer; and
- RRSP trusts, of which the most common are self-directed RRSPs where you make the investment decisions.

Within these types of RRSPs, there are two further categories: managed and self-directed. Managed RRSPs are, as the name implies, managed for you by the insurance company, mutual fund company, bank, or other financial institution. A financial institution will also hold your self-directed RRSP assets, but you are able to make your own investment decisions.

Overall, insurance companies sell RRSPs that are similar to and competitive with RRSPs sold by other financial institutions. Life insurance RRSPs usually are not protected under the CDIC, although they are self-insured by the insurance industry.

Self-Directed RRSPs

Self-directed RRSPs enable you to choose from the full complement of allowable RRSP investments. Managed accounts offer more limited choices. According to the CCRA, qualifying RRSP investments include:

- money, but not gold;
- bonds and debentures of the Government of Canada, a province, municipality, or Crown corporation, including Canada Savings Bonds and stripped bonds;
- Canadian guaranteed investment certificates (GICs);
- shares and debt obligations of Canadian public corporations listed on a Canadian exchange;
- shares listed on a specified stock exchange outside Canada;

- shares of the capital stock of certain public corporations not listed on a Canadian exchange;
- units of a mutual fund trust;
- a mortgage secured by real property inside Canada, including a mortgage on your own house (provided certain market rate interest rules are satisfied);
- real property, if it is acquired as a result of a default under a mortgage investment held by the RRSP;
- an annuity, provided that payments do not commence until the RRSP matures;
- a warrant or future listed on a Canadian exchange;
- debts issued by certain tax-exempt Canadian corporations without share capital;
- securities issued by certain community-endorsed venture capital corporations, registered employee venture capital corporations, and shares of a labour-sponsored venture capital corporation registered under the law of the Northwest Territories; and
- certain foreign stock exchange index units, including Standard & Poor's 500 Depository Receipts, units valued on the basis of the Dow Jones Industrial Average, and units for a particular country valued on the basis of the Morgan Stanley Capital Investment Index (applicable for property acquired after 1993).

Self-directed RRSPs generally provide convenient monthly reporting from one source and can help you diversify to reduce risk. As investment objectives change over time, the make-up of a self-directed investment portfolio can be updated, providing maximum flexibility.

SPECIAL SITUATIONS

RRSPs and Non-Residents

The tax consequences of becoming a non-resident can be

extremely complex. Deciding how to deal with your RRSP is just one of the many other financial and tax decisions you must make at that time. Consult with a professional advisor. In very general terms, tax is withheld from many types of payments originating in Canada and made to residents of another country. The other country also may tax the "payment," but most give credit for any Canadian taxes already paid. The Canadian tax treatment of RRSP amounts generally depends on whether the RRSP has matured, and also on your new country of residence.

> **Planning Opportunity:** If your departure from Canada is not permanent, you need not dismantle your RRSP; you can let it continue to grow on a tax-deferred basis for Canadian tax purposes. If your departure from Canada is permanent, wait until you become a non-resident before making withdrawals from your plan. As a resident, your withdrawals will be taxed at your marginal rate. As a non-resident, your withdrawals will be subject only to the Canadian withholding tax of 25 per cent or less, depending on the relevant tax treaty.

If you leave to work abroad, however, your foreign income may not qualify as earned income and you may be unable to continue to make contributions to your plan.

Creditor Access to Your RRSP

The courts have decided that creditors can gain access to a bankrupt's RRSP to settle debts. Only some insurance-type RRSPs offer any creditor protection, although recent case law may have created a chink in that armour. Creditors cannot gain access to life annuity payments, and they may have trouble seizing term-certain annuity payments or the funds in a RRIF. Switching your RRSP to an insurance company shortly before you declare bankruptcy probably will not offer any protection, because bankruptcy laws "see through" these types of transactions.

RRSPs on Death

The tax treatment of RRSP amounts on the death of the annuitant depends on whether the RRSP has matured and on the identity of the beneficiary.

> **Planning Opportunity:** To ensure that RRSP amounts go to the intended beneficiaries with as little trouble or tax consequences as possible, name specific RRSP beneficiaries in the RRSP contract or in your will.

If the RRSP has not matured, generally the fair market value of all RRSP property is included in the taxable income of the deceased in the year of death as determined in the terminal income tax return. As a result, tax may be payable before the funds can be distributed to the beneficiaries.

There are two exceptions. First, if a spouse or a financially dependent child or grandchild over age 18 who qualifies for the impairment credit is named as beneficiary, the plan can be transferred to the beneficiary's own RRSP on a tax-deferred basis. Second, if a "refund of premiums" occurs, the amount is not included in the deceased's income.

A refund of premiums, which generally includes accumulated income, is defined as either:

- any amount paid to the deceased annuitant's spouse from the RRSP, even if the spouse was not specifically named as a beneficiary; or
- amounts paid to dependent children or grandchildren who were financially dependent on the annuitant.

A spouse or a physically or mentally infirm child over age 18 may transfer a refund of premiums to his or her own RRSP or RRIF on a tax-deferred basis in the year of the annuitant's death or within 60 days after the end of that year. Alternatively, they may purchase a life annuity or term-certain annuity to age 90 with the refund of premiums. Other children who receive a refund of premiums may set up an annuity that runs until they reach 18 years of age.

The legal representative (executor) of the deceased's estate may elect for either the spouse or qualifying dependants to receive a refund of premiums.

Somewhat similar rules apply to RRIFs. If the deceased's spouse is the beneficiary, the plan is essentially transferred to the spouse on a tax-deferred basis, and the spouse receives all future payments.

MATURING YOUR RRSP

You must plan carefully for the time when your RRSP matures. Consider your retirement goals, the amount of money that will be required to achieve those goals, and the time at which the money will be required. The tax impact of arranging for your retirement income should also be examined. It is necessary to weigh RRSP retirement income options carefully. Competent professional advice is recommended to assist you in planning for your retirement income.

Maturity Options

RRSPs must be matured before December 31 of the year in which the annuitant turns age 69.

"Maturing" an RRSP simply means making arrangements for receiving a retirement income from accumulated RRSP funds. In the case of some insurance RRSPs, it is the date you begin receiving the stipulated RRSP income. With non-insurance RRSPs, there are three main maturity options. First, you can arrange to receive an annuity, of which there are several types. Second, you can transfer the accumulated RRSP funds into a RRIF from which a periodic retirement income is received. Third, you can collapse the RRSP and receive a lump sum after paying the relevant tax.

You can choose any or all of the options and have as many different types of annuities and RRIFs as you want. This flexibility allows you to arrange the type of retirement income you need to suit your expected income requirements. For example, you might consider collapsing a portion of your accumulated RRSPs to finance spending in the early years of your retirement (e.g., for extended travel), although this can also be accomplished with a RRIF. You also probably want to build in a certain amount of inflation protection by transferring some of your RRSP funds to a RRIF and/or indexed annuity.

Even after choosing your retirement income options, your plan can remain flexible. You can switch from option to option with relative freedom. For example, you can switch a RRIF to another issuer to earn a better return. As well, you can have as many RRIFs as you like. You can also withdraw any amount from any RRIF at any time, although a minimum amount must be withdrawn from each RRIF each year. You also may be able to commute RRSP annuities, depending on the terms of the contract, in which case the commuted amount becomes taxable.

You can transfer amounts withdrawn from a RRIF in excess of the required minimum amount and commuted annuity amounts on a tax-deferred basis to other annuities or a RRIF, or even to an RRSP if you are under age 70. You can also buy an impaired-health life annuity from some life insurance companies, which provides for larger payments if you can establish that your life expectancy is considerably shorter than normal.

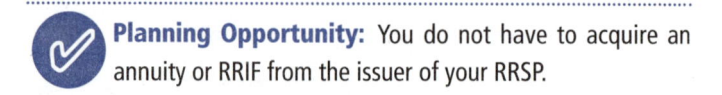

> **Planning Opportunity:** You do not have to acquire an annuity or RRIF from the issuer of your RRSP.

Shop around for the best rates on the options you want, and consider using an annuities broker or other professional advisor to search for the best rates and make arrangements for you.

> ⚠️ **Caution:** Do not miss the legislated deadline (the year in which you turn age 69); otherwise, all accumulated funds in your RRSP will be included in your taxable income in the year following the year you turn 69. You will have no recourse for correcting this oversight.

Consequence of Early Maturity

Maturing your RRSPs early can be expensive in terms of reduced income. Try to delay maturing your RRSPs until you absolutely must, or mature only a portion of your accumulated RRSP funds at any one time. If you are age 65 or older, RRSP retirement income qualifies for the pension income tax credit. See Chapter 15.

RRSP Annuities

There are essentially two types of annuities—life and term-certain. Under a life annuity, the periodic payments, which you must receive at least once a year, continue until you die. The amount payable is based on factors that include the average life expectancy for someone your age and current interest rates. Term-certain RRSP annuities are payable to age 90, or to the year your spouse turns age 90. Payments cease after your 90th year and are based primarily on current interest rates.

The table opposite illustrates the monthly income that a $50,000 investment will produce when invested in various ways at particular ages. The figures were supplied by Polson Bourbonniere Financial, a Toronto-based RRIF/annuity broker.

Monthly incomes shown commence one month after the purchase date. The listed incomes are subject to change as interest rates fluctuate, and represent the highest-yielding plan at October 24, 2003.

Comparison of Monthly Income from a $50,000 Investment

Age at Purchase	Single Life Annuity (10-Year Guarantee) Male	Single Life Annuity (10-Year Guarantee) Female	Joint Life Annuity (10-Year Guarantee) Male and Female	Term-Certain to Age 90 Male and Female	RRIF (First Year's Income Only) Minimum Payout
60	$307	$284	$263	$260	$139
61	313	288	267	263	144
62	318	293	271	267	149
63	325	299	275	272	154
64	331	304	280	277	160
65	338	311	285	283	167
66	345	317	291	289	174
67	352	323	296	296	181
68	360	330	301	303	189
69	367	337	309	311	198
70	374	344	317	320	208
71	382	352	324	330	308

When considering your retirement income options, remember that payments in the early years for indexed annuities are considerably lower than those for level payment annuities. They are much higher in later years, however, when you might require a higher income to cover increased health care costs. Carefully assess your income requirements over the long term before committing yourself to any of the options.

Registered Retirement Income Funds (RRIFs)

RRIFs have a number of advantages over annuities:

- Because you can determine the size of your annual payments to some extent, the inflation protection factor can be better controlled than with indexed annuities.

- Unusual income requirements in any year can be taken care of because you can withdraw any amount from a RRIF at any time, provided you withdraw at least the minimum amount.
- You can choose the types of investments made in the RRIF, which generate the retirement income, just as you would with a self-directed RRSP. (Of course, bad or risky investing could also dissipate your RRIF funds.)
- Your estate benefits because substantial amounts can remain in the RRIF, especially during the early years of its existence.
- You can convert amounts in a RRIF to a life annuity at any time, but the conversion cannot be reversed unless the life annuity is purchased through an RRSP and you are under age 69.

A RRIF resembles an RRSP. You can choose a managed or self-directed plan. Different plans may hold different types of eligible investments, which are similar to those allowed for RRSPs. All amounts in a RRIF remain tax-sheltered until paid out, and, as with an RRSP, investment performance affects the overall value of the plan.

A minimum amount must be paid out from each RRIF each year to the annuitant and be included in the annuitant's income for tax purposes. Since 1992, RRIF withdrawals can continue for the lifetime of the RRIF holder (or his or her spouse), instead of ceasing at age 90.

The table below compares the newer minimum withdrawal percentages to those under the former rules.

The current rules apply to all RRIFs created after the end of 1992. For most RRIFs purchased before the end of 1992, or consisting exclusively of funds transferred from pre-1992 RRIFs ("qualifying RRIFs"), the previous minimum payment percentages will continue to apply for those up to age 77. The lower minimum payment percentages for those above age 78 will apply to all RRIFs entered into after March 1986 and pre-April 1986 RRIFs that have been amended.

Comparison of Minimum Annual Withdrawals
(% of RRIF Assets)

Age	Former Rules[1] (%)	Current Rules % General	Qualifying RRIFs[2]
71	5.26	7.38	5.26
72	5.56	7.48	5.56
73	5.88	7.59	5.88
74	6.25	7.71	6.25
75	6.67	7.85	6.67
76	7.14	7.99	7.14
77	7.69	8.15	7.69
78	8.33	8.33	8.33
79	9.09	8.53	8.53
80	10.00	8.75	8.75
81	11.11	8.99	8.99
82	12.50	9.27	9.27
83	14.29	9.58	9.58
84	16.67	9.93	9.93
85	20.00	10.33	10.33
86	25.00	10.79	10.79
87	33.33	11.33	11.33
88	50.00	11.96	11.96
89	100.00	12.71	12.71
90	N/A	13.62	13.62
91	N/A	14.73	14.73
92	N/A	16.12	16.12
93	N/A	17.92	17.92
94 or older	N/A	20.00	20.00

[1] The factors in this column are equal to 1 / (90 − X), where X is the age of the annuitant or the annuitant's spouse, as the case may be.
[2] Defined as pre-1992 RRIFs.

At any point, you may withdraw any amount from any or all of your RRIFs, provided that you withdraw at least the minimum amount from each RRIF each year.

> **Caution:** By withdrawing large amounts, you will be reducing the size of payments available in future years. Keep in mind that, as you age, you will incur greater costs for medical and retirement accommodation expenses.

Withholding tax is payable on any excess amount withdrawn over the minimum amount that must be withdrawn in the year. The tax withheld becomes a credit against your tax payable for the year.

The surviving spouse of a RRIF annuitant who dies after 1990 becomes the annuitant under the fund under one of two conditions: Either the parties must have previously agreed to the ongoing payments, or the legal representative of the first annuitant consents and the carrier of the fund undertakes to make payments to the surviving spouse. Payments will then continue to the spouse, and will be taxable in the spouse's hands only as each payment is received.

Collapsing Your RRSP

Although you can choose to collapse your RRSP, this is the default option if you do not make a choice for your RRSP before you turn 69. The tax consequences of this option should provide an incentive for you to create a maturity plan. If you collapse an RRSP, the entire amount in the plan must be brought into income and taxed in that year, often at the highest personal tax rate (see "Withdrawals from an RRSP" on page 193).

If your retirement plans include moving to a foreign country and thus becoming a non-resident of Canada, you may be able to save on Canadian taxes by first establishing your non-resident status and then collapsing your RRSP. Non-resident withholding tax will apply to the funds withdrawn from your RRSP. This is likely to be at a lower rate than the rates for residents of Canada, particularly if you become a resident of a country with which Canada has a tax treaty providing for a specially reduced rate of withholding. For example, the withholding rate for periodic RRSP withdrawals under the Canada-U.S. Income Tax Treaty is 15 per cent, compared with the regular 25 per cent.

There is no withholding of provincial tax if you are a non-resident and have collapsed your RRSP after you ceased being a Canadian resident.

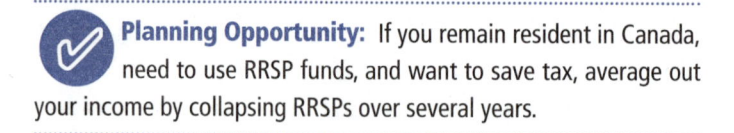

> **Planning Opportunity:** If you remain resident in Canada, need to use RRSP funds, and want to save tax, average out your income by collapsing RRSPs over several years.

The higher tax rates are difficult to avoid. Not everyone will save tax by collapsing RRSPs over several years.

Apart from paying tax at a high marginal rate when you collapse an RRSP, you also lose the tax deferral still available in the RRSP, a RRIF, or even an annuity. Of course, tax deferral is probably of little concern if the RRSP is collapsed to satisfy immediate cash requirements.

The major advantage of collapsing an RRSP is that funds can be made available in an amount to suit your needs in the early years of retirement. There does not even have to be an excessive tax cost if you are under age 69 and do not mature your other RRSPs until you absolutely must. RRIFs also provide flexible retirement income and at a much lower tax cost.

CHAPTER FOURTEEN

If You Drive a Car for Business

TAX ASPECTS FOR EMPLOYEES: EMPLOYEE-PROVIDED VEHICLES / 218
Allowances and Reimbursements You Receive / 218
Deducting Expenses from Your Income / 220
    Eligibility / 220
Deductions for Owned Vehicles / 221
Deductions for Leased Vehicles / 223
Reductions for Personal Use / 224
Purchase Assistance / 224

TAX ASPECTS FOR EMPLOYEES: COMPANY-PROVIDED VEHICLES / 225
Standby Charge / 225
    Owned Vehicles / 225
    Leased Vehicles / 226
Reimbursements to Your Employer / 227
Other Ownership and Operating Expenses / 227
Election with Respect to Operating Expenses / 227
Shareholders / 228

TAX ASPECTS FOR EMPLOYERS AND SELF-EMPLOYED INDIVIDUALS / 228
Allowances / 228
Deductible Expenditures / 229
Employer Deductions with Respect to Employee-Provided Vehicles / 229

218 ◂ If You Drive a Car for Business

>   Employer Deductions with Respect to Company-Provided
>   Vehicles / 230
>   Company-Owned Vehicles / 230
>   Leased Vehicles / 230
>
>   **PLANNING FOR BUSINESS USE OF AUTOMOBILES / 231**

This chapter highlights the principal tax rules affecting the business use of automobiles. In view of the complexity of these rules, we recommend that you seek professional advice to deal adequately with your specific situations.

TAX ASPECTS FOR EMPLOYEES: EMPLOYEE-PROVIDED VEHICLES

Allowances and Reimbursements You Receive

If you own your own vehicle, your company may compensate you for the time you use the vehicle for business or personal purposes.

One approach is for your employer to pay you an "automobile allowance." This allowance may be calculated to cover only the business-related costs of owning and operating the vehicle. Alternatively, it may be part of your total remuneration package, thereby covering more than just business-related costs.

Your employer reports allowances to the Canada Customs and Revenue Agency (CCRA) in one of two ways. First, if the allowance is not a reasonable amount for business-related purposes computed on the basis of kilometres driven, it must be reported on your T4 slip as employment income for the year.

As you would expect, the CCRA sets the standard for what qualifies as a reasonable rate. If your allowance is not reasonable, you can still generally deduct a portion of the expenses incurred if you operate the vehicle for business use. To qualify for a deduction, you must be required by contract to use the vehicle in the course of your employment, among other criteria.

Second, if the employer pays you for business use, and if the amount is a reasonable allowance for that purpose, the employer should not report this allowance as part of your taxable income. An allowance will be considered "reasonable" only if it is directly related to the number of business kilometres driven in a year and if no reimbursement is received for expenses related to the same use.

To establish that there is a direct relation between the allowance and the business kilometres driven, you may be expected to provide your employer with detailed records of your business driving distances. If you are reimbursed for the cost of additional commercial insurance for the vehicle, parking, tolls, and ferries, your allowance may still be considered reasonable provided that the allowance is determined without reference to these expenses.

The *Income Tax Act* sets a prescribed rate for what is considered a reasonable per-kilometre allowance. Your employer is entitled to deduct allowances paid to employees at the prescribed rate. The prescribed rates for 2003 are 42 cents per kilometre for the first 5,000 kilometres and 36 cents per kilometre for each additional kilometre driven. For the Yukon Territory, Northwest Territories, and Nunavut, the tax-exempt allowance is 46 cents for the first 5,000 kilometres driven and 40 cents for each additional kilometre.

Provided that the rate still qualifies as reasonable, your employer may pay you at a higher rate without reporting it as taxable income to you. Your employer will probably not pay you above the prescribed rate because your employer's deduction is limited by the rate. It is unlikely that your employer would be willing to incur a non-deductible expense. In any event, you should keep records to indicate the cost of operating your car in case you are called on to support the allowance.

The second choice for the allowance is to have it treated as taxable remuneration. If this is done, you will be permitted to deduct at least a portion of the costs of operating the vehicle for business purposes if you meet all the criteria. In many circumstances, this may be to your advantage. Moreover, you may be able to claim GST (and QST) rebates on your deductible expenses. For more details, see Chapter 6.

Specific reimbursements of direct costs incurred in the operation of your vehicle in your employer's business (e.g., gas related to identifiable business travel) are not allowances and are not considered in calculating your taxable income.

Deducting Expenses from Your Income

Eligibility. You may be allowed to claim various deductions for the ownership and operating costs of your vehicle related to its use in the course of your employment. To be eligible for these deductions, you must not receive a tax-free allowance and you must be required by your terms of employment (technically your contract of employment, which need not be written) to pay your own travel expenses. You also must be required to work away from your employer's place of business or in different places on a regular basis. A prescribed form (T2200, Declaration of Conditions of Employment, for federal purposes and TP-64.3 in Quebec) must be signed by your employer to confirm that these conditions have been met, and it must be filed with your tax return.

If you claim expenses, any payment received from your employer to cover the costs of ownership of the vehicle will be a taxable allowance. Further, any reimbursement of operating expenses by your employer must be subtracted from any deduction claimed for the same expense.

Salespeople who sell property or negotiate contracts for their employers, and who are remunerated by commission based on the volume of sales made or the contracts negotiated, may deduct part of their vehicle costs and other expenses. The deduction claim is limited to the amount of earned commissions, unless travelling expenses are the only type of expenses being claimed.

If you qualify to deduct vehicle expenses, you may deduct the business portion of the actual costs of ownership and operation, subject to the limitations discussed below for vehicles costing more than $30,000.

Deductions for Owned Vehicles

If you own the vehicle you use for business purposes, you are permitted capital cost allowance (CCA). Capital cost allowance is the rate at which the purchase cost of your vehicle can be written off against other income. The CCA can be claimed on the total cost, but cannot exceed the applicable "maximum prescribed cost." According to the *Income Tax Act*, the maximum prescribed costs for vehicles acquired are:

- after December 31, 2000: $30,000 plus GST and provincial sales tax;
- for prior acquisitions:

Acquisition Date	Limit on Cost	
1991–1995	$24,000	plus GST & PST
1996–1997	$25,000	plus GST & PST
1998–1999	$26,000	plus GST & PST
2000	$27,000	plus GST & PST

If you acquired the car from a non-arm's-length person (i.e., a related person), the cost for CCA purposes is adjusted. The adjusted cost will be the least of the maximum prescribed cost (as set out above), the fair market value immediately before the disposition, and the transferor's undepreciated capital cost (UCC) immediately before the disposition (i.e., the amount not yet claimed as CCA).

When you sell the vehicle, the terminal loss and recapture rules do not apply if the cost was in excess of the maximum prescribed cost. The result is that no recapture of CCA (i.e., no addition to taxable income) or no deduction of a terminal loss is allowed, depending on whether you sold the vehicle for a profit or loss, respectively.

For CCA purposes, the cost of each car that is less than $30,000 is included in class 10 in the Regulations under the *Income Tax Act*. This means that the rate of depreciation for CCA purposes is 30 per cent (15 per cent in the year of acquisition) on a declining balance basis.

When the cost of a car, without the applicable taxes, is $30,000 or more, it is included in a separate pool within class 10.1. The rate of depreciation for CCA purposes for a class 10.1 vehicle is also 30 per cent (15 per cent in the year of acquisition) on a declining balance basis. The difference is that you may also claim CCA at 15 per cent in the year of disposition of a class 10.1 vehicle.

For example, if the cost of your car purchased on October 1, 2003, is $35,000, the half-year rule, which will apply in the first year of ownership, will limit your claim to 15 per cent of the maximum prescribed cost in that year. Based on the maximum of $30,000 plus 15 per cent PST and GST, the claim would be $5,175. In the second and following years, you may claim 30 per cent of the excess of the maximum prescribed cost over CCA previously claimed (or $8,797.50 in the second year). In the year in which the vehicle is sold, you will not own the vehicle at year-end and no CCA can be claimed. The special rule for class 10.1 vehicles allows that one-half of the depreciation (CCA) that would have been allowed in the year of sale if the vehicle were still owned at year-end is deductible.

> **Planning Opportunity:** You are permitted to deduct interest on a loan that is directly related to the purchase of the vehicle. For vehicles acquired after December 31, 2000, the interest deduction limit is $300 per month during the period that the loan is outstanding.

> **Caution:** The reduced amounts of depreciation and interest calculated opposite are further reduced if the car is also used for personal use.

Deductions for Leased Vehicles

If you lease your car, you may deduct the least of:

- the actual lease cost;
- $800 per month plus GST and applicable provincial sales tax for leases entered into after 2000; or for prior leases:

Lease Date	Limit on Monthly Lease Expense
June 18/87–Aug. 31/89	$600
Sept. 1/89–Dec. 31/96	$650
1997	$550
1998–1999	$650
2000	$700

- the actual lease cost multiplied by the maximum prescribed amount (including GST and the applicable provincial sales tax) and divided by 85 per cent of the manufacturer's suggested list price. For leases entered into before 1991, provincial sales tax must be added to the suggested list price.

> **Caution:** The CCRA considers a lease down payment (typical of most of today's lease arrangements) as a buydown of the monthly lease payments. The buydown must be considered in the above calculation.

For example, for an Ontario resident, if your car's manufacturer's suggested list price is $42,000, and the monthly lease payment under a lease entered into on October 1, 2003, is $950, the three alternatives will be $950, $920 ($800 × 1.15; GST 7% plus PST 8%), and $918 ($950 × $34,500 / 85% of $42,000). Therefore, the maximum deduction will be $918. This example is not necessarily representative of the circumstances that will apply to this price range of car.

Reductions for Personal Use

When you determine the ratio of business kilometres to total kilometres, you will reduce your deductible ownership or lease costs.

Your deduction for operating costs (fuel, repairs, and maintenance) is also limited in the same proportion. The same rule holds true when calculating your eligible GST or QST rebate (for repairs and maintenance only).

Purchase Assistance

Your employer may assist you in the purchase of your car, for example, by providing you with an interest-free (or low-interest) loan. In this case, any reduction in interest below the government-prescribed rate of interest (set every quarter) is considered a taxable benefit. Accordingly, your taxable earnings increase by the amount of the loan outstanding multiplied by the prescribed interest rate for the period the loan is outstanding. Any interest that you pay to your employer is considered an expense, however, and you may deduct a portion of the deemed interest payment. Recall that the maximum interest deduction on a loan is an average of $300 per month for vehicles purchased after 2000.

A loan from your employer may be one of the best ways of receiving a real benefit at a relatively low tax cost. If you borrow money from a bank, you will likely pay more than the prescribed rate, while the cost to the employer (including lost investment income) is likely to approximate the prescribed rate.

TAX ASPECTS FOR EMPLOYEES: COMPANY-PROVIDED VEHICLES

If your company provides you with a car, you generally include several amounts in taxable income. Specifically, these amounts consist of a standby charge (a notional charge for making the car available to you), any benefit you receive for operating expenses paid by your employer for personal use, and taxable allowances. As mentioned earlier, the value of the benefits added to your income is subject to GST (and QST, if applicable), which is payable by your employer. Employers report the GST (and QST, if applicable) as a taxable benefit on their employees' T4s (Relevé 1 in Quebec). Specific reimbursement of out-of-pocket expenses (gasoline, parking, etc.) directly related to business use is not a taxable benefit to you.

It is to your advantage to understand how your employer calculates the taxable amount. In some cases (and assuming you have a choice), you may prefer to own your own vehicle and receive an allowance, rather than using a car provided by your employer.

Standby Charge

When you drive a company-provided car, you include in your taxable income a "standby charge," a rough measure of the benefit to you of having the car available for personal use. This charge is calculated differently depending on whether the car is owned or leased by your employer.

Owned Vehicles. If your employer owns the vehicle, the standby charge is 2 per cent of the original cost of the car (including GST and provincial sales tax) for each month the car is available to you (24 per cent for a full year). This 2 per cent applies to the full cost of the car, regardless of whether this cost is in excess of the maximum prescribed cost.

> **Planning Opportunity:** This standby charge decreases if you use the car mainly for business (interpreted by the CCRA as more than 50 per cent) and your personal use is less than 1,667 kilometres per month.

In this case, the standby charge is calculated as follows:

$$\text{Standby charge otherwise calculated} \times \frac{\text{kilometres for personal use in the year}}{1{,}667 \times \text{number of months in the year in which the car is available to the employee}}$$

For example, if your personal use is 500 kilometres per month and equivalent to 15 per cent of the total use, you will be taxed on only 30 per cent (6,000 km / 20,000 km) of the standby charge otherwise calculated. Commuting to your employer's office is personal (not business) use of the car.

An optional method applies for calculating the standby charge if you are employed principally in selling new or used cars.

The standby rules apply to members of a partnership as if they were employees.

Leased Vehicles. The standby charge included in your income for vehicles leased by your employer is two-thirds of the lease cost (including GST and provincial sales tax) and any amount included in the lease cost for repairs and maintenance, but excluding any amount included for insurance. The insurance amount is included in operating costs for the purpose of determining any operating benefit, but is excluded to establish the benefit resulting from GST and QST, if applicable. This standby charge applies on the full lease cost paid by your employer, whether or not the amount with respect to which your employer may claim deductions is the full cost.

You benefit if your employer leases the car rather than owning it. Two-thirds of the annual lease payment may work out to less than 24 per cent of the cost that would be chargeable if the employer owned the vehicle. There is also greater flexibility in a lease. Specifically, some service costs fall within the lease contract. The result is that the value of these services will be taxable benefits to you only to the extent of two-thirds of the lease cost.

If your personal use is less than 50 per cent of total use and less than 1,667 kilometres per month, this standby charge also decreases as discussed under "Owned Vehicles."

Reimbursements to Your Employer

If you reimburse your employer for part of the cost of the vehicle, you can reduce the standby charge otherwise included in your income by the amount of that reimbursement. This reduction offers you an advantage if your employer leases the vehicle. You can deduct your full lease payment against an amount that is only two-thirds of the lease cost. While you may receive a tax benefit, a reimbursement is a tax liability for your employer. Consequently, your employer may be reluctant to permit such an arrangement.

Other Ownership and Operating Expenses

When your employer also pays for such items as insurance, licence, fuel, and repairs and maintenance, you may realize an additional taxable benefit. The benefit is 17 cents per personal kilometre driven in 2003. The 17 cents-per-kilometre rate may also be used for Quebec tax purposes. This rate is revised periodically.

Election with Respect to Operating Expenses

As an alternative to calculating your taxable benefit at a rate of 17 cents per personal kilometre (14 cents per kilometre for automobile salespeople), you can make an election based on the operating expenses. If you use the car primarily for business, you can elect to include in income an amount equal to one-half of the standby charge. In this context, "primarily for business" means more than 50 per cent. If you elect to use this method, you must notify your employer in writing before the end of the applicable year that you are making the election.

Shareholders

The same rules for employee automobile benefits generally apply to a shareholder of a corporation.

TAX ASPECTS FOR EMPLOYERS AND SELF-EMPLOYED INDIVIDUALS

Allowances

A reasonable allowance paid to an employee for business purposes and based on the number of business kilometres driven in the year is not included in the employee's income. To lessen the administrative difficulty of maintaining mileage records for each employee on a regular basis, the CCRA will allow a tax-free fixed allowance to be paid to an employee during the year, provided the following conditions exist:

- There is a pre-established per-kilometre rate.
- The rate and the advance are reasonable.
- At the earlier of the calendar year-end or the date the employee ceases to be employed, the actual kilometres travelled for business purposes are calculated. If the employer has overpaid, the employee must refund the excess to the employer. If the employee was underpaid, the employer must make up the difference.
- The employee does not include the amount in income under any other provision of the *Income Tax Act*.

Deductible Expenditures

If your employees use their own cars for business, you may deduct certain allowances or reimbursements you pay them with respect to the business use. In addition, you can claim an input tax credit for GST paid on employee-reimbursed expenditures and the GST deemed to be included in the amount of paid allowances. For QST purposes, you can claim the credit for expenditures on which the QST is actually paid and on which the QST is deemed to be included in the amount of paid allowances. This eligibility may not apply to large businesses (i.e., those with $10 million or more of gross income) since July 1, 1999.

If you provide cars to your employees, your deductible amounts are limited to non-capital, "reasonable" expenses incurred for the purpose of earning income from a business, profession, or property. Accordingly, you may deduct all leasing or ownership costs, up to the maximum amounts set out above, and reasonable operating costs, parking costs, and so forth for the vehicles provided. You also may deduct the interest expense incurred on debt used to purchase the vehicles. The monthly interest expense deduction limit for money borrowed to purchase an automobile is $300 for automobiles purchased after 2000.

Employer Deductions with Respect to Employee-Provided Vehicles

As an employer, you can deduct certain distance-based car allowances paid to an employee with respect to the use of his or her car for the benefit of your business, even when these are not reported as taxable income of the employee. You may fully deduct any car allowances or similar payments that are reported on the employee's T4 as fully taxable.

You are permitted to deduct tax-free allowances to an employee to the extent that they do not exceed 42 cents for each of the first 5,000 business kilometres driven by the employee in a year, and 36 cents for each additional business kilometre. An additional four cents per kilometre is allowed in the Yukon, Northwest Territories, and Nunavut.

You may deduct payments made regarding fuel, maintenance, and repairs in full, although the part of these costs related to personal use of the car will be taxable income to the employee.

Employer Deductions with Respect to Company-Provided Vehicles

If your company purchases or leases vehicles that are provided to employees, you will be required to calculate a standby charge, as discussed above, and include the taxable benefit on your employees' T4s (Relevé 1 in Quebec). Although you are required to pay GST and QST on the benefit, you may be able to claim the GST and the QST on the purchase price or the lease cost of the car, subject to the maximum amounts prescribed.

Company-Owned Vehicles

Your company is permitted regular capital cost allowance (CCA) deductions for vehicles that it owns that are used in business. Existing CCA rules apply to vehicles costing the maximum prescribed cost or less. The vehicles will be included in the current CCA class 10, which allows a 30 per cent CCA rate. Current recapture, half-year, terminal loss, and pooling rules continue to apply for cars meeting the criteria described above.

If you purchase a car costing in excess of the maximum prescribed cost, each car must be included in a separate CCA class 10.1. The other tax measures for employees described in the section "Deductions for Owned Vehicles" also apply to employers.

Leased Vehicles

If your company provides leased vehicles to its employees, the maximum deduction regarding the lease cost is the same as the deduction available to individuals, as described earlier. To prevent indirect increases to the maximum allowable deduction, the *Income Tax Act* rules prevent your company from making refundable payments to the lessor for the purpose of reducing the monthly lease amount.

If you provide your employees with leased vehicles, any reimbursement by an employee of your lease expense will reduce the deductible portion of your cost. This can have a very punitive effect in the case of luxury cars. For example, if you pay $1,800 per month for a lease entered into on October 1, 2003, your maximum deduction before any reimbursement totals $918 (for an Ontario resident). If the employee reimbursement is $918 or greater, you obtain no deduction. If the reimbursement is less than $918, it must be deducted from the $918 allowable deduction.

PLANNING FOR BUSINESS USE OF AUTOMOBILES

In most cases, review existing policies and available alternatives to maximize tax deductions and the benefits to employees. In addition, consider the ramifications of the Goods and Services Tax.

In light of these factors, consider the following options:

- providing an interest-free loan instead of a car allowance or a company car;
- having the employer provide a leased car instead of a purchased car;
- leasing the car initially and purchasing it at a later date; or
- having a car available to you that is used more than 50 per cent for business.

Consult your professional advisor to discuss the tax consequences of particular approaches and to choose the one that suits your situation.

CHAPTER FIFTEEN

If You Are a Senior

THE TAXATION OF SENIORS / 232
Income in the Form of Benefits / 232
 Benefits from Canada and Abroad / 233

CREDITS AND DEDUCTIONS / 234
Age 65 and Over / 234
Pension Income / 234
Mental or Physical Impairment / 235
The Medical Expense Credit—Specific Issues for Seniors / 235

THE TAXATION OF SENIORS

This chapter highlights the government benefits, credits, and deductions available to seniors. For information on your RRSP, maturity options, and taxation of retirement income, refer to Chapter 13.

Income in the Form of Benefits

If you have worked in Canada and made contributions to the Canada or Quebec Pension Plan (CPP/QPP), you are likely entitled to apply for your pension benefits from those plans. You can begin collecting your CPP benefits at any age between 60 and 70. If you delay collecting your benefits after age 65, your eligible benefits will be increased to a maximum of 130 per cent (at 6 per cent per year). CPP benefits are included in your taxable income for the year they are received. In 2003, the maximum CPP or QPP retirement pension is $801.25 per month if taken at 65. The pension is adjusted for inflation every January.

Benefits from Canada and Abroad. If you have not lived and worked in Canada long enough to qualify for CPP, you can use your pension credits from your previous country of residence to help you qualify for a pension in Canada. Once you qualify for benefits, the amount of the benefit is based on your residence and contributions in Canada.

Alternatively, if you now live in Canada after having immigrated or returned from a country with which Canada has a social security agreement, you may qualify for a pension from that other country. Your former country of residence may consider the time you lived and worked in Canada to help you qualify for a pension from that country. Once you qualify, your pension will be based on your residence or contributions in that country.

If you have been a resident for at least 10 years after reaching age 18, you also may qualify to apply for Old Age Security (OAS) benefits. Residency of at least 40 years after age 18, including the 10 years immediately preceding your application, qualifies you for full benefits. If you have lived in Canada for at least 20 years after reaching age 18, you may collect the OAS pension outside Canada. You do not need a Canadian work history to qualify for OAS. Your OAS pension benefit is taxable income.

> **Planning Opportunity:** You can apply to have your CPP benefits split between you and your spouse to reduce your taxable income. You must both be at least 60 years of age and you must both have applied for retirement pensions.

While the amount of your CPP/QPP benefits depends on how much you have contributed to the plan, the benefits are not affected by the amount of your other retirement income. The OAS benefit is adjusted depending on how much you earn in retirement from other sources and has a built-in "clawback" mechanism. The OAS repayment is 15 cents for each dollar of individual net income over $57,879. For single seniors, OAS benefits are fully recovered if you earn (net) about $94,500. To avoid the clawback, optimize opportunities to split your retirement income with your spouse. Also consider postponing the receipt of retirement income, including your CPP/QPP benefits, and continue to contribute to your RRSP until you are 69.

Same-sex common-law partners have the same CPP/OAS benefits and obligations as opposite-sex common-law partners. The programs formerly called Spouse's Allowance and Widowed Spouse's Allowance are now called the Allowance and the Allowance for the Survivor.

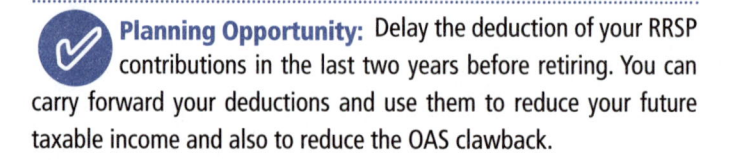

> **Planning Opportunity:** Delay the deduction of your RRSP contributions in the last two years before retiring. You can carry forward your deductions and use them to reduce your future taxable income and also to reduce the OAS clawback.

CREDITS AND DEDUCTIONS

Age 65 and Over

If you turn 65 before the end of 2003, you can claim a $606 federal tax credit. This credit is 16 per cent of the "age amount" ($3,787 currently). The age amount is reduced by 15 per cent of an individual's net income exceeding $28,193. You cannot claim this credit if you have an annual net income of $53,440 or more. If you are unable to make full use of the credit, all or a portion of it can be transferred to your spouse. The federal credit is fully indexed annually.

Pension Income

If you turn 65 before the end of 2003, you can claim a maximum federal tax credit of $160 against your pension income, provided that the income is at least $1,000. If it is less than $1,000, the maximum credit is 16 per cent of the pension income. Payments from registered pension plans, a DPSP, an

RRSP, or a RRIF will qualify as long as they are periodic payments and not lump-sum amounts.

A similar credit is available with respect to "qualified pension income" for taxpayers who are under 65 at the end of the year. Qualified pension income includes life annuity payments from a pension fund or plan and, conditionally, income that qualifies as pension income for individuals under age 65. You must be receiving the income as a result of the death of your spouse.

If you cannot make full use of your pension income tax credit, the unused portion may be transferred to your spouse. The pension income tax credit is not subject to indexing and therefore remains at its 1988 level.

Mental or Physical Impairment

If you have a severe and prolonged mental or physical impairment that has been certified by a medical doctor, optometrist, audiologist, occupational therapist, or psychologist, you can claim a federal tax credit in 2003 of $1,005. This federal credit is fully indexed annually. Any unused portion of the credit may, under certain circumstances, be transferred to a spouse or to another person who supported you.

The Medical Expense Credit—Specific Issues for Seniors

The medical expenses credit is available to all Canadians, but it has specific relevance for Canadian seniors. Refer to Chapter 5 for detailed discussion of the qualifying amounts and services covered. In addition to those services, the following expenses can be claimed:

- costs related to artificial limbs, wheelchairs, crutches, hearing aids, prescription glasses or contact lenses, dentures, pacemakers, prescription drugs, and specified prescription medical devices;
- if you or a person you support lacks normal physical development or has a severe and prolonged mobility impairment,

you can claim reasonable construction and equipment expenses associated with modifying your home to enable the individual to gain access to, or to be mobile or functional within, the home;
- guide and hearing-ear dogs, as well as signal equipment for your home if you have a hearing impairment;
- most premiums paid to a private health insurance plan; and
- rehabilitation therapy costs for individuals with speech or hearing loss.

In addition, if the required medical treatment is not available within commuting distance from your home, you may be able to claim reasonable travelling expenses for yourself and an attendant, if required.

If you claim medical expenses for yourself or your spouse, and either one of you requires attendant care or care in a facility, you may be eligible to claim those costs. Qualifying costs include full- or part-time attendant care and will be included in your medical expenses claim. Generally if you claim full-time attendant care as part of your medical expenses, you cannot also claim the mental or physical impairment credit discussed opposite. However, if the cost of attendant care does not exceed $10,000, you can also claim the mental or physical impairment credit.

CHAPTER SIXTEEN

If You Provide Care for Your Parents

CREDITS AND DEDUCTIONS / 237
Eligible Dependant / 237
Dependants / 238
Disability Amount / 239
Caregiver Tax Credit / 239
Medical Expenses Tax Credit / 239

ACCESSING PERSONAL TAX INFORMATION / 240

Numerous Canadians provide support for their elderly parents or grandparents. The government recognizes that this added responsibility results in added costs. The credits and deductions described here are available to allay some of those expenses. Some of these credits extend beyond assisting Canadians caring for elderly parents. With the exception of the eligible dependant and the caregiver tax credits, the credits and deductions listed here are available to individuals providing care to a relative or spouse suffering a physical or mental impairment.

CREDITS AND DEDUCTIONS

Eligible Dependant

You can qualify for the eligible dependant tax credit (formerly called the equivalent-to-spouse tax credit) if you support a wholly dependent person and are unmarried, or are married but do not support or live with your spouse. The federal credit is $1,054 for 2003. The credit is reduced by 16 per cent of the dependant's income over $659. If the dependant's income is $7,245 or more for 2003, the credit is nil.

To claim the credit, you must maintain a "self-contained domestic establishment in which you live with and support the dependant." You can do this on your own or with others (e.g., your siblings can assist you in the care of your elderly parent).

The dependant must be related to you, wholly dependent on you (or on you and certain others) for support, and must be resident in Canada, unless the dependant is your child. Except in the case of a parent or grandparent, the dependant must be either under 18 years of age at any time in the year or dependent by reason of mental or physical infirmity.

You can claim this credit with respect to only one other person, and no more than one individual can claim the credit for the same person or the same self-contained domestic establishment. If you and another person are both eligible to claim the credit for the same dependant or the same self-contained domestic establishment, you must agree between yourselves who will make the claim. In the absence of agreement, the credit will apparently not be allowed to anyone.

If you are entitled to claim the eligible dependant credit, neither you nor anyone else may claim a dependant tax credit for the same person. The eligible dependant federal tax credit is fully indexed annually.

Dependants

If your parent does not live with you, or if you are married, you might be eligible to claim the dependant credit if your parent meets the qualification of suffering from a mental or physical impairment. A "dependant" can include a child or grandchild of you or your spouse, or, if resident in Canada at any time in the year, a parent, grandparent, brother, sister, uncle, aunt, niece, or nephew of you or your spouse.

If a dependant is claimed under the eligible dependant tax credit described previously, that person cannot also be claimed as a dependant with a mental or physical infirmity. Details on the dependant credit are contained in Chapter 12.

If you and another person or persons claim a dependant tax credit for the same dependant, the total claimed cannot exceed the maximum allowed for one individual making the claim. The Canada Customs and Revenue Agency (CCRA) may allocate the total tax credit to the supporting individuals if they cannot agree on an allocation.

Disability Amount

If the person with a qualifying severe and prolonged mental or physical impairment cannot use all of this credit, any unused portion of the credit may, under certain circumstances, be transferred to a spouse or to another person who supported the individual. See Chapter 12 for details.

Caregiver Tax Credit

If you have not claimed the eligible dependant tax credit or the dependant tax credit for a dependant, you may be eligible to claim the caregiver credit. The caregiver tax credit can reduce federal tax up to a maximum of $586 ($3,663 × 16%) for individuals who live with and provide in-home care for a parent or grandparent (including in-laws) over the age of 65 or a dependent relative who has a mental or physical infirmity. For 2003, the credit is reduced proportionately by the dependant's net income over $12,509 and is unavailable if the dependant's net income is greater than $16,172.

Medical Expenses Tax Credit

The list of allowable medical expenses that can be claimed under the credit includes reasonable expenses for training an individual to care for a relative who has a mental or physical infirmity. The relative must live with or be dependent on you for support.

ACCESSING PERSONAL TAX INFORMATION

If you are responsible for managing the financial affairs of your parent(s), one of your main tasks will be to file annual tax returns. The CCRA will give information to an individual's representative only after they receive written authorization from the individual. Personal tax information will be released to a representative only after a completed Form T1013, Consent Form, or a letter containing the same information and signed by your parent, is submitted. Once authorization is approved, you must still provide:

- one piece of signed identification with your picture; or
- two pieces of signed identification.

In addition, the CCRA will ask for:

- your parent's Notice of Assessment, Notice of Reassessment, or other tax documents; or
- information about the contents of your parent's return.

If you call the CCRA about your parent's return before May 1, 2004, you should use the return for 2002. If you call after April 30, you should use the return for 2003.

CHAPTER SEVENTEEN

If You Make Political or Charitable Contributions

CREDITS AND DEDUCTIONS / 241
Charitable Donations / 241
Emergency Service Volunteer Allowances / 243
Political Contributions / 243
   Planning for Your Contributions / 245

Although these charitable donations and political contributions credits are in place to encourage Canadians to make gifts and contributions to aid a public purpose, the requirements and conditions are confusing. Making a contribution requires planning, and you must consider both the amount and the timing of your gift to maximize your tax benefit.

CREDITS AND DEDUCTIONS

Charitable Donations
The federal tax credit on qualifying charitable donations is 16 per cent on the first $200 donated and 29 per cent on donations above $200. For an individual in the top tax bracket in Ontario, the total credit on a $1,000 donation in 2003 will be about $416:

Calculation of the Charitable Donations Credit

Federal credit at 16% on first $200 donated	$ 32.00
Federal credit at 29% on excess ($800)	232.00
Total federal credits	264.00
Provincial tax reduction (Ontario)	151.67
Total tax reduction	$415.67

Any donation not claimed under the tax credit system in a given year can be carried forward for five years. In the carryforward year, however, the 16 per cent rate applies to the first $200 of all donations claimed, including carryforward donations. A deferral may result in a small tax cost if your donation falls short of $200 that year, but would have been part of a larger gift in another year.

The annual limit on qualifying donations to both charitable institutions and the Crown is 75 per cent of net income. Where appreciated capital property is gifted, the 75 per cent limit is further increased by one-quarter of the taxable gain arising from the gifted property. In this case, the donation limit would equal 100 per cent of the net income that arises as a consequence of the gift. Also, in the year of death and in the immediately preceding taxation year, the limit on gifts, including bequests or legacies, is 100 per cent of the individual's net income.

Retroactive to January 1, 1999, the charitable donation credit can be claimed in the final income tax return of the deceased where a direct beneficiary designation is made and RRSP, RRIF, and insurance proceeds are donated. In the case of life insurance, to qualify, the policy must either be owned by the individual or be a group policy under which the individual's life was insured.

As another incentive to encourage charitable gifting, only 25 per cent of the gain realized in the gift of publicly traded securities to a charity is added to your taxable income for the year.

If You Make Political or Charitable Contributions ▶ 243

As a result of the 2000 budget, an individual who donates publicly traded shares acquired by exercising a stock option could deduct two-thirds of the employment benefit. This relieving provision applies to shares acquired since February 28, 2000. The shares must be donated within 30 days of exercising the option. Donations to a private foundation will not benefit from this preferential treatment.

For gifts of ecological property made since February 28, 2000, the capital gains inclusion rate is reduced from one-third to 25 per cent. A taxpayer can elect to have a gift of ecological property treated as having been sold at fair market value when it is donated to a charity. This would normally result in a donation computed by reference to the fair market value, but would also require the taxpayer to include 50 per cent of the capital gain in income. Donors include only 25 per cent of the capital gain in income. This change requires the Minister of the Environment to determine the fair market value of the gift.

> **Planning Opportunity:** Pool the credit. Claiming a donation of $400 on one spouse's return (rather than each spouse claiming $200) saves tax because half the donation qualifies for the 29 per cent federal rate rather than the 16 per cent rate.

Emergency Service Volunteer Allowances

Since 1998, if you donate your time as an emergency service volunteer, you may qualify for some added tax breaks. For example, if you are a volunteer fire-fighter or other qualifying emergency service volunteer, your tax-free exemption is $1,000.

Political Contributions

A federal tax credit is available for contributions to a registered political party or an officially nominated candidate in a federal election. The credit is based on the amount contributed and is calculated on a sliding scale. The maximum credit for any one taxation year is $500.

Comparison of Credit Available for Various Amounts of Gifts

Amount Contributed	Tax Credit Available
$1–$200	75% of the contribution
$200–$550	$150 plus 50% of excess over $200
$550–$1,075	$325 plus 1/3 of excess over $550
Over $1,075	$500

All provinces and territories also permit tax credits for political contributions, but the credit is deducted from provincial tax payable and contributions must be made to provincial political parties or associations, or to candidates standing for provincial election. Most provinces and territories allow a maximum credit of $500. The maximum credit in Alberta is $750. The maximum credit in Ontario is $1,000, calculated as 75 per cent of the first $300, 50 per cent of the next $700, and 33.33 per cent of the next $1,275. In Quebec, the tax credit is calculated as 75 per cent of the first $140 for a party at the municipal level and 75 per cent of the first $400 for a party at the provincial level, for a maximum credit of $405.

Official receipts must be filed with your tax return to receive the credit. Generally, political contributions must be made in the form of cash or other negotiable instruments (cheques, money orders, etc.). However, some provinces permit the contribution of goods or services under certain conditions.

You cannot claim the credit for political contributions in excess of $1,075 federally or in Saskatchewan, Manitoba, or New Brunswick; $900 in the Northwest Territories or Nunavut; $540 in Quebec; $1,725 in Alberta; $2,275 in Ontario; and $1,150 in the remaining jurisdictions. If the tax credit exceeds your federal or provincial tax payable after the deduction of other credits, you cannot claim a refund of tax or carry forward any excess credit to a future taxation year.

Planning for Your Contributions. If you are making a large contribution, spread it over two years. You will be able to take advantage of the larger credits available. For example, if you contribute $1,000 in one year, your federal credit is $475. If you contribute $500 this year and $500 next year, your total credit is $600, giving you a $125 tax saving. This same technique should also be applied if both spouses earn taxable income, except that the spouses would split their contribution in the year (i.e., each spouse would contribute $500, instead of one spouse contributing $1,000). Splitting the contribution is beneficial because the maximum percentage credit applies at lower contribution levels.

CHAPTER EIGHTEEN

If You Live in Quebec

CREDITS AND DEDUCTIONS / 247
Employment Income / 247
Tuition Fees / 247
Child Care Expenses / 248
Charitable Gifts / 248
Medical Expenses / 248
Other Items / 248

TAX INCENTIVES / 249
Quebec Stock Savings Plan / 249
    Tax Benefit / 250
    Additional Deductions / 251
    Recovery of Deductions / 251
    Capital Gains and Dividends / 252
    QSSPs versus RRSPs / 252
Cooperative Investment Plan / 253
Quebec Business Investment Companies / 254
    Tax Benefit / 254
Mineral Exploration and Oil and Gas Sectors / 255
Fonds social Desjardins / 255

CONSEQUENCES OF MARRIAGE BREAKDOWN / 256
Family Patrimony / 256

CORPORATE TAX ISSUES / 256
Corporations Operating in Quebec / 256
    Tax Rates / 256
    Exemptions for New Corporations / 257
    Research and Development / 258

Although the Quebec government has sometimes harmonized its tax legislation with the federal legislation, there are some differences, especially with the personal income tax credits. Details of these credit amounts and a few other features particular to the Quebec system are outlined in Chapter 19.

In addition, the Quebec government has tax benefits available to its residents that are offered concurrently by the federal government or are uniquely adapted to the economic needs of the province. They are designed to promote investments in strategic sectors of industry such as mining exploration, film production, scientific research, etc.

This chapter discusses certain specific tax measures that apply to Quebec residents.

CREDITS AND DEDUCTIONS

Employment Income

Quebec provides a tax credit of 20 per cent for union and professional dues.

When employment duties are performed outside Canada in certain types of businesses (construction, engineering, etc.), federal legislation provides a tax credit, while Quebec legislation provides for a deduction in calculating taxable income. In both cases, similar conditions must be met to have access to these tax benefits.

Tuition Fees

When fees exceed $100, a tax credit equal to 16 per cent is allowed under the federal system. Where the credit is not fully claimed, it may be transferred to a spouse or parent to a maximum of $800.

Under Quebec legislation, tuition fees are eligible for a 20 per cent tax credit that can be claimed only by the student. Transfers to another taxpayer are not allowed. Moreover, examination fees charged by professional corporations mentioned in Schedule 1 of the Professional Code (i.e., exclusive professions and professions with reserved titles) are deductible when the examinations are required to become a member of one of the corporations or to practise one of the professions mentioned in the Schedule.

Child Care Expenses

Contrary to the federal legislation, which allows individuals to deduct child care expenses, the Quebec legislation provides a refundable tax credit for these expenses, based on family income, going from 26 per cent to 75 per cent. Most of the rules in both pieces of legislation are similar when it comes to determining eligible child care expenses.

Charitable Gifts

A taxpayer making a charitable gift is entitled to a tax credit, just as in the federal system, but the tax credit is different. Quebec legislation provides a flat 20 per cent credit on the first $2,000 and a 24 per cent credit on the excess. The total amount of gifts that can be deducted in a given year is limited to 75 per cent of net income. If the gift is a work of art, the tax credit is generally limited to the selling price of the work of art by the organization to which the gift is given. Moreover, the sale must take place before the end of the fifth calendar year following the year of the gift; otherwise, the tax benefit will be forfeited.

Medical Expenses

The qualifying medical expenses are similar to those under federal legislation. However, the limit of approximately $1,728 does not exist and the family net income of both spouses, instead of the net income of only one spouse, must be considered to determine the threshold of 3 per cent.

Other Items

Some items contained in the Quebec legislation do not have a federal equivalent.

For instance, a person who resides in Quebec on December 31 may be entitled to a real estate tax refund. This credit is available to both tenants and homeowners. The size of the credit depends on the individual's total income and that of the spouse, if applicable. It also depends on the aggregate of real estate taxes for the year. For 2003, the maximum credit has been set at $536.

In addition, Quebec residents can benefit from a lifetime capital gains exemption of $500,000 with respect to gains resulting from the disposal of eligible fishing property. Eligible fishing property comprises a fishing licence, an individual quota, or a fishing vessel used by an individual in a fishing enterprise. Criteria for eligible farm property—such as the 24-month holding period prior to disposal—apply with respect to eligible fishing property, with the required adaptations.

Finally, low- and middle-income families are entitled to a tax reduction. It provides a reduction of income tax, but is not refundable. The amount of the reduction depends on the household's total income. For 2003, the maximum has been set at $1,500 for a couple with at least one dependent child. Single parents who do not share an independent dwelling with another adult are also entitled to a tax reduction of $1,195.

TAX INCENTIVES

Quebec Stock Savings Plan

In 1979, the Quebec government introduced the stock savings plan (QSSP) to promote stock investments in Quebec companies and reduce the tax burden on individuals residing in the province. Although the QSSP has undergone several adjustments over the years, most making it less attractive, it nevertheless remains an interesting method of tax planning if you are prepared to acquire shares on the stock market.

> **Caution:** It is nevertheless important to note that no new issue of eligible shares can occur under the Quebec Stock Savings Plan after June 12, 2003, because on this date the government announced a moratorium during the budget speech.

Also, it is wise to keep in mind that any tax benefit achieved with a QSSP may be offset by a decline of the market value of the shares. Consequently, even when shares qualify under the QSSP, the first criterion you should investigate before purchasing shares is still their potential yield and growth. To reduce the risk associated with this type of investment, you can invest through a stock savings plan investment group or investment fund. One of the advantages of these alternative forms of investment is that you will have a share in a more diversified stock portfolio without having to make a considerable investment.

Tax Benefit. If you are a Quebec resident at the close of the tax year and have acquired qualifying shares in a stock savings plan during the year, you may deduct the adjusted cost of these shares from your taxable income, to a maximum of 10 per cent of your total income. Your "total income" is the net income amount that appears on your provincial income tax return, less the capital gains exemption used during the year. Shares must have been acquired prior to the end of the tax year and be included in the stock savings plan before February 1 of the following year to be considered qualifying shares. The allowable deduction is restricted to the "adjusted cost" of your shares; that is, to the full cost of the shares, excluding the cost of borrowing, brokers' commissions, or safekeeping fees.

These shares must be issued by "growth corporations," which means corporations with assets between $2 million and $350 million. Moreover, growth corporations can issue unsecured debentures or preferred shares that entitle the holders to a 50 per cent QSSP deduction. To meet the eligibility requirements, these securities must, in particular, be convertible at any time into common shares carrying voting rights under all circumstances.

For example, in January 2003, you purchase shares of growth corporations for $3,000. Your net income is $50,000, and you realized a taxable capital gain of $10,000 on the sale of qualified small business corporation shares for which the capital gains exemption has been used. Your QSSP deduction will amount to the lesser of the following:

- Adjusted cost of shares
  $3,000 × 100% $3,000

- 10 per cent of your total income
  10% × ($50,000 − $10,000) $4,000

Your deduction will therefore be $3,000.

Management fees for a QSSP and the cost of borrowing to purchase shares constitute financial expenses and are deductible annually.

Additional Deductions. Shares included in a QSSP entitle the holder to an additional 25 per cent deduction on the cost of the shares when they are acquired under an employee stock option plan. An employer may create a plan to encourage employees to acquire the shares issued by the employer corporation when it goes public. The plan must be available to all employees and executives with more than three months of service who own less than 5 per cent of the capital stock of the corporation immediately prior to acquiring shares in the stock option plan.

Recovery of Deductions. At the end of the two subsequent calendar years, your stock portfolio must contain shares that have an adjusted cost equal to the amount for which you obtained a deduction. Should this not be the case, you will either have to include a portion or all of the deductions previously allowed in your income for the year in which this condition is not met, or reduce the amount of the deduction that you could otherwise claim during the year.

If, for example, in 2001 you acquired $1,000 of shares, which at the time entitled you to a deduction of 100 per cent, and you sell these shares in 2003, you must, before the end of 2003, acquire replacement shares with an adjusted cost of $1,000 so that the deduction you obtained will not be added to your income during 2003. You cannot, however, benefit from a new QSSP deduction for the replacement shares.

In addition to newly issued shares, replacement shares also include the shares of growth corporations that already entitle the holder to the QSSP deduction if they are purchased on the secondary market and listed by the Commission des valeurs mobilières du Québec.

Capital Gains and Dividends. Dividends received on shares in stock savings plans are treated like any other dividend received on shares. When the shares are sold, the capital gain or loss is calculated in the usual manner. The tax benefit received does not reduce the actual cost of the shares.

QSSPs versus RRSPs. Unlike the RRSP, which only allows income tax payments to be deferred, the QSSP offers a real tax saving. The RRSP does, however, reduce your immediate income tax at both the federal and provincial levels, while the QSSP deduction can be used only in Quebec.

A share in a QSSP cannot be included under another tax plan at the same time. However, you can contribute successively to your QSSP and RRSP using the same funds and, because the deadlines for contributions are different, obtain the QSSP and RRSP deduction for the same year.

Whereas shares included in a QSSP must be acquired before year-end, it is possible to contribute to an RRSP during the first 60 days of the subsequent year. As a result, QSSP shares can be sold at the beginning of the year following the year of acquisition and the sale proceeds can be used to make a contribution to an RRSP. To avoid the recovery of deductions, QSSP shares must be replaced before the end of the year in which they are sold, unless the adjusted cost of shares held for over two years in your QSSP portfolio allows you to escape this rule. The double deduction is therefore only temporary, but may prove useful if you do not have sufficient liquid assets available at this time of the year.

Cooperative Investment Plan

To encourage investments in certain Quebec cooperatives, the provincial government introduced the Quebec Cooperative Investment Plan. This plan provides a deduction to an individual who acquires eligible securities issued by a qualified cooperative. This deduction is only available to a member or worker of the cooperative and to an employee of a partnership to which the qualified cooperative contributes more than 50 per cent of the income.

> **Caution:** It is nevertheless important to note that no eligibility certificates will be issued under this plan after June 12, 2003, because on this date the government announced a moratorium during the budget speech.

The deduction and a two-year holding period are calculated in the same manner as under the QSSP. The deduction is equal to 100 per cent (75 per cent after June 12, 2003) of the cost of the securities purchased, but not exceeding 10 per cent of total income. The basic deduction is 125 per cent (93.75 per cent after June 12, 2003) for units issued by small and medium-sized cooperatives, i.e., those with assets of less than $25 million or equity of no more than $10 million.

When a cooperative sets up a "stock ownership plan" (a plan allowing employees and officers to acquire securities in their cooperative) similar to the one discussed in the "Quebec

Stock Savings Plan" section, individuals who acquire such securities are entitled to an additional deduction of 25 per cent (18.75 per cent after June 12, 2003), for a total deduction of 125 per cent or 150 per cent (93.75 per cent or 112.5 per cent after June 12, 2003) of the cost of the shares.

Quebec Business Investment Companies

A Quebec business investment company (QBIC) is a private corporation whose primary activity is to acquire shares of other unrelated eligible private corporations, which operate in prescribed sectors. These sectors include manufacturing, tourism, export, or environmental protection in Quebec. The QBICs, which can only be incorporated in Quebec, are an intermediate financing vehicle between eligible private corporations and investors. They are private and not listed on the stock market.

Tax Benefit. Where a QBIC makes an investment in a qualified corporation, the individuals who are the shareholders may generally deduct an amount equal to 150 per cent of the value of their interest in this qualified investment. A qualified corporation is a Canadian-controlled private corporation with assets of less than $25 million that carries on business in a sector mentioned above. However, when the corporation's assets are between $25 million and $50 million, the deduction permitted is reduced to 125 per cent. If the assets exceed this ceiling, no deduction is allowed.

> **Caution:** It is nevertheless important to note that no new eligible investment can be made after June 12, 2003, because on this date the government announced a moratorium during the budget speech.

The deduction used in a given year must not exceed 30 per cent of your total income; any portion not claimed in a year due to this limit may be carried forward for five years.

Investments in a QBIC do not affect contribution limits to RRSPs and QSSPs. Unlike a QSSP, you are not required to keep your QBIC securities for at least two years. This is the responsibility of the QBIC. If a QBIC constitutes an "active business" and the other criteria prescribed by law are met, you can even benefit from the $500,000 capital gains exemption on the sale or disposal of these shares.

Mineral Exploration and Oil and Gas Sectors

The acquisition of flow-through shares, whether directly or through a limited partnership, enables the holder to benefit from tax breaks for Quebec income tax purposes.

A deduction of up to 175 per cent of surface mining exploration expenses incurred in Quebec may be allowed. An additional deduction of 25 per cent is also available after March 31, 1998, for such expenses incurred in northern Quebec. Moreover, a further exemption is granted with respect to the capital gain realized on the sale of flow-through shares, thereby enabling the holder to obtain tax breaks related to exploration.

Fonds social Desjardins

The *Taxation Act* allows a tax credit for individuals who invest in "Capital régional et coopératif Desjardins," a joint stock corporation set up to marshal venture capital for the resource regions of Quebec and cooperatives.

The tax credit granted for this type of investment is equal to the lesser of $1,250 per year or 50 per cent of the net cost of the shares acquired between March 1 of a year and February 28 of the following year. The maximum cost is therefore $2,500.

The minimum holding period of the shares is seven years, except in certain specific circumstances (death, emigration, severe illness, etc.). The tax credit is recovered prorated by the payment of a special tax when the period is less than seven years.

The shares cannot be transferred into a registered retirement savings plan. The tax credit does not reduce the adjusted cost base of the shares for purposes of calculating the capital gain. However, if the disposition of the shares triggers a capital loss, this loss is reduced by the amount of the tax credit granted.

CONSEQUENCES OF MARRIAGE BREAKDOWN

Family Patrimony

Married persons are subject to the rules on family patrimony. These relate to economic equality between spouses in the event that there is a partition of family patrimony, whether through separation, dissolution or annulment of a marriage, or death.

The partition of family patrimony may be accompanied by a partition of certain property between the spouses. Each spouse may claim a right to certain portions of the family property. A valuation is done on the basis of the total net value, not on the basis of individual property.

Property subject to partition includes the family's principal and secondary residences, household furniture, motor vehicles used for family travel, and benefits accrued during the marriage under public or private retirement plans. Any of this property that has been acquired before or during the marriage by way of succession, legacy, or gift is excluded from the family patrimony.

In the case of tax and estate planning, a spouse who makes a bequest to the other spouse should consider the implications of the partition of family patrimony. In addition to the bequest, the spouse will be entitled to 50 per cent of the net value of the property that is part of the family patrimony.

CORPORATE TAX ISSUES

Corporations Operating in Quebec

Tax Rates. In Chapter 7, we discussed the tax as well as the planning advantages available through the incorporation of a business. It was mentioned that the tax structure varies depending on the province in which the income was earned, as well as on the type and amount of income.

Under Quebec legislation, the basic corporate rate is 16.25 per cent. The active business income is subject to a tax reduction of 7.35 per cent.

The following schedule summarizes the effective Quebec corporate income tax rates and takes into account the additional surtax of 1.6 per cent that applied until March 14, 2003, on account of contributions to the Youth Fund:

Comparison of Quebec Corporate Income Tax Rates

	Before March 15, 2003		After March 14, 2003	
	Active Business Income %	Other Income %	Active Business Income %	Other Income %
Basic rate	16.25	16.25	16.25	16.25
Deduction allowed	(7.35)	(−)	(7.35)	(−)
	8.90	16.25	8.90	16.25
Contribution to the Youth Fund	0.14	0.26	(−)	(−)
Effective rate	9.04	16.51	8.90	16.25

Exemptions for New Corporations. To stimulate the formation of new firms in Quebec, provincial legislation provides certain corporations with an exemption for income tax, capital tax, and employers' contributions to the Health Services Fund. This tax exemption applies to a portion of active business income, eligible for the small business deduction, during the first five taxation years of new corporations.

A corporation qualifies for the exemption in a taxation year if:

- it is newly incorporated;
- it is not the result of an amalgamation;
- the year is one of its first five taxation years; and
- a tax return is filed within six months after the end of its first taxation year.

A corporation is not eligible for the exemption for the year if, among other things, it:

- was associated with any other corporation;
- was not a "Canadian-controlled private corporation";
- carried on a personal services business; or
- carried on an eligible business as a member of a partnership.

Research and Development. To encourage research and development (R&D) in Quebec, provincial legislation provides several refundable tax credits to certain corporations that carry out R&D in the province.

> **Caution:** It is nevertheless important to note that the deduction rates mentioned below must be reduced by 12.5 per cent if the R&D expenditures were incurred after June 12, 2003.

The basic credit is 20 per cent of wages paid in Quebec for R&D activities in Quebec. If a corporation meets certain criteria, and if the expenses are incurred pursuant to particular activities, the rate is increased to 40 per cent on the first $2 million of wages paid in Quebec for corporations whose assets are less than $25 million, and to 40 per cent of all R&D expenses incurred in Quebec pursuant to:

- a university research contract with a prescribed public research centre;
- a pre-competitive research project;
- a catalyst project recognized by the government and certified by the Technological Development Fund, with the possibility of obtaining grants equal to 50 per cent of other eligible expenditures;
- an environmental technology innovation project that has received Technological Development Fund certification (with the possibility of grants equal to 40 per cent, 50 per cent, or 100 per cent of other eligible expenditures); or
- an R&D consortium project.

The 40 per cent rate on the first $2 million of wages is progressively reduced to 20 per cent, on a linear basis, for corporations whose assets are more than $25 million and less than $50 million.

For taxation years beginning after June 30, 1999, and before June 12, 2003, a Canadian-controlled corporation having assets for the previous taxation year of less than $25 million is entitled to a refundable tax credit of 15 per cent based on the increase in R&D expenditures.

CHAPTER NINETEEN

Facts and Figures for Calculating 2003 Taxes

Maximum Combined Rates for 2003 (%)[1]

Alberta	39.00
British Columbia	43.70
Manitoba	46.40
New Brunswick	46.84
Newfoundland and Labrador	48.64
Northwest Territories	42.05
Nova Scotia	47.34
Nunavut	40.50
Ontario	46.41
Prince Edward Island	47.37
Quebec	48.22
Saskatchewan	44.00
Yukon	42.40
Non-residents	42.92

Note

[1] These rates are the combined federal and provincial rates at the top tax bracket; they include the provincial surtax and flat rate tax where applicable.

Federal Rates of Tax for 2003

Taxable Income	Tax	On Next
$0	$0 + 16%	$32,183
32,184	5,149 + 22%	32,184
64,369	12,230 + 26%	40,279
104,649	22,702 + 29%	Excess

QUEBEC PERSONAL INCOME TAX MEASURES

2003 Federal Tax – Quebec Only [1]

Taxable Income	Tax	On Next
$0	$0 + 13.36%	$32,183
32,184	4,300 + 18.37%	32,184
64,369	10,212 + 21.71%	40,279
104,649	18,958 + 24.22%	Excess

Note

[1] The table takes into account the 16.5% federal tax abatement for residents of Quebec.

2003 Quebec Provincial Tax

Taxable Income	Tax	On Next
$0	$0 + 16%	$27,095
27,096	4,335 + 20%	27,100
54,196	9,755 + 24%	Excess

2003 Quebec Personal Tax Credits

	Quebec Credit	Federal Tax Credit[1]
Basic	$1,230	$1,036
Person living alone[2]	219	N/A
Spouse[3]	1,230	880
Dependent children[4,5]		
first child	542	N/A
each additional child	500	N/A
attending post-secondary school[6]		
—credit per term (max. 2 per year)	344	N/A
Single-parent family[5,7]	271	N/A
Other dependants[5,8]		
general	500	N/A
mentally or physically infirm	1,230	489
Age exemption[9]	440	506
Mentally or physically infirm[10]	440	839
Pension income[11]	200	134
Lump-sum amount[12]	574	N/A

Notes

[1] Federal credits for Quebec residents reflect only the 16.5% federal abatement.

[2] The credit for an individual living alone is allowed to a single person who maintains a self-contained domestic establishment, or, if married, who lives alone or with dependent children. The equivalent-to-spouse credit, which still exists as the eligible dependent credit for federal tax purposes, is replaced in the Quebec system by a combination of the credits for the head of a single-parent family, the credit for

the first dependent child, and the credit for a person living alone in a dwelling. Quebec also provides tax reductions for families in addition to these credits, eligibility for which is based on their income.

3 In Quebec, this credit is reduced by 20% of the spouse's net income. The federal tax credit is reduced by 16% of the spouse's net income exceeding $659. The word "spouse" includes a common-law spouse of the opposite sex or the same sex.

4 Dependent children include children, grandchildren, sisters, brothers, nieces, and nephews under age 19 at the end of the year or over 18 and studying full-time.

5 For all Quebec credits claimed in respect of a dependant or a spouse, the income amount (i.e., the amount before the 20% factor is applied) is reduced dollar for dollar by the dependant's or spouse's net income. Where the additional credits are claimed (e.g., post-secondary studies in addition to basic dependant claim or spouse credit plus transfer of credit for age 65 or over from a spouse), net income is deducted only once from the combined amounts.

6 This additional credit is allowed when a dependant is in full-time attendance in a post-secondary educational program.

7 The credit for a single-parent family is available in respect of the first dependent child if the spouse credit is not claimed and the taxpayer does not live with a common-law spouse, is unmarried, or, if married, does not live with the spouse and is neither supported by nor supports that spouse. This credit may be claimed for one dependant only.

8 Other dependants include anyone over 18 years of age who is related to the taxpayer by blood, marriage, or adoption.

9 The federal age tax credit is reduced by 15% of the taxpayer's net income exceeding $28,193 at the federal level and by 15% of the family net income in excess of $27,095 in Quebec.

10 The disability credit may also be transferred in certain circumstances to a spouse and other dependants.

11 The definition of "pension income" differs for persons age 65 and over, as compared to those under age 65. CPP/QPP benefits and OAS or GIS payments do not qualify for this credit, regardless of the taxpayer's age.

[12] Individuals are able to choose to use a simplified taxation system that replaces many credits and deductions by a lump-sum non-refundable tax credit of $574, or 20% of $2,870.

OTHER QUEBEC CREDITS AND DEDUCTIONS

Union, professional and artist's dues, Quebec Pension Plan and unemployment insurance contributions: 20% of contributions.

Charitable donations: 20% on the first $2,000; 24% on the excess, not exceeding 75% of net income.

Health Services Fund contributions: 20% of contributions, not exceeding $200.

Medical expenses: 20% of expenses in excess of 3% of combined net income of both spouses.

Adults housing a parent: a refundable tax credit of $550 per person.

Tuition fees: 20% of fees paid in respect of post-secondary-school level courses in excess of $100.

Home support of older persons: 23% of eligible expenditures, limited to $12,000 a year ($2,760).

COMBINED FEDERAL AND PROVINCIAL PERSONAL INCOME TAX RATES FOR 2003[1]

Taxable Income	Newfoundland/Labrador Taxes Payable Other Income	Marginal Rate on Other Income	Dividend	Prince Edward Island Taxes Payable Other Income	Marginal Rate on Other Income	Dividend	Nova Scotia Taxes Payable Other Income	Marginal Rate on Other Income	Dividend
10,000	633	26.6%	2.6%	363	25.8%	0.0%	359	24.3%	0.0%
12,000	1,164	26.6%	7.0%	879	25.8%	0.0%	845	25.8%	0.0%
14,000	1,696	26.6%	7.0%	1,395	28.3%	0.0%	1,360	28.3%	0.0%
16,000	2,227	26.6%	7.0%	1,961	30.8%	0.0%	1,926	30.8%	0.0%
18,000	2,758	26.6%	7.0%	2,577	30.8%	0.0%	2,541	30.8%	0.0%
20,000	3,290	26.6%	7.0%	3,193	25.8%	0.0%	3,157	28.3%	0.0%
22,000	3,821	26.6%	8.1%	3,709	25.8%	0.0%	3,722	25.8%	0.0%
24,000	4,353	26.6%	14.0%	4,225	25.8%	0.0%	4,237	25.8%	2.6%
25,000	4,618	26.6%	14.0%	4,483	25.8%	2.6%	4,495	25.8%	9.1%
26,000	4,884	26.6%	14.0%	4,741	25.8%	7.6%	4,753	25.8%	9.1%
28,000	5,415	27.7%	17.9%	5,257	25.8%	11.5%	5,268	26.8%	13.0%
30,000	5,970	32.2%	24.8%	5,773	28.3%	18.5%	5,805	31.0%	19.9%
32,000	6,613	37.6%	24.8%	6,339	35.3%	18.5%	6,424	36.4%	19.9%
34,000	7,365	38.2%	24.8%	7,044	35.8%	18.5%	7,152	37.0%	19.9%
35,000	7,747	38.2%	24.8%	7,402	35.8%	18.5%	7,521	37.0%	19.9%
36,000	8,128	38.2%	24.8%	7,760	35.8%	18.5%	7,891	37.0%	19.9%
38,000	8,892	38.2%	24.8%	8,476	35.8%	18.5%	8,630	37.0%	19.9%
40,000	9,655	38.2%	24.8%	9,192	35.8%	18.5%	9,369	37.0%	19.9%
42,000	10,418	38.2%	24.8%	9,908	35.8%	18.5%	10,108	37.0%	19.9%
44,000	11,181	38.2%	24.8%	10,624	35.8%	18.5%	10,847	37.0%	19.9%
45,000	11,563	38.2%	24.8%	10,982	35.8%	18.5%	11,216	37.0%	19.9%
46,000	11,944	38.2%	25.5%	11,340	35.8%	18.5%	11,586	37.0%	20.6%
48,000	12,708	38.2%	27.1%	12,056	35.8%	19.9%	12,325	37.0%	22.0%
50,000	13,471	38.2%	28.4%	12,772	35.9%	23.3%	13,064	37.0%	23.3%
52,000	14,234	38.2%	32.1%	13,489	37.2%	27.1%	13,803	37.0%	27.0%
54,000	14,997	38.2%	32.1%	14,233	37.2%	27.1%	14,542	37.0%	27.0%
55,000	15,379	38.2%	32.1%	14,605	37.2%	27.1%	14,911	37.0%	27.0%
56,000	15,760	38.2%	32.1%	14,977	37.2%	27.1%	15,281	37.0%	27.0%
58,000	16,524	40.0%	32.1%	15,720	37.2%	27.1%	16,020	37.7%	27.0%
60,000	17,324	41.6%	32.1%	16,464	38.0%	27.1%	16,773	38.7%	27.0%
62,000	18,157	41.6%	32.1%	17,223	40.4%	27.1%	17,546	38.7%	27.0%
64,000	18,989	44.9%	32.9%	18,031	43.6%	27.1%	18,320	41.9%	27.0%
66,000	19,888	45.6%	33.6%	18,903	44.4%	27.1%	19,158	42.7%	27.0%
68,000	20,800	45.6%	33.6%	19,791	44.4%	27.1%	20,012	42.7%	27.0%
70,000	21,713	45.6%	33.6%	20,678	44.4%	27.1%	20,865	42.7%	27.0%

	Newfoundland/Labrador			Prince Edward Island			Nova Scotia		
Taxable Income	Taxes Payable Other Income	Marginal Rate on Other Income	Dividend	Taxes Payable Other Income	Marginal Rate on Other Income	Dividend	Taxes Payable Other Income	Marginal Rate on Other Income	Dividend
72,000	22,626	45.6%	33.6%	21,565	44.4%	27.1%	21,719	42.7%	27.0%
74,000	23,539	45.6%	33.6%	22,453	44.4%	27.1%	22,572	42.7%	27.0%
76,000	24,452	45.6%	33.6%	23,340	44.4%	27.1%	23,425	42.7%	27.0%
78,000	25,365	45.6%	33.6%	24,228	44.4%	27.4%	24,279	43.1%	27.0%
80,000	26,277	45.6%	33.6%	25,115	44.4%	28.2%	25,140	44.3%	27.0%
82,000	27,190	45.6%	34.1%	26,002	44.4%	28.7%	26,027	44.3%	27.6%
84,000	28,103	45.6%	37.3%	26,890	44.4%	32.0%	26,914	44.3%	30.8%
86,000	29,016	45.6%	37.3%	27,777	44.4%	32.0%	27,800	44.3%	30.8%
88,000	29,929	45.6%	37.3%	28,665	44.4%	32.0%	28,687	44.3%	30.8%
90,000	30,842	45.6%	37.3%	29,552	44.4%	32.0%	29,574	44.3%	30.8%
92,000	31,754	45.6%	37.3%	30,439	44.4%	32.0%	30,461	44.3%	30.8%
94,000	32,667	45.6%	37.3%	31,327	44.4%	32.0%	31,347	44.3%	30.8%
96,000	33,580	45.6%	37.3%	32,214	44.4%	32.0%	32,234	44.3%	30.8%
98,000	34,493	45.6%	37.3%	33,102	44.4%	32.0%	33,121	44.3%	30.8%
100,000	35,406	47.2%	37.3%	33,989	46.0%	32.0%	34,008	45.9%	30.8%
110,000	40,131	48.6%	37.3%	38,587	47.4%	32.0%	38,602	47.3%	31.0%
120,000	44,995	48.6%	37.3%	43,324	47.4%	32.0%	43,335	47.3%	31.9%
130,000	49,859	48.6%	37.3%	48,061	47.4%	32.0%	48,069	47.3%	31.9%

	New Brunswick			Quebec			Ontario		
Taxable Income	Taxes Payable Other Income	Marginal Rate on Other Income	Dividend	Taxes Payable Other Income	Marginal Rate on Other Income	Dividend[2]	Taxes Payable Other Income	Marginal Rate on Other Income	Dividend
10,000	359	16.0%	0.0%	670	29.4%	0.0%	359	23.2%	0.0%
12,000	679	27.0%	4.3%	1,257	29.4%	0.0%	823	27.5%	0.0%
14,000	1,219	30.7%	13.7%	1,844	29.4%	0.0%	1,373	22.1%	0.0%
16,000	1,833	30.7%	11.7%	2,431	29.4%	0.0%	1,814	22.1%	0.0%
18,000	2,447	30.7%	7.5%	3,019	29.4%	7.3%	2,255	22.1%	0.0%
20,000	3,060	29.9%	7.5%	3,606	29.4%	8.3%	2,696	22.1%	0.0%
22,000	3,658	25.7%	7.5%	4,193	29.4%	12.5%	3,137	22.1%	0.0%
24,000	4,171	25.7%	7.5%	4,780	29.4%	12.5%	3,578	22.1%	0.0%
25,000	4,428	25.7%	9.1%	5,074	29.4%	12.5%	3,799	22.1%	0.0%
26,000	4,685	25.7%	13.9%	5,367	31.2%	11.8%	4,019	22.1%	0.0%
28,000	5,199	25.7%	17.8%	5,991	33.4%	14.7%	4,460	22.1%	3.9%
30,000	5,712	25.7%	24.7%	6,658	33.4%	20.5%	4,901	22.1%	15.7%
32,000	6,226	35.8%	24.7%	7,325	37.9%	20.5%	5,342	29.9%	17.4%
34,000	6,942	36.8%	24.7%	8,083	38.4%	20.5%	5,941	31.2%	15.9%
35,000	7,310	36.8%	24.7%	8,467	38.4%	20.5%	6,252	31.2%	15.9%

Facts and Figures for Calculating 2003 Taxes ▶ 267

Taxable Income	New Brunswick Taxes Payable Other Income	Marginal Rate on Other Income	Marginal Rate on Dividend	Quebec Taxes Payable Other Income	Marginal Rate on Other Income	Marginal Rate on Dividend[2]	Ontario Taxes Payable Other Income	Marginal Rate on Other Income	Marginal Rate on Dividend
36,000	7,678	36.8%	24.7%	8,851	38.4%	20.5%	6,564	31.2%	15.9%
38,000	8,415	36.8%	24.7%	9,618	38.4%	20.5%	7,187	31.2%	15.9%
40,000	9,151	36.8%	24.7%	10,386	38.4%	21.2%	7,810	31.2%	15.9%
42,000	9,887	36.8%	24.7%	11,153	38.4%	23.1%	8,433	31.2%	15.9%
44,000	10,624	36.8%	24.7%	11,920	38.4%	26.5%	9,056	31.2%	15.9%
45,000	10,992	36.8%	24.7%	12,304	38.4%	26.5%	9,367	31.2%	15.9%
46,000	11,360	36.8%	24.7%	12,688	38.4%	26.5%	9,679	31.2%	15.9%
48,000	12,097	36.8%	24.7%	13,455	38.4%	26.5%	10,302	31.2%	15.9%
50,000	12,833	36.8%	26.5%	14,223	38.4%	27.6%	10,925	31.2%	17.3%
52,000	13,569	36.8%	31.9%	14,990	38.4%	30.7%	11,548	31.2%	23.4%
54,000	14,306	36.8%	31.9%	15,757	41.6%	30.7%	12,171	31.2%	23.4%
55,000	14,674	36.8%	31.9%	16,173	42.4%	30.7%	12,482	31.2%	23.4%
56,000	15,042	36.8%	31.9%	16,597	42.4%	30.7%	12,794	32.0%	23.4%
58,000	15,779	36.8%	31.9%	17,444	42.4%	30.7%	13,433	33.0%	23.4%
60,000	16,515	36.8%	31.9%	18,292	42.4%	30.7%	14,093	33.0%	23.4%
62,000	17,251	36.8%	31.9%	19,139	42.4%	30.7%	14,752	33.0%	23.4%
64,000	17,988	41.5%	31.9%	19,987	45.1%	30.7%	15,412	37.6%	23.4%
66,000	18,817	42.5%	31.9%	20,889	45.7%	30.7%	16,164	40.8%	23.4%
68,000	19,668	42.5%	31.9%	21,803	45.7%	30.7%	16,980	43.4%	23.4%
70,000	20,518	42.5%	31.9%	22,717	45.7%	30.7%	17,849	43.4%	23.4%
72,000	21,368	42.5%	31.9%	23,631	45.7%	30.7%	18,717	43.4%	23.4%
74,000	22,219	42.5%	31.9%	24,545	45.7%	30.7%	19,585	43.4%	23.4%
76,000	23,069	42.5%	31.9%	25,460	45.7%	30.7%	20,453	43.4%	23.4%
78,000	23,920	42.5%	31.9%	26,374	45.7%	30.7%	21,321	43.4%	23.4%
80,000	24,770	42.5%	31.9%	27,288	45.7%	30.7%	22,189	43.4%	23.4%
82,000	25,620	42.5%	32.6%	28,202	45.7%	31.1%	23,058	43.4%	23.9%
84,000	26,471	42.5%	37.3%	29,116	45.7%	33.8%	23,926	43.4%	27.1%
86,000	27,321	42.5%	37.3%	30,031	45.7%	33.8%	24,794	43.4%	28.1%
88,000	28,172	42.5%	37.3%	30,945	45.7%	33.8%	25,662	43.4%	28.6%
90,000	29,022	42.5%	37.3%	31,859	45.7%	33.8%	26,530	43.4%	28.6%
92,000	29,872	42.5%	37.3%	32,773	45.7%	33.8%	27,399	43.4%	28.6%
94,000	30,723	42.5%	37.3%	33,687	45.7%	33.8%	28,267	43.4%	28.6%
96,000	31,573	42.5%	37.3%	34,602	45.7%	33.8%	29,135	43.4%	28.6%
98,000	32,424	42.5%	37.3%	35,516	45.7%	33.8%	30,003	43.4%	29.1%
100,000	33,274	44.8%	37.3%	36,430	47.1%	33.8%	30,871	45.0%	31.3%
110,000	37,757	46.8%	37.3%	41,135	48.2%	33.8%	35,373	46.4%	31.3%
120,000	42,441	46.8%	37.3%	45,957	48.2%	33.4%	40,014	46.4%	31.3%
130,000	47,125	46.8%	37.3%	50,778	48.2%	32.8%	44,655	46.4%	31.3%

	Manitoba			Saskatchewan			Alberta		
	Taxes Payable	Marginal Rate on		Taxes Payable	Marginal Rate on		Taxes Payable	Marginal Rate on	
Taxable Income	Other Income	Other Income	Dividend	Other Income	Other Income	Dividend	Other Income	Other Income	Dividend
10,000	402	28.9%	3.3%	579	27.0%	0.0%	7	26.0%	0.0%
12,000	980	28.9%	6.8%	1,119	27.0%	0.0%	527	26.0%	0.0%
14,000	1,558	28.9%	9.4%	1,659	27.0%	0.0%	1,047	26.0%	0.0%
16,000	2,136	28.9%	8.6%	2,199	27.0%	0.0%	1,567	26.0%	0.0%
18,000	2,714	28.4%	7.4%	2,739	27.0%	0.0%	2,087	26.0%	0.0%
20,000	3,282	27.9%	7.4%	3,279	27.0%	0.0%	2,607	26.0%	0.0%
22,000	3,840	27.2%	7.4%	3,819	27.0%	1.0%	3,127	26.0%	0.0%
24,000	4,383	26.9%	10.2%	4,359	27.0%	3.8%	3,647	26.0%	0.0%
25,000	4,652	26.9%	12.4%	4,629	27.0%	3.8%	3,907	26.0%	0.0%
26,000	4,921	26.9%	12.4%	4,899	27.0%	3.8%	4,167	26.0%	0.0%
28,000	5,459	26.9%	16.3%	5,439	27.0%	10.2%	4,687	26.0%	3.8%
30,000	5,997	29.8%	23.2%	5,979	27.0%	17.1%	5,207	26.0%	15.3%
32,000	6,593	36.4%	23.2%	6,519	32.5%	17.1%	5,727	31.5%	15.3%
34,000	7,320	36.9%	23.2%	7,168	33.0%	17.1%	6,356	32.0%	15.3%
35,000	7,689	36.9%	23.2%	7,498	35.0%	17.1%	6,676	32.0%	15.3%
36,000	8,058	36.9%	23.2%	7,848	35.0%	17.1%	6,996	32.0%	15.3%
38,000	8,796	36.9%	23.2%	8,548	35.0%	17.1%	7,636	32.0%	15.3%
40,000	9,534	36.9%	23.2%	9,248	35.0%	17.1%	8,276	32.0%	15.3%
42,000	10,272	36.9%	23.2%	9,948	35.0%	17.1%	8,916	32.0%	15.3%
44,000	11,010	36.9%	23.2%	10,648	35.0%	17.1%	9,556	32.0%	15.3%
45,000	11,379	36.9%	23.2%	10,998	35.0%	17.1%	9,876	32.0%	15.3%
46,000	11,748	36.9%	23.2%	11,348	35.0%	17.1%	10,196	32.0%	15.3%
48,000	12,486	36.9%	23.2%	12,048	35.0%	17.1%	10,836	32.0%	15.3%
50,000	13,224	36.9%	24.5%	12,748	35.0%	18.3%	11,476	32.0%	16.6%
52,000	13,962	36.9%	31.3%	13,448	35.0%	22.1%	12,116	32.0%	20.3%
54,000	14,700	36.9%	31.3%	14,148	35.0%	22.1%	12,756	32.0%	20.3%
55,000	15,069	36.9%	31.3%	14,498	35.0%	22.1%	13,076	32.0%	20.3%
56,000	15,438	36.9%	31.3%	14,848	35.0%	22.1%	13,396	32.0%	20.3%
58,000	16,176	36.9%	31.3%	15,548	35.0%	22.1%	14,036	32.0%	20.3%
60,000	16,914	36.9%	31.3%	16,248	35.0%	22.1%	14,676	32.0%	20.3%
62,000	17,652	36.9%	31.3%	16,948	35.0%	22.1%	15,316	32.0%	20.3%
64,000	18,390	41.4%	31.3%	17,648	38.3%	22.1%	15,956	35.3%	20.3%
66,000	19,218	43.4%	31.3%	18,413	39.0%	22.1%	16,661	36.0%	20.3%
68,000	20,086	43.4%	31.3%	19,193	39.0%	22.1%	17,381	36.0%	20.3%
70,000	20,954	43.4%	31.3%	19,973	39.0%	22.1%	18,101	36.0%	20.3%
72,000	21,822	43.4%	31.3%	20,753	39.0%	22.1%	18,821	36.0%	20.3%
74,000	22,690	43.4%	31.3%	21,533	39.0%	22.1%	19,541	36.0%	20.3%
76,000	23,558	43.4%	31.3%	22,313	39.0%	22.1%	20,261	36.0%	20.3%

Facts and Figures for Calculating 2003 Taxes

	Manitoba			Saskatchewan			Alberta		
	Taxes Payable	Marginal Rate on		Taxes Payable	Marginal Rate on		Taxes Payable	Marginal Rate on	
Taxable Income	Other Income	Other Income	Dividend	Other Income	Other Income	Dividend	Other Income	Other Income	Dividend
78,000	24,426	43.4%	31.3%	23,093	39.0%	22.1%	20,981	36.0%	20.3%
80,000	25,294	43.4%	31.3%	23,873	39.0%	24.6%	21,701	36.0%	20.3%
82,000	26,162	43.4%	31.9%	24,653	39.0%	25.1%	22,421	36.0%	20.9%
84,000	27,030	43.4%	35.1%	25,433	39.0%	28.3%	23,141	36.0%	24.1%
86,000	27,898	43.4%	35.1%	26,213	39.0%	28.3%	23,861	36.0%	24.1%
88,000	28,766	43.4%	35.1%	26,993	39.0%	28.3%	24,581	36.0%	24.1%
90,000	29,634	43.4%	35.1%	27,773	39.0%	28.3%	25,301	36.0%	24.1%
92,000	30,502	43.4%	35.1%	28,553	39.0%	28.3%	26,021	36.0%	24.1%
94,000	31,370	43.4%	35.1%	29,333	39.0%	28.3%	26,741	36.0%	24.1%
96,000	32,238	43.4%	35.1%	30,113	39.0%	28.3%	27,461	36.0%	24.1%
98,000	33,106	43.4%	35.1%	30,893	39.0%	28.3%	28,181	36.0%	24.1%
100,000	33,974	45.0%	35.1%	31,673	42.6%	28.3%	28,901	37.6%	24.1%
110,000	38,475	46.4%	35.1%	35,934	44.0%	28.3%	32,661	39.0%	24.1%
120,000	43,115	46.4%	35.1%	40,334	44.0%	28.3%	36,561	39.0%	24.1%
130,000	47,755	46.4%	35.1%	44,734	44.0%	28.3%	40,461	39.0%	24.1%

	British Columbia			Northwest Territories			Nunavut		
	Taxes Payable	Marginal Rate on		Taxes Payable	Marginal Rate on		Taxes Payable	Marginal Rate on	
Taxable Income	Other Income	Other Income	Dividend	Other Income	Other Income	Dividend	Other Income	Other Income	Dividend
10,000	461	22.1%	0.0%	199	17.8%	−1.6%	159	17.7%	−1.8%
12,000	902	22.1%	0.0%	555	22.0%	−1.6%	513	18.5%	−1.9%
14,000	1,343	22.1%	0.0%	994	22.0%	−1.6%	883	18.5%	−1.9%
16,000	1,784	22.1%	0.0%	1,433	22.0%	−1.6%	1,253	18.5%	−1.9%
18,000	2,225	22.1%	0.0%	1,872	22.0%	−1.6%	1,623	18.5%	−1.9%
20,000	2,666	22.1%	0.0%	2,311	22.0%	−1.6%	1,993	18.5%	−1.9%
22,000	3,107	22.1%	0.0%	2,750	22.0%	−1.6%	2,363	18.5%	−1.9%
24,000	3,548	22.1%	0.0%	3,189	22.0%	−1.6%	2,733	18.5%	−1.9%
25,000	3,769	22.1%	0.0%	3,409	22.0%	−1.6%	2,918	18.5%	−1.9%
26,000	3,989	22.1%	0.0%	3,628	22.0%	−1.6%	3,103	18.5%	−1.9%
28,000	4,430	22.1%	5.6%	4,067	22.0%	2.3%	3,473	18.5%	2.0%
30,000	4,871	22.6%	15.9%	4,506	22.0%	9.3%	3,843	18.5%	9.0%
32,000	5,323	30.6%	15.9%	4,945	29.9%	9.3%	4,213	26.7%	9.0%
34,000	5,935	31.2%	15.9%	5,543	30.7%	13.4%	4,746	27.5%	9.0%
35,000	6,247	31.2%	15.9%	5,849	30.7%	14.1%	5,021	27.5%	9.0%

	British Columbia			Northwest Territories			Nunavut		
	Taxes Payable	Marginal Rate on		Taxes Payable	Marginal Rate on		Taxes Payable	Marginal Rate on	
Taxable Income	Other Income	Other Income	Dividend	Other Income	Other Income	Dividend	Other Income	Other Income	Dividend
36,000	6,558	31.2%	15.9%	6,156	30.7%	14.1%	5,296	27.5%	12.7%
38,000	7,181	31.2%	15.9%	6,769	30.7%	14.4%	5,846	27.5%	14.6%
40,000	7,804	31.2%	15.9%	7,382	30.7%	14.5%	6,396	27.5%	14.6%
42,000	8,427	31.2%	15.9%	7,995	30.7%	14.5%	6,946	27.5%	14.6%
44,000	9,050	31.2%	15.9%	8,608	30.7%	14.5%	7,496	27.5%	14.6%
45,000	9,362	31.2%	15.9%	8,914	30.7%	14.5%	7,771	27.5%	14.6%
46,000	9,673	31.2%	15.9%	9,221	30.7%	14.5%	8,046	29.0%	14.6%
48,000	10,296	31.2%	15.9%	9,834	30.9%	14.5%	8,626	29.0%	14.6%
50,000	10,919	31.2%	19.3%	10,452	30.9%	16.3%	9,206	29.0%	16.5%
52,000	11,542	31.2%	24.1%	11,070	30.9%	22.5%	9,786	29.0%	22.1%
54,000	12,165	31.2%	24.1%	11,688	30.9%	23.0%	10,366	29.0%	22.1%
55,000	12,477	31.2%	24.1%	11,997	30.9%	23.0%	10,656	29.0%	22.1%
56,000	12,788	31.2%	24.1%	12,306	30.9%	23.0%	10,946	29.0%	22.1%
58,000	13,411	31.2%	26.4%	12,924	30.9%	23.0%	11,526	29.0%	22.1%
60,000	14,034	31.2%	26.6%	13,542	30.9%	23.0%	12,106	29.0%	22.1%
62,000	14,657	32.0%	26.6%	14,160	30.9%	23.0%	12,686	29.0%	22.1%
64,000	15,298	37.0%	26.6%	14,778	35.6%	23.0%	13,266	33.9%	22.1%
66,000	16,037	37.7%	26.6%	15,490	37.7%	23.0%	13,944	35.0%	22.1%
68,000	16,791	37.7%	26.6%	16,244	37.7%	23.0%	14,644	35.0%	22.1%
70,000	17,545	37.7%	27.5%	16,998	37.7%	23.0%	15,344	35.0%	22.1%
72,000	18,299	39.0%	27.8%	17,752	37.7%	23.0%	16,044	35.0%	22.1%
74,000	19,079	39.7%	27.8%	18,506	37.7%	23.0%	16,744	35.0%	22.1%
76,000	19,873	39.7%	27.8%	19,260	37.7%	23.0%	17,444	35.0%	22.1%
78,000	20,667	39.7%	27.8%	20,014	37.7%	23.0%	18,144	35.0%	22.1%
80,000	21,461	39.7%	27.8%	20,768	37.7%	23.0%	18,844	35.0%	22.1%
82,000	22,255	39.7%	28.4%	21,522	37.7%	23.7%	19,544	35.0%	23.1%
84,000	23,049	39.7%	31.6%	22,276	37.7%	28.4%	20,244	35.0%	29.0%
86,000	23,843	39.6%	31.6%	23,030	37.7%	28.4%	20,944	35.0%	29.0%
88,000	24,635	40.7%	31.6%	23,784	37.7%	28.4%	21,644	35.0%	29.0%
90,000	25,449	40.7%	31.6%	24,538	37.7%	28.4%	22,344	35.0%	29.0%
92,000	26,263	40.7%	31.6%	25,292	37.7%	28.4%	23,044	35.0%	29.0%
94,000	27,077	40.7%	31.6%	26,046	37.7%	28.4%	23,744	35.0%	29.0%
96,000	27,891	40.7%	31.6%	26,800	37.7%	28.4%	24,444	35.0%	29.0%
98,000	28,705	40.7%	31.6%	27,554	37.7%	28.4%	25,144	35.0%	29.0%
100,000	29,519	42.3%	31.6%	28,308	40.0%	28.4%	25,844	37.9%	29.0%
110,000	33,749	43.7%	31.6%	32,311	42.1%	28.4%	29,638	40.5%	29.0%
120,000	38,119	43.7%	31.6%	36,516	42.1%	28.4%	33,688	40.5%	29.0%
130,000	42,489	43.7%	31.6%	40,721	42.1%	28.4%	37,738	40.5%	29.0%

Facts and Figures for Calculating 2003 Taxes

		Yukon			Non-Resident	
Taxable Income	Taxes Payable Other Income	Marginal Rate on Other Income	Dividend	Taxes Payable Other Income	Marginal Rate on Other Income	Dividend
10,000	391	17.4%	0.0%	531	23.7%	0.0%
12,000	739	20.0%	0.0%	1,005	23.7%	0.0%
14,000	1,139	24.5%	0.0%	1,479	23.7%	0.0%
16,000	1,629	26.0%	0.0%	1,952	23.7%	0.0%
18,000	2,150	26.0%	0.0%	2,426	23.7%	0.0%
20,000	2,671	26.0%	0.0%	2,899	23.7%	0.0%
22,000	3,192	26.0%	0.0%	3,373	23.7%	0.0%
24,000	3,713	26.0%	0.0%	3,847	23.7%	0.0%
25,000	3,973	23.0%	0.0%	4,083	23.7%	0.0%
26,000	4,203	23.0%	0.0%	4,320	23.7%	0.0%
28,000	4,664	23.0%	5.7%	4,794	23.7%	5.8%
30,000	5,125	23.0%	15.6%	5,267	23.7%	16.0%
32,000	5,586	30.9%	15.6%	5,741	31.7%	16.0%
34,000	6,204	31.7%	15.6%	6,376	32.6%	16.0%
35,000	6,520	31.7%	15.6%	6,702	32.6%	16.0%
36,000	6,837	31.7%	15.6%	7,027	32.6%	16.0%
38,000	7,471	31.7%	15.6%	7,678	32.6%	16.0%
40,000	8,104	31.7%	15.6%	8,330	32.6%	16.0%
42,000	8,738	31.7%	15.6%	8,981	32.6%	16.0%
44,000	9,372	31.7%	15.6%	9,632	32.6%	16.0%
45,000	9,688	31.7%	15.6%	9,958	32.6%	16.0%
46,000	10,005	31.7%	15.6%	10,283	32.6%	16.0%
48,000	10,639	31.7%	15.6%	10,934	32.6%	16.0%
50,000	11,272	31.7%	17.4%	11,586	32.6%	17.9%
52,000	11,906	31.7%	22.8%	12,237	32.6%	23.4%
54,000	12,540	31.7%	22.8%	12,888	32.6%	23.4%
55,000	12,856	31.7%	22.8%	13,214	32.6%	23.4%
56,000	13,173	31.7%	22.8%	13,539	32.6%	23.4%
58,000	13,807	31.7%	22.8%	14,190	32.6%	23.4%
60,000	14,440	31.7%	22.8%	14,842	32.6%	23.4%
62,000	15,074	31.7%	22.8%	15,493	32.6%	23.4%
64,000	15,708	36.4%	22.8%	16,144	37.4%	23.4%
66,000	16,435	37.4%	22.8%	16,892	38.5%	23.4%
68,000	17,184	37.4%	22.8%	17,661	38.5%	23.4%
70,000	17,933	37.4%	22.8%	18,431	38.5%	23.4%
72,000	18,682	37.4%	22.8%	19,201	38.5%	23.4%
74,000	19,430	37.9%	22.8%	19,970	38.5%	23.4%
76,000	20,188	38.0%	22.8%	20,740	38.5%	23.4%

	Yukon			Non-Resident		
	Taxes Payable	Marginal Rate on		Taxes Payable	Marginal Rate on	
Taxable Income	Other Income	Other Income	Dividend	Other Income	Other Income	Dividend
78,000	20,948	38.0%	22.8%	21,509	38.5%	23.4%
80,000	21,708	38.0%	22.8%	22,279	38.5%	23.4%
82,000	22,468	38.0%	23.6%	23,049	38.5%	24.2%
84,000	23,228	38.0%	28.2%	23,818	38.5%	29.0%
86,000	23,989	38.0%	28.2%	24,588	38.5%	29.0%
88,000	24,749	38.0%	28.2%	25,357	38.5%	29.0%
90,000	25,509	38.0%	28.2%	26,127	38.5%	29.0%
92,000	26,269	38.0%	28.2%	26,897	38.5%	29.0%
94,000	27,030	38.0%	28.2%	27,666	38.5%	29.0%
96,000	27,790	38.0%	28.2%	28,436	38.5%	29.0%
98,000	28,550	38.0%	28.2%	29,205	38.5%	29.0%
100,000	29,310	40.4%	28.2%	29,975	40.9%	29.0%
110,000	33,346	42.4%	28.4%	34,061	42.9%	29.0%
120,000	37,586	42.4%	28.6%	38,353	42.9%	29.0%
130,000	41,826	42.4%	28.6%	42,645	42.9%	29.0%

Note

[1] Rates shown include surtaxes and flat rate taxes where applicable. The basic personal tax credits were taken into consideration when calculating taxes payable on Other Income. The marginal rates for capital gains are one-half of the rates shown for Other Income. The rates shown do not take minimum tax into account.

[2] For Quebec, the contribution to the Health Service Fund has been considered for dividend income.

Index

accrual rules
    planning around, 136
alimony and maintenance
    agreements, 171–72
allowable business investment loss
    (ABIL), 134
Alternative Minimum Tax (AMT), 56
annuities, 21
asset freeze, 61
attribution rules, 25, 165–68
audit, tax, 73
automobiles, 217
    allowances and reimbursements, 218–20
    business use, planning, 231
    company-provided, 225–28
    employee-provided, 218–24
    expense deduction, 220, 227
    personal-use reductions, 224
    purchase assistance, 224
    reimbursing employer, 227
    standby charge, 225–27
    tax aspects for employer, 228–31
    tax aspects for self-employed, 228–31

benefits, 19
    from employee loans, 77
    fringe, 76–77

buy–sell agreement, 63–65

Canada Child Tax Benefit, 175, 177
Canada Education Savings Grant, 183
Canada Pension Plan (CPP), 105, 232–34
Canadian-controlled private
    corporation (CCPC), 107–9, 126–27
capital cost allowance (CCA), 141
capital gains, 124
    cumulative net investment losses, 129–32
    deemed disposition on death, 37, 41
    exemptions, 125–32
    identical properties, 133–34
    reserves, 135
    special cases, 135
capital losses, 124
    cumulative net investment losses, 129–32
    superficial, 133
capital property, 124
charitable donations, 241–43
child care expenses, 176–77
children. *See also* grandchildren; income splitting
    attribution rules, 25, 165–70

Canada Child Tax Benefit, 175
child care expenses, 176–77
education of, 46–47, 179–82
eligible dependant credit, 175
farm property, 42–43, 55–57,
   178–79
gifting assets to, 44–46, 49
loans made by parents to adult,
   166–69
paying salaries to, 105
RESP contribution on behalf of,
   182
sale of asset to, 49–50
share ownership in company,
   122
with special needs, 46–47
child support, 171–73
child tax benefit, 175
corporation, 105
   basic tax, 106
   Canadian-controlled private,
      107–9
   large, 109
   setting up, 110
cottage, 51, 152–53
cumulative net investment losses
   (CNIL), 129–32

death
   deemed dispositions, 37, 41–43
   estate taxes, 40–44
   foreign death taxes, 44
   optional tax returns, 43
   RRSPs, 208
   taxation of estate, 43
   without a will, 39
deemed disposition rules, 37, 41,
   45, 49, 55
deferred income. *See* Income deferral
deferred profit sharing plans
   (DPSPs), 89

dividends, 26, 138–39
due dates for tax payments, 13

eligible dependant credit, 175
emergency service volunteers, 243
employee benefit plans, 92
employee loans, 86–87, 93–94
employee stock options, 87
employment
   northern residents deduction, 85
   remote work location, 84
   special work site, 84
entertainment expenses, 103
estate planning, 30–37, 65
   advisor's requirements, 33
   business assets, 54–65
   buy–sell agreements, 63–65
   early in life, 35
   freezes, 49–50
   gifting, 44–46
   income splitting, 46
   life insurance, 53–54
   middle age, 36
   objectives, 32–35
   pre-retirement, 36
   principal residence exemption,
      42, 50–51
   rollovers, 42, 52–53
   RRSPs, 51
   succession planning, 54
   taxation on death, 40
   techniques, 44
   use of trusts, 46–49
   wills, 37
executor, 38
expenses
   automobile, 220–23
   child care, 176
   child support, 172
   deductible employment, 81–83
   deductible small business, 102–5

Index ▶ 275

eligible for GST/HST/QST
  rebate, 96
golf and entertainment, 103
medical, 67–71
moving, 83
rental, 140

farming, as tax shelter, 149
farm property, 42, 45, 57, 127–29, 178–79
films, Canadian, 145
foreign asset reporting, 146–49
freeze, estate, 49–50

gambling, 22
gifting, 37, 44–46
gifts, 22
golf expenses, 103
Goods and Services Tax (GST), 72
  credit, 72
  rebate, 95–97
grandchildren, 179

Harmonized Sales Tax (HST), 72
  rebate, 95–97
holding company, 59
Home Buyers' Plan, 153, 194
home office expenses, 102, 154
home purchase loans, 78
home relocation loans, 79

income
  alimony and maintenance, 171–72
  annuity, 21
  business, 20, 99–101
  employee loans, 77–79
  exempt, 22
  fringe benefits, 76
  gifts, 22
  inheritance, 22
  investment, 130–31, 136, 138

  prize winnings, 22
income deferral, 24, 27
  accrual rules, 136
  deferred income plans, 27, 87–92
  DPSP contributions, 89
  employee benefit plans, 92
  employee stock options, 87
  RCAs, 91
  retiring allowances, 87–89
  salary deferral arrangements, 90
  shareholder loans, 93
  unpaid remuneration, 92
income splitting, 25
  attribution rules, 25, 167–70
  business income, 158
  Canada Child Tax Benefit, 177
  estate planning, 46
  family expenses, 161, 163
  farm property, 178
  interest expense, 163
  interest on interest, 159
  leverage, 163
  non-arm's-length loan, 168
  personal residence, 155
  professional management
    companies, 164
  salary to family, 105, 118, 161–62
  spousal business partnership, 162
  spousal loans, 163
  spousal RRSPs, 160
  spouse's taxes, 161
  transferring property, 162, 177–78
incorporation, 105
  advantages and disadvantages, 114
inheritance, 22
insurance, 53, 63–65
  corporate-owned, 64
  criss-cross, 64
  split-dollar, 65
interest, 27
  deduction, 85, 103, 139

internal freeze, 61
intestacy, 39
investing. See also tax shelters
   business investment losses, 134
   cumulative net investment
      losses, 129–32
   dividends, 138–39
   income from, 130–31
   offshore, 146
investment deductions, 139
investment selection, 24, 28

large corporations tax (LCT), 109
limited partnerships, 143
loopholes, 16
lotteries, 22

marginal tax brackets, 23
marriage breakdown, 170
matrimonial property, 60
medical expenses, 67–71
mineral exploration tax shelters, 144, 255
money, time value of, 16
moving expenses, 83
multiple-unit residential buildings (MURBs), 144

oil and gas tax shelters, 144
Old Age Security (OAS), 233–34
owner-manager
   capital gains exemption, 115
   deductions, 102–5
   distributions from corporation, 110
   estate planning, 35–37, 44–50
   family considerations, 122
   incorporating business, 101, 105, 110
   private health service plan, 104
   salaries to family members, 105
   salary/dividend trade-offs, 118
   selling business, 62, 120–21

   taxation of income from business, 99, 106
   taxation year, 101
   tax deferral, 109
   tax integration, 111–13

parents, providing care for, 237
partnership, spousal business, 162
political contributions, 243–45
principal residence
   designating property as, 150–52
   exemption, 20, 42, 50, 150
   renting during absence, 155
   taxable portion of gain on sale of, 152
prizes, 22
professional management companies, 164

Quebec Pension Plan (QPP), 232–34
Quebec Sales Tax (QST), 72
   rebate, 95–97
Quebec taxation, 246–59, 261–64
   cooperative investment plan, 253
   corporate tax issues, 256–59
   credits and deductions, 247–49, 264
   family patrimony, 256
   mineral exploration, 255
   oil and gas, 255
   Quebec business investment companies, 254
   Quebec Stock Savings Plan, 249
   simplified tax system, 264

Registered Education Savings Plan (RESP), 182
Registered pension plan (RPP), 36, 190
Registered retirement income fund (RRIF), 212–15

Index ▶ 277

Registered retirement savings plan (RRSP), 136–37, 185–216
  annuities, 211
  borrowing to contribute, 199
  Canada deposit insurance, 204
  carryforward rule, 193
  for child, 182, 189
  collapsing, 215
  collateral for loan, 202
  contribution limits, 189–91
  contribution types, 198
  creditor access, 207
  death, 208
  deregistration, 200
  earned income, 192
  estate planning, 35–37, 51
  excess contributions, 200
  fees, 139
  foreign investments, 201
  Home Buyers' Plan, 153
  investments, 201–206
  locked-in, 198
  maturity options, 209
  non-qualified investments, 201
  non-residents, 206
  past-service pension adjustment, 190
  pension adjustment, 190–92
  pension adjustment reversal, 190–91
  self-directed, 205
  spousal, 160, 170, 195–97
  transfers, 199
  types, 205
  withdrawals, 193–95
rental expenses, 140
retirement compensation arrangement, 91
retirement planning, 36
retiring allowances, 87, 199
returns
  amending previous years', 73
rollovers, 42, 52, 57
"Rule of 72," 33
salary deferral arrangements (SDAs), 90
second home, 152
self-employed. *See* owner-manager
seniors
  Canada or Quebec Pension Plans (CPP/QPP), 232–34
  caregiver tax credit, 239
  credits and deductions, 234
  Old Age Security (OAS), 233
settlement date, 133
shareholder loans, 93
small business deduction (SBD), 107–8
spousal business partnerships, 162
spousal loans, 163
spousal trust rollovers, 52
spouse. *See also* income splitting
  common-law relationship, 157
  definition of, 157
  preparation of will, 37
  same-sex couples, 157
  tax credit, 157
statistical tables for calculating 2003 taxes, 16, 260–72
substituted property, 168
succession planning, 54

tax brackets, marginal, 23, 260
tax calendar, 13
tax credits, 66–72,
  age 65 or over, 234
  caregiver, 239
  charitable donations, 241–43
  child tax benefit, 175
  CPP/QPP/EI, 80
  eligible dependant, 175, 237
  federal education, 180
  federal tuition fee, 179
  medical expenses, 67, 235

mental or physical impairment, 184, 235
pension income, 234
single status, 67
spouse, 157
student loan interest, 182
tax deductions, 66
tax information
   accessing personal, 240
tax integration, 111–13
tax planning
   defined, 15
   initial steps, 16
   key concepts, 24
   for owner-managers, 99–102
   record-keeping, 73
tax shelters, 24, 28, 142–46
   Canadian films, 145
   farming, 145
   limited partnerships, 143

mineral exploration, 144, 255
multiple-unit residential buildings, 144
oil and gas, 144, 255
provincial, 146, 249
T4s, 19, 76
trusts, 46–49
   attribution rules, 167–70
   deemed disposition rule, 49
   preferred beneficiary election, 47
   spousal, 52
tuition fees, 179

will
   consulting spouse when preparing, 37
   dying without, 39
   executor, 38
   reviewing, 39

Deloitte Offices

British Columbia
Langley	(604) 534-7477
Prince George	(250) 564-1111
Vancouver	(604) 669-4466

Alberta
Calgary	(403) 267-1700
Edmonton	(780) 421-3611

Saskatchewan
Prince Albert	(306) 763-7411
Regina	(306) 525-1600
Saskatoon	(306) 343-4400

Manitoba
Winnipeg	(204) 942-0051

Ontario
Guelph	(519) 822-2000
Hamilton-Halton	(905) 523-6770
Hawkesbury	(613) 632-4178
Kitchener	(519) 576-0880
London	(519) 679-1880
Ottawa	(613) 236-2442
St. Catharines	(905) 688-1841
Toronto	(416) 601-6150
Windsor	(519) 967-0388

Québec
Alma	(418) 669-6969
Amos	(819) 732-8273
Baie-Comeau	(418) 589-5761
Chicoutimi	(418) 549-6650
Dolbeau	(418) 276-0133
Farnham	(450) 293-5327
Granby	(450) 372-3347
Grand-Mère	(819) 538-1721
Jonquière	(418) 542-9523
La Baie	(418) 544-7313
Laval	(450) 978-3500
Longueuil	(450) 670-4270
Matane	(418) 566-2637
Montréal	(514) 393-7115
Québec	(418) 624-3333
Rimouski	(418) 724-4136
Roberval	(418) 275-2111
Rouyn-Noranda	(819) 762-0958
Saint-Hyacinthe	(450) 774-4000
Sept-Îles	(418) 962-2513
Sherbrooke	(819) 823-1616
St-Félicien	(418) 679-4711
Trois-Rivières	(819) 691-1212

New Brunswick
Saint John	(506) 632-1080

Nova Scotia
Halifax	(902) 422-8541

Newfoundland
St. John's	(709) 576-8480

National Offices
Montréal	(514) 393-7115
Toronto	(416) 874-3874